GREAT BRITISH COMICS

CELEBRATING A CENTURY OF RIPPING YARNS AND WIZARD WHEEZES

Paul Gravett
& Peter Stanbury

This book is dedicated to The Rescuers who have saved and studied our Great British Comics and made this book possible: First, foremost and particularly, Denis Gifford and Alan Clark, but also Derek Adley, Mick Anglo, David Ashford, Martin Barker, Mary Cadogan, Alan and David Coates, Walter Dexter, P.R. "Doc" Garriock, Melinda Gibson, Arthur Harris, Mike Higgs, Steve Holland, W.O.G. Lofts, Ray Moore, Barry Ono, Leonard Packman, George Perry, David Roach, Roger Sabin, Jenni Scott, Dez Skinn, Lew Stringer, A & B Whitworth, Norman Wright and to all other Rescuers, past, present and yet to come—and perhaps that will include you?

Cover design by Peter Stanbury
Front cover: Korky the Cat by Charles Grigg
Back cover, top to bottom: Tank Girl by Jamie Hewlett; Dan Dare by Frank Hampson; Judge Dredd by Brian Bolland; Rupert by Alfred Bestall; Modesty Blaise by Jim Holdaway; and Jonah by Ken Reid. All images © their respective copyright holders.

First published 2006 by
Aurum Press Limited
25 Bedford Avenue
London WC1B 3AT
www.aurumpress.co.uk

Copyright © 2006 Paul Gravett and Peter Stanbury
Design by Peter Stanbury
www.paulgravett.com
www.greatbritishcomics.com

The moral right of Paul Gravett and Peter Stanbury to be identified as the authors of this work has been asserted by them in accordance with the Copyright Designs and Patents Act 1988.

A catalogue record for this book is available from the British Library.

ISBN-10 1 84513 170 3
ISBN-13 978 1 84513 170 8

10 9 8 7 6 5 4 3 2 1
2010 2009 2009 2007 2006

Printed in Slovenia

Other books by Paul Gravett and Peter Stanbury

Manga: Sixty Years of Japanese Comics

Laurence King Publishing, 2004. ISBN 1-85669-391-0.

Graphic Novels: Stories to Change your Life

Aurum Press, 2005. ISBN 1-84513-068-5.

Dear Reader—Some Notes

Original artwork: Where indicated, several pages of comics presented here have been photographed from the original artwork, drawn half as big again, or sometimes twice as big or more as the final printed size. These artworks may have some corrections, blemishes or instructions on them and their artboard may be faded, but they show the artists' work more clearly, revealing their thinking, techniques and drawing before it was printed.

Annuals: British annuals are usually dated one year ahead of their actual publication.

Your cheery chums, The Authors

PS: For lots more fun and facts, visit:
www.greatbritishcomics.com

PREVIOUS PAGE: Girls reading comics at the Oasis open-air swimming pool, Endell Street, in the heart of London in May 1956 (when the average temperature was 19.8°C (67.7°F in old money) maximum). *The Beezer* that the girl on the left is reading, dated 12 May 1955, was a new weekly giant-size title launched in January 1956.

CONTENTS

Lost Worlds of Topsy-Turvy

"WHATEVER HAPPENED TO BRITISH COMICS?" "DO THEY STILL MAKE THEM ANY MORE?" "HAVE YOU GOT MY ABSOLUTE FAVOURITE IN? NOW WHAT WAS IT CALLED?"

THESE WERE SOME OF THE questions we were asked many times while writing this book. With a spot of prompting, we found the topic sparked a reverie of warm memories. We quickly learnt that any character, no matter how obscure or undistinguished, can become somebody's all-time favourite if they read it at the right time and in the right circumstances. It's been said that the "Golden Age" of comics is ten, or twelve, or whatever age in our lives when their magic worked its spell. This book comes with no guarantee that you'll find your favourite in these pages, because an exhaustive, if not exhausting, encyclopedia of every British comic that ever existed would have grown into an unfeasibly massive tome.

Hopefully, you'll find a few familiar faces here and also meet some new faces and future favourites for the first time.

So let's start by taking in a deep breath and savouring the air, because there is no escaping the heady scent of nostalgia that permeates comics. In his 1987 graphic novel *Watchmen*, a very British paean to America's fading superheroes, writer Alan Moore named a perfume range "Nostalgia", selling it with the slogan, "Oh, how the ghost of you clings", and filling the final, tender love scene with its fragrance. Moore knew that a touch of nostalgia was no bad thing, as long as

you don't start dwelling entirely in the past but look back to learn from the past and build something new out of it. When it comes to "these foolish things" called comics, their subtle blend of fading newsprint and smudgy ink with a soupçon of rusty staple can transport us back to those supposedly simpler, happier days curling up with our weekly comic bought hot off the press from the local newsagent or dropped onto the doormat. Like connoisseurs sampling a vintage wine, I've seen collectors open a long-lost comic and inhale its bouquet, so evocative you could bottle it as the very essence of childhood.

Nostalgia, however, can be an intoxicating aroma, so powerful that it can cloud all judgement and hinder a clearer-headed appreciation of the essential qualities of comics, their humour, fantasy, excitement, joy, and the artistry and storytelling behind them. Just as we can still be entertained and enlightened by old movies, plays, music or books, we don't need to have grown up reading the comics of yesteryear to enjoy them afresh as both timely and timeless, helping us to feel closer to the past and perceive its echoes around us still. Like watching restored newsreels online or unearthed silent movies on television, looking into British comics from before our time is like seeing our former selves staring back at us, so different yet so similar, wrapped up like us in all their manners and preoccupations, fears and foibles.

RIGHT: One newsboys' perk was being the first to read the latest comics before delivering them. From the uncredited cover of *Boys' World*, 16 February 1963.

BELOW: The same robust figure of Robin Hood by Derek Eyles used on the advertising poster for *Sun* opposite also appeared on the cover of *Thriller Comics* 44 on 6 August 1953.

TOLD IN PICTURES
THRILLER COMICS Library No. 44
8D
KING OF SHERWOOD

OPPOSITE: So many comics to choose from at this West Kensington newsagent in 1957. Posters promote *The Oracle*, one of the first women's magazines to run romance comics, *School Friend* and *Sun*.

ABOVE: A vendor selling comics and papers on the street at Ludgate Circus, London, on the sunny afternoon of 7 or 8 June 1893. He may have been selling them for a few days by the time this photograph was taken. He displays among other comics and story papers *Chums* 39 of Monday 5 June and *Snap-Shots* 148 of 3 June, the previous Saturday. *Chums*, a boys' story paper, not a comic, only began in September 1892 and became a staple for adventure stories of all kinds. *Snap-Shots* had been reprinting sixteen pages entirely of American cartoons and strips for one penny since July 1890.

Directly or indirectly, the writers and artists behind the comics cannot help but reflect their era, sometimes as sharply in focus as a documentary film, more often distorted, or turned upside down, like a funfair hall of mirrors. In this topsy-turvy realm, storytellers are freed from the limits of reality and able to highlight their absurdities all the more: a little girl is strong enough to pull a ship out of the sea; animals walk, talk, go to school or save the world; impossibly wealthy bumpkins find their money a burden; and in a future police state, littering becomes a criminal offence, sugar a banned drug, and ugliness and obesity competitive honours. Nobody famous, especially those in authority, escapes from being knocked off their pedestals. We relish seeing the pecking order overturned, our superiors reduced to cruelly exaggerated grotesques. What better title could there be for the first weekly journal of caricatures and strips than *The Looking Glass*, published in Glasgow in 1825? Like Alice stepping through her looking glass in 1871, comics can let us enter realms where imagination reigns supreme.

Sniff the air once again, however, and you'll detect another whiff strongly associated with British comics: the telltale smell of burning paper and artboard turning to ashes. Seen merely as another stage in the production process by many publishers, pages of original artwork would be used by them to prop up a wobbly table, mop up a spillage or be casually disposed of to save space and expense. One employee can still chuckle to himself at the memory of his consigning most of the artwork from the weekly comic *Battle* into a flaming brazier. At least Scottish publishers D.C. Thomson have always maintained their own archives. The majority of other companies never thought to return the artworks to the artists; in fact, some artists cranking work out anonymously saw no value in their own drawings, didn't want them back, and were even ashamed of them. Norman Pett was able to recover his originals from his *Daily Mirror* newspaper strip *Jane* that ran from 1932 to 1948 (spotlighted in Chapter 7). After his death, however, a neighbour and lawyer for Pett's estate, who disapproved of the risqué strips, set all the art on fire in Pett's garden where the artist used to sketch his nude model. As accomplished an illustrator as David Wright, who went on to draw the moody *Daily Mail* strip *Carol Day*, could throw his three sons' imported

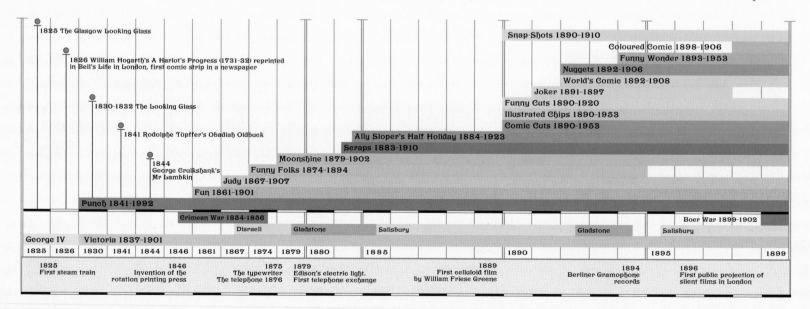

American "horror comics" onto a bonfire in 1955, because American psychologist Dr Fredric Wertham's scare-mongering book *Seduction of the Innocent* had convinced him of their corrupting influence. Despite, or perhaps because of this, the three boys adored comics all the more: Nicky collected and wrote a study about them, while Paul and Patrick grew up to be comic artists too.

So it is a miracle that the original artworks reproduced here in their hand-drawn glory exist at all, and that their fragile newsprint forms have weathered the years. Despite their often massive print runs, you might be surprised how few copies of comics remain after the ravages of being read and re-read to pieces and then usually thrown away. Apparently, a mere handful or two survive of the thousands of first issues of *The Dandy* and *The Beano*, for example. Because condition is everything, and it's also vital to have their accompanying free gifts, a genuine modern antique like *The Dandy* 1 with its Express Whistler sold for £20,350 in 2004, not a bad return for a weekly comic that cost only two (old) pennies in 1937, though still thousands of pounds below the stratospheric prices commanded by American comic books of a similar vintage. Whether trash or treasure, the real value of comics is not monetary but cultural, yet for all their popularity, social relevance and visual and verbal creativity what survives has primarily been down to devoted collectors.

Modern kids have so many other distractions, but comics were once key sources of cheap and cheerful chuckles and thrills. For decades, another black-and-white penny weekly popped out every day except Sunday from Amalgamated Press (AP) on different coloured papers—*Chips* in pink, *Comic Cuts* in white, *Funny Wonder* in blue, *Butterfly* in green—and were traded like

From largest to littlest, British comics come in a wide variety of shapes including big tabloids; middle-sized weeklies measuring 290 x 230 mm (11 x 9 inches); slightly smaller hardback Christmas annuals; titles in an American comic-book format; and "Picture Libraries", 175 x 135 mm (7 x 5.5 inches).

THE TIMELINE: Alongside world events, prime ministers and monarchs, this timeline charts the sometimes surprisingly long lifespans of some of Britain's popular comics and magazines. For example, in 2007 *2000AD* reaches 30, *The Dandy* 70. You can also see which titles came out in any year. So when were your earliest comic-reading experiences?

Title/Event			
Snap-Shots 1890-1910		The Kinema Comic 1920-1932	
Puck 1904-1940			
Lot-O'-Fun 1906-1929			
Coloured Comic 1898-1906	Big Comic 1914-1918		
Funny Wonder 1893-1953			
Nuggets 1892-1906	Chuckles 1914-1923		
World's Comic 1892-1908	Favourite Comic 1911-1917		
Funny Cuts 1890-1920	Film Fun 1920-1962		
Fun-1901	The Jester 1902-1920	The Jester 1924-40	
Illustrated Chips 1890-1953			
Comic Cuts 1890-1953			
Ally Sloper's Half Holiday 1884-1923			
Scraps 1883-1910	Rainbow 1914-1956		
Moonshine-1902	The Butterfly 1904-1940		
Judy 1867-1907	Tiger Tim's Weekly 1910-1940		
Punch 1841-1992			
Boer War 1899-1902	World War One		
Salisbury	Balfour	Campbell-Bannerman	Asquith	Lloyd George	Law	Baldwin
Victoria	Edward VII	George V		

1900	1905	1910	1915	1920	1925
1903 Wright Brothers' aeroplane		1910 63 large music halls in London	1914 Chaplin's first films Around 3,000 cinemas in UK Ford's Model T motor car	1918 Votes for women over 30 Influenza epidemic kills more people than WWI	1922 176,000 households with telephone	1924 580,000 motor cars in use

9

ABOVE AND OPPOSITE: *The Champion* was not a comic but a boys' story paper, but anything would do while Fred Brown, second in line, was queuing up in Eltham for his ration of comics on a rather wet morning on Saturday 21 August 1943. This photo appeared in the *Daily Mirror* the following Monday. This edition with *Red Fury in the Wild West* on the cover and Rockfist Rogan battling the Nazis inside had been passed around since the previous Saturday. Even with the war raging they found enough paper to get some comics printed.

Pokémon or *Yu-Gi-Oh!* cards today. "Comic-swapping was a recognised street activity like marbles and French cricket," recalled writer Keith Waterhouse. "It doubled the enjoyment you got out of your comic. First you read it (and what a lot there was to read—acres of eye-ruining small type) and then you had the pleasure of hunting a bargain swap." The revolution of *The Dandy* in 1937 and *The Beano* in 1938 "...blew the roof off the comic exchange. With its clean, bright, modern format, a *Dandy* was worth three *Jokers* at least. Suddenly the old-style tabloid comics with their fuzzy line drawings and blurred type on vile green, blue or pink newsprint, looked like the dud currency they now were."

Swapping became vital during the bleakest years of the Second World War, when those titles that managed to keep going were published in limited quantities due to paper rationing and *Dandy* and *Beano* were forced to alternate as fortnightlies. There was even a shortage of red ink. So that every family could get a fair share of comics, one south London shop in 1943 sold them only at 9.30 on Saturday mornings. Young Fred Brown woke up extra early to be at the front of the queue for the two new editions apportioned to him and to ensure his pals bought other ones so that over the week they could swap and read them all.

So how to define British comics for the purposes of this book? It might seem straightforward, perhaps British characters created and published in Britain by and for the British, thus excluding all imported reprints, but as this book reveals, that definition needs some defining. Both major comics publishers, Amalgamated Press in London and its subsequent incarnations and the Dundee-based D.C. Thomson, used non-British artists since the 1950s via Spanish, Italian and Argentinian agencies, so several beloved series were never drawn in Britain but in Barcelona, Bologna or Buenos Aires. In the reverse direction, Barry Windsor-Smith blazed a trail by daring to fly to New York in 1968, almost penniless, scraping by and sleeping on park benches until he convinced Stan Lee at Marvel to hire him. The 1980s brought a "British Invasion" of American comics by artists and writers head-hunted from *2000AD* and *Warrior*, whose irreverent outsider's view and conceptual daring continue to re-energise the industry. A few of those comics are included that are unmistakeably British through and through, except that they happen to have been published in America. Also on the radar are foreign icons from Mickey Mouse to Sonic the Hedgehog and Marvel's superheroes when they have been published here and written and drawn entirely by British talent.

Kinema Comic 1920-1932
Dazzler 1933-1939
Knockout 1939-1963
The Beano 1938
Radio Fun 1938-1961
Mickey Mouse Weekly 1936-1957
The Joker 1927-1940
Eagle-Volume One 1950-1969
Film Fun 1920-1962
Rainbow 1914-1956
Tiger Tim's Weekly 1910-1940
Sun 1947-1959
Lot-O'-Fun 1929
The Dandy 1937
The Butterfly 1904-1940
Slick Fun 1940-1945
Comet 1946-1959
Puck 1904-1940
Cute Fun 1940-1951
Girl 1951-1964
The Jester 1924-40
Thrill Comics 1940-1950
School Friend 1950-1965
Funny Wonder 1893-1953
Illustrated Chips 1890-1953
Comic Cuts 1890-1953
Punch 1841-1992

World War Two

Baldwin | MacDonald | Baldwin | Chamberlain | Churchill | Attlee | Churchill
George V | Edward VIII George VI | Elizabeth II
1927 | 1930 | 1935 | 1940 | 1945 | 1950

1928
First talking pictures
Votes for women on the same terms as men

1932
32% of homes wired for electricity

1936
First regular TV broadcasts

1939
71% of homes own a radio

1941
First British jet flight
The era of antibiotics begins

1951
Festival of Britain

In case British comics are alien to you, their formats boil down to a few: the anthology traditionally runs short strips, complete or serials, on half, whole or double pages, occasionally longer, at a tabloid or smaller size, sometimes on tinted paper, sometimes with a second colour or even four colours, mainly on the front cover and perhaps the back and centre spread. With anything from 64 to a meagre 4 pages, they come on the cheapest of newsprint or on quality paper if printed on photogravure presses or as a modern glossy. Many titles spin off into hardback annuals as Christmas gifts, always dated the following year and sold off cheap in January, and, since 1963, into summer specials for holiday reading. Compact Picture Libraries offer long, self-contained complete stories of up to 64 pages with mostly two panels a page. Slow to start compared to the Americans, popular strips in newspapers and magazines also get compiled into paperbacks for the Christmas market.

The characters in these comics are part of our national psyche and one aim of this book is to dust off and revisit their lost worlds. We also want to acknowledge the men and women who produced them but this isn't always easy. Aside from a few exceptions, most artists and writers worked anonymously. The publishers' excuse for this was that credits would confuse their little readers and stop them believing the characters were "real". Keeping creators' names secret also prevented rival publishers from poaching them. Artist Kevin O'Neill's first office junior job in comics in the late 1960s was to white out artists' signatures, often cunningly disguised in rocks or shrubbery. Earlier humour comics can be even harder to tell apart as artists were instructed to imitate each other, right down to the lettering and balloon styles, and were sent pages of original art to copy from. It's only thanks to experts' eyes that some artists are named here for the first time. To divide and rule, editors kept writers and artists apart; many had never met until the first British Convention, Comics 101, was set up by historian Denis Gifford in 1975.

Each chapter of this book shows how these creators have responded to and influenced the previous century's turbulent decades and still do so today. Far from being "dead in the water" or "down the tubes", British comics are still being made today, albeit in more diverse forms and formats. Current newsstands carry about the same number of titles as those in say 1966, around 100, but with the exception of weeklies like *Dandy*, *Beano* and *2000AD*, they tend to come out less frequently (every two weeks or monthly), usually include more editorial than comics (girls' monthly *It's Hot!* bills their comics as "cartoons"), and cost £2 or so, more parental than pocket-money buys. Pre-schoolers and youngsters are spoilt for choice and given comics, seem to love them as much as ever, but there's little for older children to graduate to. Whereas once free gifts were something special for launches or promotion, these days they seem to come with every issue; you wonder if people are buying a comic with a gift attached, or a gift with a comic attached. Homegrown titles like *Toxic* and *Dr. Who Adventures* claim respectable sales of over 50,000 but can they ever approach the half million or more copies most weeklies routinely sold in the 1950s and 1960s, when Britain was one of the world's biggest comics producers? How can the newsstand become an outlet for a vibrant variety of comics again, when it is dominated by one wholesaler-retailer that can dictate terms, reject a title or charge for merely testing it and rent out prime shelf space only to the biggest payers?

A richer future may lie away from the cut-throat newsstands. Since the 1960s, the underground, alternative and small press scenes have been fertile seedbeds for innovators like Bryan Talbot, *Viz*, Eddie Campbell, Steven Appleby and Jamie Hewlett, once ahead of their time and marginalised, who later reached a more mass audience. Instead of short-lived annuals,

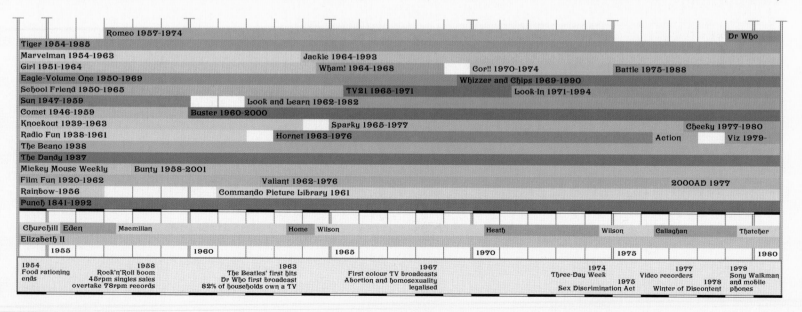

more British comics are being kept in print as perennial graphic novels in bookshops, libraries and new specialist comic shops. By cutting out middlemen and going direct to readers, webcomics are as wide open as the "unlimited canvas" of cyberspace. The internet and print-on-demand can also rescue gems left to languish in newsprint limbo.

It's a time of revolution and opportunity, but historically so many British comic publishers have avoided change for as long as possible. By the early 1950s, ageing AP editors would break down in tears whenever their failing 19th-century weeklies faced the axe; repeatedly reprieved, they folded only once those veterans legally had to retire. It took total novices Marcus Morris and Frank Hampson to overhaul the industry in *Eagle* in 1950. Hampson's aspirations were compromised, however, by two corporate take-overs that plunged him into despair. He later confided to interviewer Alan Vince, "Towards the end I was treated like an office boy. I tried to commit suicide... but Dorothy came home, she'd forgotten her gloves or something." By the 1970s, upstart Pat Mills had to cut through the old-boy complacency with *Battle*, *Action* and *2000AD*. Indie magazines *Warrior*, *Escape* and *Deadline* pointed ways forward in the 1980s, but by the mid-1990s the bigger publishers had left it too late to innovate, losing most of a generation to the multiple endings and flashy effects of computer games and the glitz of pop stars and celebrities. British comics seem to need a regular kick up the backside; whether it comes from Japan's long, complex manga comics, cartoon bands like Gorillaz, Alan Moore and company's *Albion* revivals of classic characters, the urban vinyl cult or comics for mobile phones, iPods or whatever comes next, that kick will definitely come.

ABOVE: Faced with new competition from *The Dandy* and *The Beano*, Amalgamated Press promoted their long-running *Chips*, originally *Illustrated Chips*, with free gifts. This big, rare newsagents' poster (730 x 480mm or 29 x 18.5 inches) is part of a New Year promotion from the late 1930s with art probably by Bertie Brown.

Dr Who Weekly/Monthly 1979-
Judge Dredd Megazine 1992-
Viz 1979-
2000AD 1977
Battle 1975-1988 · Deadline 1988-1995 · Dr Who Adventures 2006-
Look-In 1971-1994 · Warhammer 1997-2004 · It's Hot! 2004-
Whizzer and Chips 1969-1990 · Sonic the Comic 1993-2005
Jackie 1964-1993 · Wallace & Gromit 2005-
Look & Learn · Escape 1983-1989 · Electric Soup · Scenes from the Inside 1992-97 · Striker 2003-2005
Commando Picture Library 1961-
Buster 1960-2000 · Jetix 2004-
Bunty 1958-2001 · Toxie 2004-
Tiger 1954-1985 · Oink! 1986-88 · Revolver · Red Dwarf 1992-94 · A.T.O.M. 2005-
The Beano 1938
The Dandy 1937
Punch 1841-1992 · Punch 1996-2002
Gulf War · Iraq War
Thatcher · Major · Blair
Elizabeth II
1981 · 1985 · 1990 · 1995 · 2000 · 2005

| 1982 ZX Spectrum computer | 1984 Apple Macintosh Nintendo Game Boy launched | 1990 Poll Tax riots | 1991 Sony Playstation World Wide Web goes public | 1994 Channel Tunnel opens | 1997 Death of Princess Diana | 2000 44% of homes have at least one mobile phone | 2001 9/11 | 2002 Over half of households have a home computer | 2005 53% of households have an internet connection |

The CD player

more British comics are being kept in print as perennial

GREAT BRITISH COMICS
A Series of 250   No. 78

FRANK HAMPSON

(1918–85) Nobody before him had created such a painstakingly illustrated vision of the future. His *Dan Dare* assured *Eagle*'s success from its nearly million-selling launch on 14 April 1950. Working from his detailed layouts, he and his studio staged photo-references by casting his family and friends as characters and building models of space-craft, sets and aliens like the Mekon. Hampson left *Eagle* in 1961, denied any share in *Dare*'s success. When none of his strip proposals found a publisher, he quit comics entirely. Rediscovered in 1975, he enjoyed acclaim first in Italy and finally Britain.

Issued by
GRAVETT & STANBURY
LONDON . . . . ENGLAND
PRINTED IN ENGLAND

GREAT BRITISH COMICS
A Series of 250   No. 86

SYDNEY JORDAN

(b. 1931) From 15 February 1954, Jordan's solid scientific grounding and rich invention of alien cultures set his *Daily Express* strip about RAF pilot Jeff Hawke apart from the formula SF of the day. From 1956 to 1969, he worked with his long-time pal, writer Willie Patterson, whose wit lifted their stories to new heights. After *Jeff Hawke* was dropped in 1975, Jordan devised *Lance McLane* for the Scottish *Daily Record* and revived *Dan Dare* for the first and only edition of the *Planet on Sunday* in 1996. His current colour SF serial *Hal Starr* appears in *Spaceship Away*.

Issued by
GRAVETT & STANBURY
LONDON . . . . ENGLAND
PRINTED IN ENGLAND

GREAT BRITISH COMICS
A Series of 250   No. 37

NORMAN PETT

(1891–1960) Creator of Forces Sweetheart Jane, he first drew her as a "Bright Young Thing" whose diary began in the *Daily Mirror* on 5 December 1932. Like Pett, Jane had a dachshund named Fritzi. After basing Jane on his wife Mary, he spotted Christabel Leighton-Porter at a life-drawing class, who posed as his nude model from 1938 on. After he was "retired" from the strip in May 1948, he created lookalike *Susie* for the *Sunday Dispatch*, illustrated strip versions of *Animal Farm* and the Errol Flynn film *Don Juan*, and drew for *Comet, Knockout, Girl* and romance comics.

Issued by
GRAVETT & STANBURY
LONDON . . . . ENGLAND
PRINTED IN ENGLAND

GREAT BRITISH COMICS
A Series of 250   No. 81

LEO BAXENDALE

(b. 1930) Since his debut *Beano* feature *Little Plum* in 1953, the ever-evolving style and humour of this strong-willed maverick have influenced British children's funnies to this day as much as *The Goons* and *Monty Python* influenced TV comedy. After creating *Minnie the Minx, Bash Street Kids, Banana Bunch* and *Three Bears*, he left Thomson in 1964 for Odhams Press to create *Wham!*, home to *Eagle-Eye Junior Spy, Grimly Feendish* and more. He left weekly comics in 1976 to create three solo *Willy the Kid* Annuals. Since settling his copyright lawsuit against Thomson in 1987, he runs his own company, Reaper Books.

Issued by
GRAVETT & STANBURY
LONDON . . . . ENGLAND
PRINTED IN ENGLAND

GREAT BRITISH COMICS
A Series of 250   No. 93

DON LAWRENCE

(1928–2003) Hired in 1954 by Mick Anglo, Lawrence first wrote and drew *Marvelman* before taking on historical epics *Olac the Gladiator* for *Tiger* and *Karl the Viking* for *Lion*. In 1965 he painted the first of 950 pages of Mike Butterworth's *Trigan Empire*, part Roman saga, part SF fantasy, in *Ranger* and then *Look & Learn*. Frustrated at his work being sold across Europe with no royalties paid to him, he resigned. Within hours Dutch publisher Oberon offered him the contract he wanted. From 1977 his 23 *Storm* books sold two million copies and earned him the rewards and recognition he richly deserved.

Issued by
GRAVETT & STANBURY
LONDON . . . . ENGLAND
PRINTED IN ENGLAND

GREAT BRITISH COMICS
A Series of 250   No. 141

ALAN MOORE

(b. 1953) Being born with no useful sight in his left eye and no hearing in his right ear, being expelled from school and denied all but the most menial jobs, has not stopped him from becoming the most brilliant living writer of comics in the English language. He began in 1979 by both writing and drawing strips for rock paper *Sounds* and his local paper, before selling scripts to *Dr Who Weekly*, *2000AD* and *Warrior*. His *Marvelman* revival and *V for Vendetta* political thriller led to *Swamp Thing, Watchmen* and more for US publishers. From Ripper-ology in *From Hell* to sex in *Lost Girls*, he brings new life to every genre.

Issued by
GRAVETT & STANBURY
LONDON . . . . ENGLAND
PRINTED IN ENGLAND

GREAT BRITISH COMICS
A Series of 250   No. 53

ALFRED BESTALL

(1892–1986) Bestall was an established, versatile illustrator for *Punch, Tatler* and other magazines by the time he succeeded Mary Tourtel on *Rupert* in the *Daily Express* in 1935. Under his pen, the world of the little boy bear was enriched with clever stories and fresh characters for thirty years. From 1936, his tales were collected and coloured in annuals, which peaked at nearly a million-and-a-half copies sold. He contributed to them up to his ninetieth year, providing endpapers, origami and "magic painting" pages. He was awarded the MBE in 1985.

Issued by
GRAVETT & STANBURY
LONDON . . . . ENGLAND
PRINTED IN ENGLAND

GREAT BRITISH COMICS
A Series of 250   No. 64

TOM BROWNE

(1870–1910) Inspired by cartoonist Phil May, Tom Browne set a new style of British comic art with his economy of line and solid black accents, perfect for cheap printing, with his tramps *Weary Willie and Tired Tim* in *Illustrated Chips* on 16 May 1896. His other duos included junior versions *Little Willie & Tiny Tim, Don Quixote & Sancho Panza*, and *Airy Alf & Bouncing Billy*. His drawing for postcards, adverts, magazines, his own annual, and paintings in oils and water-colours made him the most famous and honoured artist of the Edwardian age. He was only 39 when he died of cancer.

Issued by
GRAVETT & STANBURY
LONDON . . . . ENGLAND
PRINTED IN ENGLAND

GREAT BRITISH COMICS
A Series of 250   No. 167

BRYAN TALBOT

(b. 1952) Britain's pioneering graphic novelist began his book-length projects in the 1970s underground press with the *Chester P. Hackenbush* trilogy for *Brainstorm Comix*. Thanks to patron Serge Boissevain, he completed his multi-layered, award-winning *Adventures of Luther Arkwright* after a decade in 1989. His Beatrix Potter-inspired *Tale of One Bad Rat* marked a high point in 1995 in his sensitive exploration of parental abuse. He has worked on such major characters as Batman, Sandman and Nemesis. 2007 brings *Alice in Sunderland*, his most ambitious epic yet.

Issued by
GRAVETT & STANBURY
LONDON . . . . ENGLAND
PRINTED IN ENGLAND

GREAT BRITISH COMICS
A Series of 250   No. 178

POSY SIMMONDS

(b. 1945) A sharply observant, ambidextrous observer of British manners, she started cartooning for *The Times* in 1968 and the *Sun* in 1969 on her daily feature, *Bear*. In May 1977, she began her weekly *Guardian* strip about the Weber family, initially called *The Silent Three*. Her first graphic novel *True Love* in 1981 was followed in 1999 by *Gemma Bovery*, an adulterous English rose in Normandy whose fate seems to mirror that of Madame Bovary. Her latest in colour, *Tamara Drewe*, also serialised in the *Guardian*, will be collected in 2007. In a parallel career she creates children's books in colour strip form.

Issued by
GRAVETT & STANBURY
LONDON . . . . ENGLAND
PRINTED IN ENGLAND

These twenty tea cards come from Gravett & Stanbury's first set of 250 artists, writers, editors and publishers which can be viewed on the site www.greatbritishcomics.com

GREAT BRITISH COMICS

A Series of 250 No. 52

KEN REID

(1919–87) Master of grotesque bodily humour and warped intensity, Reid began on the *Manchester Evening News*, creating *Fudge the Elf* from 1938, a far stranger children's strip than *Rupert*. He drew *Roger the Dodger* and enhanced Walter Fearne's scripts on nautical jinx *Jonah* at Thomson before switching in 1964 to Odhams to write and draw *Frankie Stein, Queen of the Seas, The Nervs, Jasper the Grasper* and *Faceache*. Some of his work proved too far-out for kids' comics, notably a suppressed *Dare-A-Day Davy* and a suicidal character whose attempts to kill himself endlessly backfire.

Issued by
GRAVETT & STANBURY
LONDON . . . . ENGLAND
PRINTED IN ENGLAND

GREAT BRITISH COMICS

A Series of 250 No. 44

DUDLEY WATKINS

(1907–69) Joining the Thomson family firm in 1925, his big-chinned, big-hearted cartooning and robust adventure art came to define the company's clear, friendly style still in use today. He drew the *Sunday Post* series *The Broons* and *Oor Wullie* from 1938, *Desperate Dan* and *Lord Snooty* in *The Dandy* from 1938, and *The Shipwrecked Circus* and *Jimmy and his Magic Patch* for *The Beano*. A deeply religious man, he worked next to a huge Bible open at his drawing desk, which he annotated and hoped to adapt into comics. He died at this desk, leaving his last *Desperate Dan* half-finished.

Issued by
GRAVETT & STANBURY
LONDON . . . . ENGLAND
PRINTED IN ENGLAND

GREAT BRITISH COMICS

A Series of 250 No. 20

MARY TOURTEL

(1874–1978) An accomplished children's book illustrator adept at drawing animals, she created the daily adventures of Rupert Bear in the *Daily Express* for nearly fifteen years from 8 November 1920. She had help on the stories and rhyming couplets from her husband Henry, who was a sub-editor on the paper until his death in 1931. When her failing eyesight forced her to retire in 1935, she was granted the copyright to her drawings. She sold these for £50 to publishers Sampson Low, who issued thick *Monster Rupert* books of her stories from 1931 to 1950.

Issued by
GRAVETT & STANBURY
LONDON . . . . ENGLAND
PRINTED IN ENGLAND

GREAT BRITISH COMICS

A Series of 250 No. 78

DAVID LAW

(c.1907–1971) The arrival of Law's *Dennis the Menace* in a half-page in *The Beano* on 17 March 1951 heralded a major shift towards a wilder brand of humour closer to real life that boosted sales to over two million a week. *Dennis* grew out of another cheeky kid, *The Wee Fella*, whose strips Law drew in *The People's Journal* in the early 1930s. In 1953, he took on *Beryl the Peril* in *The Topper* and in 1960 the colour spread *Corporal Clott* in *The Dandy*, which he drew until 1970. Pressure of work caused his art to elongate and loosen but he never lost his vigorous comedic inventiveness.

Issued by
GRAVETT & STANBURY
LONDON . . . . ENGLAND
PRINTED IN ENGLAND

GREAT BRITISH COMICS

A Series of 250 No. 72

FRANK BELLAMY

(1917–76) *Dan Dare* in *Eagle*, *Robin Hood* in *Swift*, *Thunderbirds* in *TV21* and *Garth* in *The Mirror* are four iconic series to benefit from Bellamy's dynamic, design-oriented draughtsmanship since his strip career began in 1952. *The Happy Warrior*, Churchill's life story in comic form, brought him national fame in 1957. Also in *Eagle*, he painted the classical *Heros the Spartan* across full-width centre spreads and *Fraser of Africa*, his favourite, in a subtle, sun-bleached palette. In 1972, he was the first British artist to be honoured by the American Academy of Comic Book Arts.

Issued by
GRAVETT & STANBURY
LONDON . . . . ENGLAND
PRINTED IN ENGLAND

GREAT BRITISH COMICS

A Series of 250 No. 19

AUSTIN BOWEN PAYNE

(1876–1959) In 1919, after a decade drawing for weekly comics, Welsh cartoonist Payne created Pip the dog and Squeak the penguin with journalist Bertram Lamb ('Uncle Dick') for the *Daily Mirror*'s revived children's supplement. Payne added a baby bunny, naming him Wilfred on 7 February 1920, who said only "Gug!" or "Nunc" for uncle. Animated in short films in 1922, the pets were joined by Auntie, an elderly penguin who only spoke words like "Oogle" and "Oomsk", and bearded Bolshevik Wtzkoffski and his pup Popski. Payne drew the strip until 1940 and revived it from 1947 before retiring.

Issued by
GRAVETT & STANBURY
LONDON . . . . ENGLAND
PRINTED IN ENGLAND

GREAT BRITISH COMICS

A Series of 250 No. 185

CHRIS DONALD

(b. 1960) In 1979, with his younger brother Simon and his friend Jim Brownlow, Chris Donald created the first twelve-page issue of *Viz*, a rude parody of *The Beano* and trashy tabloids. He paid £42.35 to print 150 copies. Contrary to legend, they did not sell out of them on the first night, but by 1985 with sales in Newcastle alone growing to over 5,000, he agreed to let Virgin Books, and later John Brown, publish it across the country. Donald edited *Viz* until 1999, its sales peaking in 1991 at 1.2 million copies. The over-the-top characters created by him and his team continue to influence British comedy.

Issued by
GRAVETT & STANBURY
LONDON . . . . ENGLAND
PRINTED IN ENGLAND

GREAT BRITISH COMICS

A Series of 250 No. 161

PAT MILLS

(b. 1949) As writer and editor, Mills was the upstart outsider who, with ex-Thomson cohort John Wagner, rescued IPC's boys' adventure comics from terminal decline with a hat-trick of harder-hitting weeklies: *Battle* (1975); the infamous, censored *Action* (1976); and *2000AD* (1977), still "the galaxy's greatest comic". His outstanding epics include the damning WWI diary *Charley's War*, alien freedom fighter *Nemesis the Warlock* and warping Celtic warrior *Sláine*. He has also written American comics such as superhero-killer *Marshal Law* with Kev O'Neill and French series *Sha*, *Requiem* and others.

Issued by
GRAVETT & STANBURY
LONDON . . . . ENGLAND
PRINTED IN ENGLAND

GREAT BRITISH COMICS

A Series of 250 No. 41

ROY WILSON

(1900–65) As Browne before him and Baxendale after, Wilson defined the look of humour comics of his era, in his case the 1930s, and beyond. After assisting Don Newhouse in the 1920s, he began his solo career in 1931. Both prodigious and perfectionist, he produced many exuberant pages for *Merry & Bright, Funny Wonder* and other weeklies, and watercolour covers and frontispieces for annuals. Streamlining his style in the 1950s, he drew comics starring popular comedians for *Film Fun* and *Radio Fun*, ending with his favourites, Eric Morecambe and Ernie Wise, in *Buster*.

Issued by
GRAVETT & STANBURY
LONDON . . . . ENGLAND
PRINTED IN ENGLAND

GREAT BRITISH COMICS

A Series of 250 No. 201

EDDIE CAMPBELL

(b. 1955) Campbell was a prime mover in the early 1980s self-publishing scene and pioneered autobiography in British comics in the reflective *Alec*, serialised from 1984 by *Escape* through to 2005's *The Fate of The Artist*. His other solo series, *Bacchus*, god of wine grown old in the modern world. In 2000 he completed a 576-page dissection of the Ripper murders, *From Hell*, written by Alan Moore, and then adapted Moore's performance pieces, *The Birth Caul* and *Snakes & Ladders*, into comics. His next graphic novel is the detective story, *The Black Diamond Agency*.

Issued by
GRAVETT & STANBURY
LONDON . . . . ENGLAND
PRINTED IN ENGLAND

For Richer, For Poorer

"I AM UPPER CLASS AND I LOOK DOWN ON HIM." "I AM MIDDLE CLASS AND I LOOK UP TO HIM, AND I LOOK DOWN ON HIM." "I AM LOWER CLASS, AND I KNOW MY PLACE."

RIGHT: **Bert Codman, a descendent of the original nineteenth-century Punch and Judy showmen called "professors", performs the puppet show in 1968 at Colwyn Bay, Wales. Mr Punch's dog Toby is on stage.**

BELOW: **Among the mass of often unlicensed merchandise of Ally Sloper, Britain's first comics superstar, was this iron door-stop, c. 1880.**

THE STUDIO AUDIENCE watching the live satirical television show *The Frost Report* in 1966 may have laughed out loud at this sketch by Marty Feldman and John Law, but what were they laughing at? Before them was a line-up of three comedians. In descending height, from left to right, stood the imposingly lofty John Cleese in bowler hat and suit; the average-height Ronnie Barker in a trilby; and the small Ronnie Corbett in overalls. The way they each looked, dressed and spoke revealed their class instantly, as well as their likely jobs and wealth. Even the trio's relative heights correspond to research which has found that the top two classes of professionals and managers measure around three centimetres (just over one inch) taller than workers in the bottom two classes. The audience's laughter was full of recognition that this succinct observation summed up the hierarchy between the classes. Depending on which class an audience member belonged to, their laughter was perhaps also laced with unease or frustration: while this status quo still held true, the swinging Sixties might bring an unstoppable wind of change.

Attitudes in Britain between the various classes had been shifting for decades. At least since the carnage of the First World War, the working class's deference towards their supposed superiors had been irreversibly eroded, while a good many among the aristocracy saw their financial security begin to decline. Over time, respect for the once

venerable institutions of monarchy, church, government, police and marriage itself would also diminish. For the majority of Britons, the last 50 years or so had brought greatly improved standards of living and individual freedoms, to the point where the old formalities of "knowing your place" and the hidebound pecking order and confined class and gender opportunities that came with this code held less sway. Nevertheless, despite calls for "a classless society", the differences and divisions between "the haves and the have-nots" never entirely vanished, and they underpin a lot of British comedy and drama in their many forms, including comics.

Punch and Judy, for instance, hardly presented a model married couple, and yet the puppet shows about them still draw young and old who join in on the beach or at travelling fairs. Kids and adults would shout, "Look behind you!" to aid and abet the squeaking, hook-nosed Mr Punch in the multiple murders of his child, his wife, a policeman and a hangman, before he outwitted the devil himself. In 1841, this gleefully amoral, immortal psychopath was softened into the cheery jester and figurehead of *Punch,* a mildly radical new magazine of satire and cartoons. His subversiveness, though, was shortly subsumed by a creeping respectability that made this weekly fit for all the best drawing rooms. Only certain forms of comics were permitted in its pages, such as the later silent comedies of manners and social gaffes perfected by H.M. Bateman. Mr Punch's true puppet persona was too shrill and disturbing to appear in

OPPOSITE: **The whole family gathers round the table for tea, biscuits and bacon and eggs on the cover of the 1952 *Broons* annual painted by Dudley Watkins, the Norman Rockwell of Scottish everyday life.**

THE BRITISH WORKING MAN.

PHASE FOURTH.—A LITTLE WORK FOR THE NEXT-COMER.

The party who does the gutters and undoes the slates.

The party who does the slates and undoes the garden.

The party who does the garden and undoes the paint.

The party who does the paint and undoes the furniture.

The foreman who says,—Bless his soul! ought to be ashamed of 'emselves. Disgraceful! ain't it? He'll let 'em know what's what.

Letting 'em know what's what.

ABOVE: James Sullivan's popular series of strips in *Fun* started with *The British Working Man, by One who does not Believe in him* in 1875, in which he catalogued the laziness and trickery of builders, plumbers, female domestics and other workers, a theme that would recur in many later cartoons and comics. Here, each labourer leaves behind him another job that needs attending to.

comics in *Punch*. As tastes changed, even the scripts for the puppet shows were watered. It was left to Neil Gaiman and Dave McKean in their 1994 graphic novel to restore Mr Punch's original story and evoke its echoes in a present family's un-spoken shames.

Catering for the aspiring upper middle classes secured *Punch* magazine's longevity, but left open the expanding market for those increasingly literate and prosperous classes below them, of both sexes, in the lower labour and service sectors. Undercutting *Punch* by a penny came twopenny rivals such as *Fun* from 1861 and *Judy* from 1867. With their more knowing and "low-life" humour, which often focused on the cheats, rogues and idlers all too familiar to their readers, these magazines confirmed their readers' prejudices while also engendering self-recognition in some. In *Fun*, for example, James Sullivan's outspoken strips in his "big-head" style are not so different from today's television exposés of dubious builders caught on hidden cameras, suggesting that distrust of labourers goes back a long way.

Another stinging satire of the Victorian work ethic in the pages of *Judy* produced Britain's earliest popular comic celebrity, Ally Sloper. In his initial form, conceived in 1867 by Charles Ross and developed by his French-born artist wife Marie Duval, Sloper was decrepit, balding, gawky and unmistakably lower-class. In the

manner used by Dickens and others before him that a person's name should reveal their nature—a British tradition that lives on in the punning names given to characters in humour comics to this day—the name Ally short for Alexander Sloper signalled his habit of "sloping" down an alley to avoid the rent collector or the angry victims of his hopeless money-making schemes. However hard he tried to keep up appearances, his crumpled clothes, stovepipe hat and umbrella gave away his lack of funds and his tell-tale swollen nose was a beacon to his partiality for drink. If he looks similar to W.C. Fields, that is because Sloper may well have inspired the American vaudeville and film comedian. Compared to the homicidal Mr Punch, Sloper was merely a minor reprobate in London's East End and, even in cahoots with his cleverer Jewish cohort Isaac Moses or "Iky Mo", he never came out on top.

Sloper evolved significantly when he graduated in 1884 to his own one-penny weekly, *Ally Sloper's Half-Holiday*, named after the workers' leisure time recently introduced on Saturday afternoons. In tune with his public's changing tastes and fortunes, Sloper smartened up his wardrobe and, shaking off his criminal leanings and working-class roots, became the "Friend of Man" or a man of the people, and something of a gent. Elevated to single-panel cover cartoons as lavish as his fantasy *arriviste* status, the laughs came from Sloper no longer "knowing his place" and somehow gaining access to the most exclusive society events, seaside resorts, even Parliament and the Royal family. That this Sloper appealed across the classes is borne out by a book of 273 letters from celebrity readers who were granted a "Friend of Sloper" award. Among them were artists John Everett Millais, Lawrence Alma-Tadema and John Singer Sargent, Gilbert and Sullivan impresario Richard D'Oyly Carte and assorted variety artists including cowgirl Annie Oakley, who wrote, "Am grateful for the honer [sic]... and shall give it a place in my little tent." Sloper was made into such a widely merchandised brand that he and his wife were imitated in musical halls, circuses and pantomimes and were cast in the roles of Punch and Judy in puppet shows of their own.

Slopermania did not go unnoticed. When Alfred Harmsworth, the future press magnate Lord Northcliffe and "Napoleon of Fleet Street", was unable to buy *Ally Sloper's Half-Holiday*, he cobbled together his own weeklies, *Comic Cuts* and *Illustrated Chips*, in 1890. By charging only a halfpenny, he trounced his competitors. His burgeoning empire, united in 1901 under the Amalgamated Press banner, would virtually monopolise Britain's comics market until it was seriously challenged by D.C. Thomson. Harmsworth owed much of his success in comics to the Nottingham-born cartoonist Tom Browne. His crisp, economical line and adeptly placed accents of solid black heralded a refreshingly modern style, influenced by the elegant essentials of cartoonist Phil May and a far cry from *Punch*'s frequent excesses of ornate rendering. Also worlds away from *Punch*'s genteel social circles were Browne's pair of tramps, Weary Willie and Tired Tim, inspired in 1896 partly by Miguel de Cervantes's spindly, bearded Don Quixote and Sancho Panza, his squat, rotund sidekick. Far from being pitiable failures, tramps were seen by many as dignified dropouts in an era when industrialisation rewarded millions with poor pay, working conditions and health. The public loved the notion of tramps as rebels flouting the system and they became stock characters in comics. After only a year or so in print, Browne's duo were swiftly adapted in 1897 into the first of several live short films. Among their admirers was London-born Charlie Chaplin, who once remarked, "I started the little tramp simply to make people laugh and because those other old tramps, Weary Willie and Tired Tim, had always made me laugh."

Cheery down-and-outs were possibly less amusing once the Depression and mass unemployment took hold between the Wars. In 1936, for D.C. Thomson's *Sunday Post*, Dudley Watkins drew the first of over 30 years' worth of *The Broons*, portraying a boisterous extended family, eleven in all, living under one tenement roof and always smiling through. They are still together in the *Post* 70 years on, a romanticised Scottish institution striking a balance between old and new. Staying true to Watkins' style comes naturally to current *Broons* illustrator Peter Davidson, because, as a young pal of the great man's son, he never forgot watching him draw, nor the heady smell of his black Indian ink.

Not everyone felt as warmly about such tales of tramps, scoundrels or a humble family's cheery survival. George Orwell wrote in the left-wing paper *Tribune* in 1944, "... this business about the moral superiority of the poor is one of the deadliest forms of escapism the ruling class have evolved. You may be downtrodden and swindled, but in the eyes of God you are superior to your oppressors, and by means of films and magazines you can enjoy a fantasy existence in which you constantly triumph over the people who defeat you in real life. In any form of art designed to appeal to large numbers of people, it's an almost unheard-of thing for a rich man to get the better of a poor man. Film magnates, press lords and the like amass quite a lot of their wealth by pointing out that wealth is wicked. The formula 'good poor man defeats bad rich man' is simply a subtler version of 'pie in the sky'."

1. After their gallant exploits last week Willy and Tim hurried back to form a "Tramp Army" to take out to the Transvaal. And here they are enlisting the merry Out-of-work Brigade. "Now then, me 'andsome pal!" chirped Tim, "wot d'yer say to that? Free drinks, mind you!" "Free gargles!" whistled the Wanderer; "why I'd die twice a week for that!"

2. Such a tempting offer could not be resisted, and straight away the great Army of Weary Unwashed Wanderers was formed. "Now then, skinny Willy," quoth Tim, as he inspected the corps, "why can't you chuck a chest, and look proud?" "Carn't, old pal!" giggled Willy; "me muvver's sent it to the wash, and it ain't come back!"

TOP: Down but never out, Charlie Chaplin's tramp symbolised that spirit of plucky optimism, of bouncing back from defeat, shown here in *The Kid* from 1921.

ABOVE: Weary Willie and Tired Tim do their patriotic duty and enlist their fellow unwashed into a "Tramp Army" to "spifflicate" the Boers in South Africa. These two panels opened the story on the cover of *Illustrated Chips* for 23 December 1899. Tom Browne's lively clarity set the style of British humour comics for the new century.

RIGHT: From 1904 to his death in 1962, Donald McGill produced 12,000 designs for postcards, whose sauciness he varied according to a private scale from "mild" or "medium" to "strong". The strong ones sold best. His caption here reads: "I think I shall click, if I stick it out a few days more." In 1906 McGill tried telling a story in a series of six postcards, but his idea did not catch on.

BELOW: Among the tangled web of families in Posy Simmonds' *Guardian* newspaper strip *The Silent Three* are the Webers, headed by moustached Liberal Studies lecturer George and children's book writer Wendy, the couple in glasses, with their six children and one cat.

Orwell would not have appreciated the custom in comics of endless rivalries between the classes, kept up by the likes of The Toffs and the Toughs, Swots and Blots, Snobs and Scruffs, Upper Crusts and Lazy Loafers, or schoolkids Ivor Lott and Tony Broke and Milly O'Naire and Penny Less, which tended to show the poor usually coming out on top over the rich. Orwell's concerns, however, suggest that readers of such comics are easily indoctrinated, their minds empty vessels waiting to be filled. Today it is a different story. Contemporary media researcher Martin Barker argues persuasively that a comic can offer multiple messages and each reader can enter into a dialogue with them, comparing and questioning how they relate to their own experiences.

Class-consciousness, however it is learnt, remains fundamental to British people and to many of the comics they read in which they themselves appear. So, expensive, well-printed, educational comics such as *Eagle*

(1950–69) or *Look and Learn* (1962–82) were clearly aimed at the kids, and at the parents who bought them, from the middle classes. Most of the comical weeklies, however, for a long time lower in price and print quality, mostly centred around concerns of their principal target readership, the working class. Through all kinds of signals, the characters in many of the comics, both old and contemporary, featured in this book, convey assumptions about which rung they occupy on the social ladder, from Lord Snooty "slumming it" with his poor pals to Dan Dare and Digby's officer-and-batman working relationship.

In modern newspapers too, each daily caters to its own through the strips it prints inside, so that in many ways "you are what you read". Posy Simmonds' Weber family supply acute portrayals of a good proportion of the *Guardian*'s liberal-minded, professional readership, while liberated George and Lynne's innuendos and sex drives in the *Sun* tap into the populist taste for the brand of saucy humour used in *Carry On* films and Donald McGill's postcards. At its peak, the milder, middle-class *Daily Express* enjoyed broad appeal by running both Giles' topical single-panel cartoons of his down-to-earth family, headed by the formidable Grandma, and strips of chirpy

20

1932   1949   1960   1982   1997   2005

newly-weds The Gambols. Teenage school-leavers thrust onto the job market and stuck working in supermarkets responded in their droves in 1982 to the novel soap opera of *Checkout Girl* in the *Daily Star*. Scriptwriter Les Lilley found that "each letter contains the same claim, that we accurately depict the type of life being lived in Belfast, Liverpool, Manchester or London, comments that have led me to believe that most people, no matter where they come from, are obsessed with the same small worries".

Few readers of the left-leaning *Daily Mirror* would admit to recognising themselves in the work-shy, football-loving boozer Andy Capp, but a few might admit to knowing someone like him. His creator, Reg Smythe in Hartlepool, certainly did, as he based Andy partly on a recognisable but exaggerated version of his working-class father, a good footballer who wore a cap at all times. Smythe's mother Florrie was the exact model for Andy's long-suffering wife Flo. In one strip, when a census gatherer asked Flo how many children she had, she replied, "Just the one." This is an insight into why Flo has thrown Andy out on several occasions, only to take him back in. Smythe says, "There is a very special relationship that grows between a childless couple. The man will come to represent the child and, in some strange way, the woman becomes his mother. I started to draw [Florrie] in a more buxom and motherly way, I also made Andy a little smaller. It works more easily for me when the pair look like mother and child." What began in 1958 as single-panel gags intended purely for local readers of the *Mirror*'s northern editions transformed into a strip only when it had to be syndicated in American papers. Who would have thought that such typical "Geordie" humour from the northeast of England would go on to make the whole world laugh?

By the late 1960s and the rise of the counterculture and women's, gay and lesbian liberation, Andy Capp's attitudes were looking very old-fashioned and, to many, chauvinistic. Alternative values and lifestyles needed alternative outlets in which to get an airing and found them in the British underground press. Almost a precursor to these adults-only "comix" was the scandal-mongering *Private Eye* in 1961, though its stance was anti-establishment for the sake of it, with no sympathy with any pro-drugs, "free love" or other alternative agendas. In the *Eye*'s short, sharp single-gag strips, any type is still fair game, whether crooked *Directors*, wafer-thin *Supermodels* or vain *YBAs* (Young British Artists).

In a far more scatological lineage going back at least to cartoonist James Gillray's savage eighteenth-century prints came Newcastle's rude, crude, punk-inspired rag *Viz* in 1979, another product of northeast humour. During Chris Donald's twenty-year editorship, a high turnover of over 500 characters and, from 1985 to 2002, only six issues per year have kept the dense, detailed whole-page skits in *Viz* alert to Britain's ever-changing types and tribes. From Ally Sloper to today's loutish "chavs" in Tony Husband's *Yobs* in *Private Eye* or the crumbling gentry in Annie Tempest's *Tottering-by-Gently* for *Country Life*, cartoonists are among our keenest social observers, incisive and only as offensive as Britain's eternally classifying society they witheringly record. A topsy-turvy 2006 poll revealing middle class builders and working class bank managers only shows how important it still is to "know your place".

ABOVE: On the front cover of this 32nd *Giles Cartoons* collection from 1978, Giles' Grandma, seated far right in the earmuffs, passes a pound note to her grandchildren for sabotaging a dreaded recital. Only by turning to the back cover do we see what some characters have already spotted through the window: the stolen violin dangling from a telephone pole.

BELOW: Over-the-top, overweight and oversexed, Sandra and Tracey are the controversial *Fat Slags*, first devised by Graham Dury and Simon Thorp for *Viz* 36 in 1989. Their outrageous exploits divided public opinion and boosted sales of *Viz* to over a million copies.

SLOPER A MAN SANDWICH

The sandwich trade has its bright sides, particularly when such a pretty idea as this is adopted.

This was an enormous idea of ALLY's.

Only, when the candle burnt down in its socket * * *!

This isn't a nice situation when somebody is calling "Mad Bull!" at the other end of the lane.

And it's not always pleasant to have to walk on the Embankment on a windy day.

Generally speaking, an advertiser likes his boards shown the right way up.

After all, then, it would appear that ALLY's umbrella was not made to open, or else, why didn't he use it?

This is the advertiser who searched in vain for ALLY and his boards.

At last he found the boards with their faces to the wall.

And when he found ALLY, goodness knows what happened!

They say that ALLY retired from business, after cooking his supper with the timber.

ABOVE: Marie Duval was the *nom de plume* of Emilie de Tessier, French wife of writer Charles Ross. She drew their original version of Ally Sloper in *Judy* magazine in a consciously naive style. This tale follows the character's inevitable failure working as an advertising sandwich-board man.

22

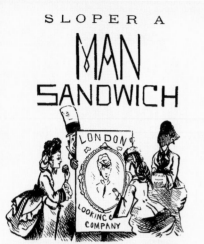

ABOVE: Ally Sloper was partly inspired by Charles Dickens' Mr Micawber from *David Copperfield* in 1850, drawn by Hablot "Phiz" Browne and played by American comedian W.C. Fields in the 1935 film. It seems Fields aspired to be a cartoonist in the early 1900s when he toured widely in Europe, so Ally Sloper may well have inspired his act.

THE CATTLE SHOW.

The EMINENT'S REDISTRIBUTION BILL, *introduced in the Agricultural Hall with the sole object of advertising* "ALLY SLOPER'S CHRISTMAS HOLIDAYS," *ready December 16th. Sixteen Pages and a Special Plate. Price Twopence.*

ABOVE: Ally Sloper was reinvented as a far more respectable gent in his own weekly, *Ally Sloper's Half-Holiday*. Here he meets King Edward VII himself, at the Agricultural Hall, while shamelessly advertising his periodical.

Another fat and thin comedy duo like Weary Willie and Tired Tim were "saucy salts" Pitch and Toss, who sailed into disaster in *Funny Wonder* from 1922 to 1944. Out of cash to pay for his ship's anchor, Captain Codseye has to pawn poor Pengy the Penguin. But his two seamen save the day when they haul up Occy the Octopussie and get the public to pay to watch him perform his eight-legged jigs. It all ends happily with a big slap-up feed. Roy Wilson drew this for the 21 August 1937 issue.

LEFT: This down-and-out goes up-and-away in his one-man mini-plane *The Flying Flea*. In this wartime romp drawn by John Jukes for 7 April 1940, Alfie the Air Tramp "digs for Victory" and grows a giant marrow on board that he slices in half to change his vehicle into a seaplane. Notice his dog Wagger has a fan tied to his tail to help with steering. And in the tradition of the slap-up feed at the end, Alfie concludes, "Nothing suits me better than a bit of grub when I come to picture twelve each week." In 1940, after ten years on *The Joker*, Alfie flew off into *Chips* till 1952.

ABOVE: Bathing beauties enjoy the "What The Butler Saw" picture peep shows (or mutoscopes) on the pier at Llandudno, North Wales on 27 June 1935.

RIGHT: G.M. Payne's bow-tied Portland Bill (a pun on the Dorset island prison) was an ex-convict always looking for work on the front cover of *The Butterfly* from 1907. A decade later, in a bid to clean up the comics, he was renamed *Butterfly Bill* and his criminal record erased. In these six final panels from 28 October 1922, he narrates how he gives two lazy loungers their comeuppance for cheating him out of a wealthy toff's two-shilling tip. Finding them in the free public library, Bill is forced to leave, but with the help of comedians the Brothers Patter and a gramophone record of their "Paviseum" double-act (a reference to the Palaseum Theatre), Bill gets the rascals ejected. The artist has not been identified.

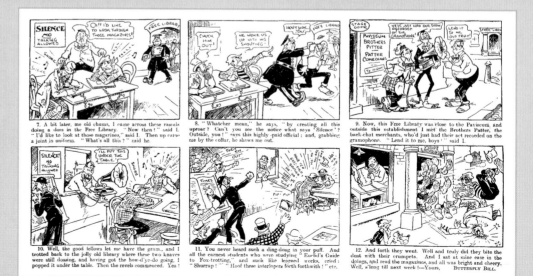

Summer is here at the seaside resort of Pebblesea and Constable Cuddlecook is called in to find the thief breaking into the penny amusement machines on the pier. Judging on appearances, the PC spots the culprit with a tin-opener. Cuddlecook was on the beat from 1909 to 1940 in *The Jester* with "terrier 'tec" Bobbie with a little policeman's helmet on his head and a truncheon tied to his tail. Don Newhouse drew the first 11 panels and Bertie Brown the 12th for the 28 July 1928 issue.

LEFT: An admirer of Caran d'Ache, French master of the wordless comic strip, Henry Mayo Bateman excelled at this himself in *Punch* with a forte for depicting the shocking social blunder. In this 1920 strip *Familiarity Breeds Contempt*, facial expressions and body language convey a first conversation between a moustached, cigar-smoking toff and a just-introduced commoner, whose outbursts cross the line of polite behaviour.

RIGHT: William Heath Robinson's cartooning specialised in over-complicated contraptions that perform simple, often silly tasks. In this case, in a strip dating from 1922, he devises a machine for tailors to measure up a client for a new suit.

RIGHT: Following in the Bateman "pantomime" vogue, David Langdon in *Punch* shows a salesman's unsuccessful attempt to woo a housewife into buying a vacuum-cleaner, something every home would soon have. From his 1952 collection *Look At You*.

FAR RIGHT: The modernist style adopted in the 1950s transformed urban dwellings and saw the rise and rise of large blocks of flats. In a page called *Living Room*, Fougasse, the pen-name of Kenneth Bird, points out the contrast between their cavernous entrance lobbies and the cramped passenger lift and flats themselves. Drawn for *Punch*, this appeared in the 1958 collection *Between the Lines* and shows Fougasse paring his own lines down to their sophisticated essence.

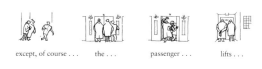

LIVING ROOM

At the vast new Minkhampton House . . .

everything's large and lavish . . .

except, of course . . .   the . . .   passenger . . .   lifts . . .

and also . . .   the . . .   flats . . .   themselves.

DOMESTIC ECONOMY

SOMEONE SENT THE JONESES AN AWFULLY JOLLY LITTLE CUSHION FOR THEIR DRAWING-ROOM AS A CHRISTMAS PRESENT

IT MADE THE OLD CHINTZ LOOK VERY DULL, OF COURSE, BUT THAT WAS SOON REMEDIED.

THE OLD CURTAINS CERTAINLY SEEMED TO PUT THE SCHEME OUT RATHER, BUT NEW ONES PULLED THE ROOM TOGETHER WONDERFULLY.

IT WAS GREAT FUN GETTING A NEW CARPET, MORE IN KEEPING WITH THE CHARACTER OF THE ROOM.

CHOOSING A NEW WALL-PAPER TO CARRY OUT THE MOTIF WAS ALSO VERY EXCITING. AND NOW THAT THEY'VE REMOVED A

CUSHION (WHICH DIDN'T HARMONISE VERY WELL) THEY'VE REALLY GOT A MOST CHEERY LITTLE ROOM.

Long before make-over television programmes, one modernist cushion leads to a total transformation of this comfortable couple's decor.
Fougasse drew this one-off strip for *Punch* and it was compiled into the hardback *P.T.O.* in 1926.

TOP RIGHT: Featuring in a daily strip of the same name, Pop debuted in the *Daily Sketch* in 1921. He lost his glasses, moustache and finally his mouth (except when he shouts) to became the practically bald, portly upper-class paterfamilias loved by the public and King George himself. Cartoonist John Millar Watt soon arrived at unique refinements in his techniques, avoiding outlined speech balloons and carefully timing his jokes. He was perhaps the first to unfold his gags in adjacent pairs of panels or "panning" across four as one continuous scene, as in this hand-coloured print from 1921.

BELOW RIGHT: Watt drew *Pop* for over 25 years, and these 1930s examples reveal Pop's posh circles, overhearing the maids after a grand dinner party and escaping a night at the theatre.

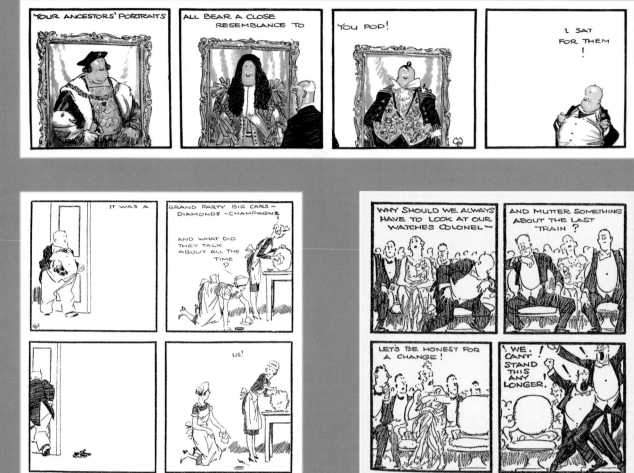

ABOVE: Other more grotesque upper-class types filled Bernard Graddon's madcap *Just Jake* strip for the *Daily Mirror* from 1938 to 1952, which began as a British answer to Al Capp's hillbilly *L'il Abner*. Like comedy cad Terry-Thomas, Captain Reilly-Ffoull was the ineffectual tyrant at the stately pile of Arntwee Hall, which was riddled with secret passages and skeletons in the closet.

It's 1950 and Hogmanay, Scotland's celebration of New Year's Eve. It's also "Gran'paw" Broon's 80th birthday, so he has two reasons to drop in on friends for a drink. Worse for wear, Gran'paw uses lampposts to help him walk straight, unaware that they have been skewed by passing buses, and gets spooked when he thinks he sees a midget policeman. A power cut strikes on his arrival at The Broons' Glebe Street tenement, but his 80 birthday-cake candles save the day in this Dudley Watkins gem.

29

RIGHT: Graham Laidler, famed as the *Punch* and *British Character* cartoonist Pont, began his career while still a student on the rather twee *Twiff Family* strip in the weekly *Woman's Pictorial* from 1930 to 1937. In this example from 8 February 1936, the couple rush to get to a party, only to arrive unfashionably early. Pont died tragically young from polio aged 32 in 1940.

RIGHT: Inspired by Sidney Smith's phenomenally popular American strip *The Gumps*, Steve Dowling and his writer and brother Fred cooked up the long-running *Mirror* comedy strip *The Ruggles* in 1935 and it ran till 1957. Here, Gladys comes to agree with hubby John about trying to get rid of an aunt who is outstaying her welcome, when she blocks everyone's view of the live BBC TV broadcast of the 1953 Coronation. This was written by Ian Gammidge.

30

RIGHT: Gammidge also wrote *The Flutters*, all about a family who were always ready for a "flutter" or gamble, whether losing money at the races with lodger Bert Cert or entering a cheese contest in this glimpse from 1950. They were right at home on the sports page on the *Daily Mirror*'s back cover from 1947 to 1971. And, would you believe it, the artist on this strip was named Len Gamblin and it was not a pseudonym!

RIGHT: Meet George and Gaye Gambol, named because like *The Flutters* they enjoyed a gamble. In *The Gambols* the couple soon settled down to married life. Cartoonist Barry Appleby and his wife Dobs (Doris) produced the feature for the *Daily Express* for 46 years, first as a single panel in 1950, then as a strip from 1951. This gag from the sixth paperback compilation in 1957 combines George's home-movie hobby with Gaye's fashion-victim anxieties.

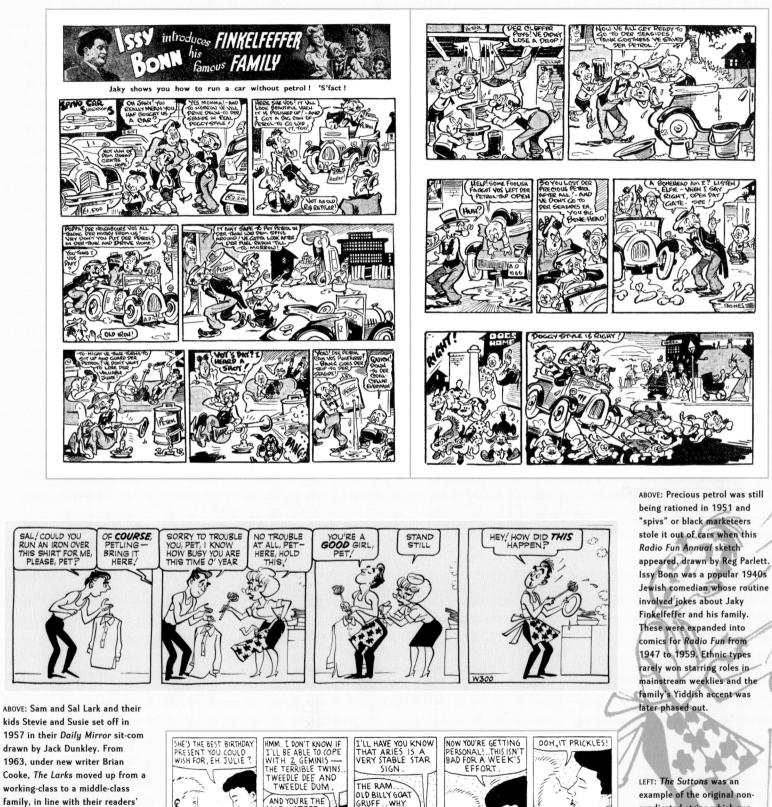

31

ABOVE: Precious petrol was still being rationed in 1951 and "spivs" or black marketeers stole it out of cars when this *Radio Fun Annual* sketch appeared, drawn by Reg Parlett. Issy Bonn was a popular 1940s Jewish comedian whose routine involved jokes about Jaky Finkelfeffer and his family. These were expanded into comics for *Radio Fun* from 1947 to 1959. Ethnic types rarely won starring roles in mainstream weeklies and the family's Yiddish accent was later phased out.

ABOVE: Sam and Sal Lark and their kids Stevie and Susie set off in 1957 in their *Daily Mirror* sit-com drawn by Jack Dunkley. From 1963, under new writer Brian Cooke, *The Larks* moved up from a working-class to a middle-class family, in line with their readers' aspirations, here taking the battle of the sexes into the kitchen. The family's stories ended in 1985.

LEFT: *The Suttons* was an example of the original non-syndicated strips which run only in a local paper, in this case the weekly *Maidstone Star* from 1985 to 1991. It was a warm, whimsical portrait based on the artist Phil Elliott's family life, here marking the arrival of their daughter.

ABOVE LEFT: In his 1998 graphic novel *Ethel & Ernest* Raymond Briggs tells the biography of his parents through nearly a century of social and technological upheaval. It's washing day, usually a Monday, and proper and extremely class-conscious Ethel thinks the newfangled invention of television "might be all right for the gentry" while she slaves over the laundry in the scullery with a mangle and a gas copper to boil the sheets.

ABOVE RIGHT: When young Raymond joins the Army, Ethel wants her son to be an officer, but he knows that as a "grammar school oik" he stands little chance of promotion.

ABOVE: The evolution of Andy and Florrie Capp's relationship is clear from these two strips by Reg Smythe in the *Daily Mirror*, from its early years when it was still in the rectangular two-by-two format. In the earlier example c. 1958 on the left, Andy is about the same height as Florrie, while in the slightly later strip on the right Andy has grown shorter and behaves more like Florrie's naughty, work-shy son than her grown husband.

LEFT: Pretty blonde dreamer Dot and plain, practical Carrie took their names from the shorthand typist's phrase to "dot and carry on" and their office-based comedy was inspired by the American working-girl strip *Somebody's Stenog* (short for stenographer) by A.E. Hayward. James Francis Horabin was hired to create them for London evening paper the *Star* in 1922 and drew the pair's run-ins with their tetchy boss Mr Spilliken for nearly 40 years until his death in 1962.

LEFT: Bristow was the old-fashioned office man in bowler hat and pin-striped suit, a fixture in the London *Evening Standard* for 35 years. Unlike his desk-bound character, Frank Dickens could rustle up five strips in an hour or two in his informal style and spend the rest of the week as he pleased.

LEFT: Alex is the swinish city banker co-created by writer Russell Taylor and artist Charles Peattie, initially in 1983 for the *Independent*'s financial pages before being headhunted by the *Telegraph*. Alex's road has been a bit bumpy over the years, here coping in his usual boorish way with the aftermath of a little fling with his secretary Wendy in the 1993 collection, *Alex Calls the Shots*.

LEFT: *Marlon du Bois: The New Black Man* by Gary Coley appeared in the mid-1990s in the *Weekly Journal* newspaper in response to "buppies", or black yuppies. In this example from a 1995 collection, Marlon and his hip brother experience some institutional racism when they attend the Wimbledon Tennis Championships.

34

ABOVE: Like a British *Beverly Hillbillies*, *The Bumpkin Billionaires* were simple country yokels who won a huge fortune on the football pools. Here, finding the mansion they have bought is too huge for their needs, they will pay anything for a cosier place. These pages from *Whoopee!*, 31 August 1974, were drawn by Mike Lacey. Their money worries lasted from 1974 till 1991.

CENTRE: Set in the county of Whimshire, *Colonel Pewter* by Arthur Horner began in the *News Chronicle* in 1956 and continued in the *Guardian* until 1970. In 1967 Pewter persuaded Lord and Lady Terminus to add a visitor attraction to help pay their bills.

RIGHT: In 1971, *The Fosdyke Saga* took its name from *The Forsyte Saga*, John Galsworthy's trilogy adapted on TV at the time. For fifteen years in the *Daily Mirror*, Bill Tidy transposed its affluent middle-class genealogy to the Lancashire mining town of Griddlesbury and the penniless, banished Josiah Fosdyke, whose luck improves in Manchester.

LEFT: In 1972, after four years of communal living, Clifford Harper began *Class War Comix*, a projected six-part graphic novel about how an anarchic, alternative society might develop that rejects capitalist relationships. Left unfinished, only the first part was published in 1974 and reissued in the USA in 1979. Here, despite their self-sufficiency, some communards find the "acorn brew" a poor substitute for coffee.

BELOW: In *Alice's Alternative Adventures with ATman* by Jo Nesbitt, a housewife saved from her domestic prison finds her lot is no better in an alternative squat, in the feminist anthology *Sour Cream* in 1980.

RIGHT: Like some seedy, greedy Groucho Marx, Mr White easily fobs off one of his disgruntled workers, Hose, when he asks him for a raise. Captain Stelling, alias Mike Weller, created *The Firm* for the third solo special issue of *Oz* magazine's *cOZmic Comics* in 1972. The following year, Britain would be brought almost to a standstill by union strikes and the three-day week.

RIGHT: Rampant property speculation and unscrupulous local authorities and developers went largely unchecked under Margaret Thatcher's government. In *Downside*, Hackney-based writer Dave McNamara and artist Peter Ketley imagined the inner-city devastation this policy might lead to and showed how one group of activists, single mothers, punks, lesbians and others defend their homes and community. This was self-published from 1989 and compiled into a graphic novel in 1993.

ABOVE: "It occurred to me that the cartoon form had the potential for something wider-ranging than the three patterns in current usage: the political cartoon, the single joke, the strip cartoon." One-of-a-kind John Glashan composed all sorts of new patterns for *Genius* every week in *The Observer Magazine* from 1978 to 1983, watercolouring frameless landscapes and architecture which dwarfed his sketchy miniature figures. Here, wealthy Lord Doberman has hired bearded genius Anode Enzyme (IQ 12,794) to build a mad TV-projecting apparatus.

RIGHT: From 1977 until 1987 on the weekly women's page of the *Guardian*, Posy Simmonds would elegantly skewer the chattering professional classes. In this example from 1986, a discussion by George Weber with two priggish American visitors about the British taste for "dirdy yumor" descends into a free-for-all on different classes' terms for "toilet".

ABOVE: In a departure from his usual highly finished heroics, Brian Bolland adopted a looser style for *Mr Mamoulian*, starting in *Escape* in 1987 and continuing intermittently in *Negative Burn*. Here, nothing can stop the steamy hype of fashion ads rattling through his repressed misfit's head.

ABOVE: *The Greens* in *Electric Soup* was Frank Quitely's affectionate spoof of *The Broons*. Here Paw Green learns from the twins' report-card of their poor performance in school, which the teacher blames on "behaviour problems" in the home. Furious, Paw Green gets a bad court report, too.

ABOVE: The Fat Slags will stoop to anything to grab a bargain mink coat in the sale, from sleeping overnight and shagging outside the department store to assaulting a granny and shoplifting the fur, in this riot from *Viz 94*, February 1999, by Graham Drury, Simon Thorp and Chris and Simon Donald. Drury dropped the duo after the universally slated live-action film in 2004, but more recently they have stormed back into the pages of *Viz* once more.

BELOW: Also from *Viz*, John Fardell's brilliant satire *The Modern Parents* began in 1991 and still appears. Here they meddle in their young son Tarquin's simple friendship with a girl.

RIGHT: In *The Adventures of Barry McKenzie*, Barry or "Bazza" embodied the worst prejudices of the "Poms" or British in the 1960s towards expatriate Australians. As one himself, these attitudes were all too familiar to writer and actor Barry Humphries, who pushed the boundaries of taste in *Private Eye* from 1964 with cartoonist Nicholas Garland. With his Desperate Dan chin, Barry McKenzie lived mainly for the simple pleasures of urination, inebriation and copulation, for which Humphries coined memorably colourful slang terms. Humphries is famed for playing Dame Edna Everage, including an appearance as McKenzie's aunt in the 1972 film of the strip. Humphries and Garland finally went too far by adding nudity and lesbians and the strip was axed in 1974.

RIGHT: Recycling "found" comics and commercial illustrations of the past, Chris Garratt and Mick Kidd give them a novel and often ironic sting. Their cut-ups appeared in alternative 1970s magazines before they turned them into badges, postcards, T-shirts and more and sold them at London's Camden Market. They worked under the name Biff, short for Biffo, which was Mick's nickname because he looked, dressed and danced like *The Beano*'s famous bear. From 1985 to 2005, they were published in the *Guardian*. This 1987 example splices girls' comics, romance art and adverts to skewer the "Opportunity 2000" goal to improve women's equality.

ABOVE: Since 1972, Paul Sample's *Ogri* has summed up the call of the open road and biker lifestyle in *Bike* magazine.

LEFT: In her weekly *Millennium Basin* strip in the *Guardian* from 1994 to 1996, Kate Charlesworth developed an eclectic, engaging ensemble of late twentieth-century urban types. Among them were her "truly ghastly" couple Sushi and Filo Feisty and her regular star, Clarrie the dog. This episode about Sushi's search for an approved child substitute shows off Charlesworth's sparkling repartee and surprise twists.

BELOW LEFT: Created in 2000 by Andi Watson, the graphic novel *Breakfast After Noon* reflects the 1990s decline in the pottery industries where he lives in the Midlands. Here, unemployment puts extra strains on Rob and Louise, a young, soon-to-be-married couple, as Louise discloses to her wedding-dress maker.

ABOVE AND LEFT: A father, who is a spin doctor for a London mayor, falls out with his politicised teenage daughter over the arrival, literally in their back yard, of gypsy travellers and their caravans in *The Birthday Riots*, a graphic novel from 2001 by Nabiel Kanan.

BELOW: Raconteur and romantic Eddie Campbell recalls his circle of pub-going mates and his first insecure forays into dating via his alter ego *Alec*, serialised from 1984 by *Escape*. Here he has to keep a low profile at The King Canute Pub while his new lady friend Penny deals with another admirer. Alec can't help wondering if he can compete with him, as well as her estranged husband.

RIGHT: Among several strips in the gay press, *Dick* by Ilya showed a range of ages and relationships. Here, our innocent hunk, the aptly named Dick Coxwell, is invited to dinner with a mature gay couple. Laced with frissons and double entendres, this instalment ran on 8 September 2001 in *Boyz*.

ABOVE: It's 1973, "clackers" are all the rage and Miss Buchanan is trying her best to make a fresh start teaching in a new district at the Catholic Our Lady of Fatima school. Under pressure, both from strict Sister Scholastica and from being stalked by religious motorcyclist Brendan Cass, she confides in her hairdresser at Curly Birds. John Bagnall recreates the atmosphere, setting and turns of phrase in this slice of the past entitled *Our Lady of the Tower Block*, one of several short stories in his 2003 collection *Don't Tread on My Rosaries*.

ABOVE: In 1990, with one in three marriages ending in divorce, Carol Swain captured one divorcée's conflicting feelings on a kids' trip to the zoo with her prospective new man, portrayed as being almost predatory, like the shark in a tank behind them. Suppressed emotions seethe in Swain's charcoal drawings for her contribution to the anthology *Seven Ages of Woman*.

ABOVE: The violent original story of *Mr Punch* acquires deeper significance to a young boy as he uncovers his family's secrets in Neil Gaiman and Dave McKean's 1994 graphic novel. The term "bottler" here refers to a young lad employed by the puppeteer to get the audience to join in.

RIGHT: Contrasting types currently being skewered in *Private Eye* include Tony Husband's anti-social *Yobs* and Knife and Packer's trendy urbanites in *It's Grim Up North London*.

FAR RIGHT: In his 2006 graphic novel *Little Star*, Andi Watson uses his own experience to express with candour the pressures and pleasures of being a young modern father.

Spitting Images

"DEAR SIRS, NO IT ISN'T A BIT—NOT THE LEAST LITTLE BIT LIKE ME. SO JOLLY WELL STOW IT! SEE! CHARLES. P." THIS UNUSUAL LETTER OF COMPLAINT FROM A READER IN LONDON ARRIVED IN THE New York offices of the satirical comic magazine *Mad* in 1958. It was written by hand on triple-cream laid paper with a copper engraving of the Duke of Edinburgh's crest and the simple address: Buckingham Palace. Franked at a post office near the Palace, this looked for all the world like a letter from Charles. P., for *Princeps*, or Prince Charles himself. Ten at the time, he could well have taken exception to his photo being printed in *Mad* 48 next to a reader's remark on his resemblance to *Mad*'s inane, big-eared mascot, the "What, me worry?" kid Alfred E. Neuman. Instead of "stowing it", *Mad* poked fun some more by having Wally Wood draw the Prince's photo into a feature by Frank Jacobs, *Comic Strip Heroes (Taken from Real Life)*. In their four-panel *Bringing Up Bonnie Prince Charlie*, a parody of *Bringing Up Father* and *Mary Worth*, Charles complains, "Why can't I go out with ordinary boys and have fun for once in a while!", to which the Queen replies, "Hold your tongue, Charlie! You're beginning to sound like your father!" There it might have ended, if this skit had not so infuriated one loyal Canadian subject, that he sent it to the British newspaper, the *Sunday Pictorial*, who plastered it across their front page of 31 May 1959 stating, "Thousands may laugh at this, but we call it—A Stupid Insult."

Goodness knows what they would think of the caricatures of the Royal family soon to follow, as the tradition of scurrilous satire, previously well established in cartoons and comics, returned during the next decade. Today, surrounded by our anything-goes media of trashy tabloids, gossip magazines and degrading "reality" TV shows, celebrity-obsessed Britons can forget how much respect the monarchy and other authority figures once commanded. True, that respect might have been built on fear, wealth and repression, but by 1780 and the dawn of Britain's Golden Age of Caricature, no royal, political or social scandal could escape the cartoonist's pen; not only was it mightier than the sword but sometimes deadlier. In 1821, after three years of being humiliated in George Cruikshank's cartoons, King George IV offered him a substantial £100 bribe to "show him no more in immoral situations". For a while Cruikshank complied, but it was not long before he was back on the attack, much to the British public's delight.

There is a direct line of descent from the contorted caricatures and unbridled farting and scatology in the work of James Gillray (1756–1815) and his peers, to those of Gerald Scarfe and Ralph Steadman, who first cut loose in *Private Eye* from 1961 and paved the way for newspaper cartoonists like Steve Bell, Martin Rowson and Peter Brookes, as well as Peter Fluck and Roger Law's *Spitting Image* puppets on television.

RIGHT: James Gillray caricatures British prime minister William Pitt and France's emperor Napoleon carving up the globe in this 1805 coloured etching of *The Plum Pudding in Danger*.

BELOW: A female pot-washer climbs the ladder to celebrity in William Heath's *The Life of an Actress* in *The Northern Looking Glass*, 11 November 1825.

OPPOSITE: Big-hearted Arthur Askey steps up to the large microphone to introduce his wireless co-stars on the cover of the 1943 *Radio Fun Annual* illustrated by Alexander Akerbladh.

42

ABOVE: The first halfpenny issue of *Dan Leno's Comic Journal* from 26 February 1898, drawn by Tom Browne, is a milestone as it shows the first real-life comedian (see photo, top right) to star in his very own comic. The cover shows him in the editor's office, his rings sparkling, smoking a cigar, with a wastepaper basket full of "old chestnuts" and a trunk of new jokes.

Topical satire and caricature also came to flourish in comic form in adults-only features such as *Penthouse*'s racy *Oh Wicked Wanda*, and in national newspaper strips such as Peter Maddocks' *No. 10* in the *Sunday Express* and Bell's daily *If...* serial for the left-wing *Guardian*. Many comic creators found a still stronger, clearer voice during Margaret Thatcher's years in office from 1979 and were some of her most outspoken critics within the often complacent mass media. The *Sun* on 19 March 1990 reported, "'Death to Maggie' book sparks Tory uproar." In fact, the "book" was the comic *St Swithin's Day*, based on author Grant Morrison's teen diaries, in which he explored one angry, alienated boy's fantasy of assassinating the prime minister. In reality, all the boy does is get close enough to point his accusing finger at her, but that act of defiance was enough to alarm Conservative Party officials, especially after the Brighton Conference bombing of 12 October 1984.

One sign of a nation's freedom of expression, or to some its moral decadence, may be that its cartoonists go unpunished for criticising those in authority. In some countries, they still risk prison, execution or assassination. In Britain, the risk that cartoonists might be convicted of libel by an offended public figure arose in 2000. Steve Bell was sued for £200,000 by Christian millionaire business-man Brian Souter, who was backing a campaign to keep Section 28 to regulate any references to homosexuality in Scottish schools, and whom Bell had caricatured in his *If...* strip. If Souter won, the cartoon profession was concerned it could severely inhibit their freedom. The offending *sub-judice* strips had to be blacked out when they were compiled into a book. Finally, in 2002, Souter withdrew his lawsuit and had to pay all costs. The freedom to vent, mock and cajole is vital. In 2003, the crude, childish scrawl and bad spelling in *Tony and Me by Georg* [sic] *Bush* purported to come from a disturbingly deranged President's art-therapy sessions. More extreme pages in "Dr" James Parsons' sequel *This is War* had to be censored, though some saw print regardless in the anthology *Sturgeon White Moss* (2003). The need for cartoonists to deal with the sensitivities and taboos heightened after September 11, the Iraq War and the 2006

| 1941 | 1955 | 1963 | 1978 | 1986 | 2003 |

furore about Danish cartoons depicting the Prophet Muhammad should be balanced with their responsibility as the court jester to get away with speaking many a truth in jest that others dare not say.

Away from the spheres of royalty and political spin, a parade of names and faces from history, art, sport and especially entertainment—movie, radio and television stars, comedians, pop idols and all manner of celebs—have cavorted through comics. Such is the fleeting fickleness of fame that some are quickly forgotten, while others endure as cultural icons. Some stars make one-off promotional appearances, such as Geri Halliwell meeting her heroine Minnie the Minx or Tina Turner teaming up with Garth. Instead of just their songs inspiring stories, some pop stars got personally embroiled in unexpected exploits, from Tommy Steele's match-making to Adam Ant's travels in time. Biographies were usually flattering, whether in *Eagle*'s and *Girl*'s exemplars, *Valentine*'s true confessions of how star couples met and married, or *Look-in*'s well-researched, photo-referenced pop-idol documentaries.

The first real-life celebrity to star in his own comic was Dan Leno in 1898, who was phenomenally popular in his day. This also happened in reverse, with acts from the comics being brought to life on the stage. In 1906, the Casey Court gang in *Illustrated Chips* toured the vaudeville circuit and their leader Billy Baggs was played by a young Charlie Chaplin. When his film career took off, he became the exclusive cover attraction on *The Funny Wonder* from 1915. Tastes were changing and despite the appeal of adapting music-hall turns like George Robey and Nellie Wallace into strips for *Merry and Bright*, its young editor Frederick Cordwell could not ignore how the cinemas were stealing away the mostly working-class music-hall audience. In January 1920 Cordwell conceived *Film Fun,* the first weekly comic devoted to movie comedies. It was such an instant hit that a companion,

The Kinema Comic, was released only four months later. Both offered adolescent and adult picture-goers the equivalent of a programme of new two-reelers of their favourite stars, most of whom were initially Hollywood's global exports like Laurel and Hardy or Brits working there like Chaplin. These incarnations set firmly in Britain were not always done with the stars' knowledge. *Film Fun* grew into the period's best-selling comic in the British Empire and its formula worked again in *Radio Fun* in 1938 and *TV Fun* in 1953, comics providing a handy way to commune with the stars whenever and wherever you liked before video recorders became available.

Not everyone has been as respectful of celebrities. In strips like *Justin Timberlake Laid My Laminate*, Lucy Sweet lampoons girls' comics' impossible dream dates with pop heart-throbs. Meanwhile, Rob Dunlop, co-creator of *Tozzer*, an uninhibited assault on Hollywood, sees today's stars as "our modern equivalent of aristocracy, in fact they wield more influence. In many people's eyes, they are god-like, untouchable, and it's high time they were brought down a peg or two." Maybe Jamie Hewlett and Damon Albarn have hit on one way to subvert the ego system by manufacturing cartoon band Gorillaz. Technology has let them take on a life of their own, doing real-time interviews and multi-media performances, their histories being written and rewritten in a graphic autobiography. Who needs flesh-and-blood celebrities when you can have wild and woolly virtual ones?

ABOVE: Peter Brookes cleverly mimicked Frank Hampson's characters, Dan Dare and the Mekon, in a weekly full-colour political satire pitting Tony Blair against William Hague and "the Toreens" for *The Times* from September 1997 to January 1999. This is the original artwork for 4 April 1998.

BELOW: Jamie Hewlett and Damon Albarn devised the ultimate collusion and collision between music and comics in cartoon band Gorillaz. Noodle (guitar) sits in front of (LEFT TO RIGHT) Murdoc (bass), Russel (drums) and 2D (vocals).

45

ABOVE: Stan and Ollie again, on the beach and getting the better of some disagreeable types, in this colour page from the 1956 *Film Fun Annual* which reprints and colours an old story by George Wakefield from the *Film Fun* weekly.

ABOVE: Several *Film Fun* artists drew their panels on separate, identically sized pieces of card. These three originals by George Wakefield conclude a fifteen-panel wheeze from 27 September 1941, in which barefoot coppers Laurel and Hardy trick two crooks by leaving their boots sticking out from behind a corner. Within nine months, Wakefield would be dead aged only 54.

RIGHT: Best remembered today for his closing line in the film *Some Like it Hot*—"Nobody's perfect"—the American star Joe E. Brown first appeared in strip form in *Film Fun* in 1933 and lasted twenty years.

LEFT: A one-page Arthur Askey sketch casts him in a western and ends up with him riding a milk cart. The "Chalk and Water Milk Company" is a dig at swindlers who doctored milk supplies. Drawn by Reg Parlett for the 1952 *Radio Fun Annual*.

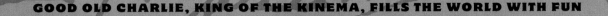

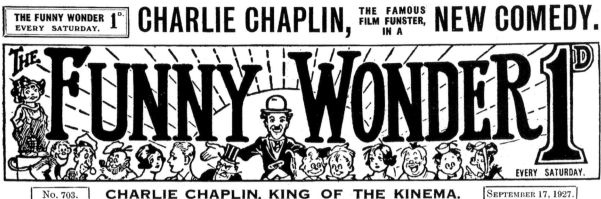

Hold the front page for Charlie Chaplin, appearing here on 17 September 1927 in *The Funny Wonder*, the only British comic to feature his antics. This makes topical references to flappers in Susie Sweetly and the Charleston dance craze. The simple slapstick story is clearly understandable from the pictures and balloons alone, but readers enjoyed Charlie's narration underneath for the extra gags and dialogue. The cartooning here is by Bertie Brown.

ABOVE: Norman Wisdom "serves up double helpings of laughter" as a waiter who impresses his new boss when he apprehends a tricky customer who runs up a huge bill and leaves without paying. This was the opening comic, drawn by Reg Parlett, of the 1956 *Radio Fun Annual*, which spotlighted Norman on the cover.

ABOVE: Hapless, hopeless magician Tommy Cooper appears in the 1959 *Film Fun Annual*. This was recycled from an archive story by the late George Wakefield, originally starring George Formby, by drawing Cooper's head onto Formby's body. Wakefield's son Terry designed the new title.

LEFT AND ABOVE: Larger-than-life wrestler Big Daddy arrives in his own strip and on the cover in *Buster*, 13 February 1982, art by Mike Lacey.

BELOW: Terry-Thomas's gap-toothed grin and cigarette holder feature on the photographic cover of the 1959 *Film Fun Annual*.

In this front-pager from *Film Fun*, 6 July 1957, Terry-Thomas winds up handcuffed to a grand piano, resulting in the sort of visual lunacy only comics could pull off. Terry Wakefield drew this page in four separate strips. The areas shaded in non-reproductive blue pencil showed printers where to add different grey screen tones. Each original used to be stamped with a file number, sometimes within the panels themselves, and usually with a date on the back.

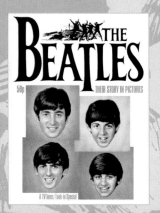

ABOVE: A 1982 compilation of Angus P. Allen and Arthur Ranson's *Look-in* strip biography of The Beatles.

RIGHT: Marty Wilde's hotel bathroom provides the perfect echo chamber in a tale from *Romeo*, 23 January 1960, art by Norman Lee.

BELOW: An early strip appearance, *So You Want To Know Our Story?*, revealed the secrets of The Beatles in *Jackie*, this page from issue 12, March 1964, art by Brian Delaney.

ABOVE: The perfect romance between American hunk Troy Donahue and Lili Kardell hits a rough patch. The secret is out in *Cherie*, 9 March 1963, illustrated by Len Batch.

ABOVE: In *The Vince Eugene Story* in 1973's *Rock'n'Roll Madness* Mick Farren and Dave Gibbons parody an Elvis Presley type who stages a comeback by having his rivals bumped off.

ABOVE: Lou Reed, Alice Cooper, Elton John, David Bowie and Mick Jagger pose on the wraparound cover of *It's Only Rock & Roll Comix* by Joe Petagno, 1975.

BELOW: Taking after his Victorian namesake Adam Adamant, dandy popster Adam Ant plays the eternal hero in his fantastic time-travelling adventures in *Tops*, D.C. Thomson's answer to *Look-In*, 1 October 1981, illustrator unknown.

ABOVE: The Small Faces acquire their keyboard player Ian "Mac" McLagan in their bio-comic drawn by Jim Baikie for *Valentine*, 20 January 1968. Squealing girl groupies don't faze him, as he's used to practising with the noise of planes flying overhead.

ABOVE: *It's Madness* was billed as "An hilarious new picture strip starring the craziest pop group around!" A suitably mad comic by *Mad* artist Harry North for *Look-in*, 12 September 1981.

51

ABOVE: Horatio Nelson's seafaring exploits are recaptured by the bravura brushwork of Eric Parker in this centre spread from *Valiant*, 24 November 1962.

ABOVE: The regular series *Real Life Stories* offered life stories of women in history to inspire readers of *Girl*. In the 14 July 1954 issue, Barbara Wace and Laurence Houghton condense the story of Anna Lenowens, remembered as the governess of the King of Siam in the musical *The King and I*.

RIGHT: General George Custer deals with "the painted demons" besieging Fort Riley in this episode from *Jag*, 24 August 1968. This original art shows off Geoff Campion's skill at drawing men and horses in action.

BELOW: Who better to draw sports comics than *Roy of the Rovers* artist Barrie Mitchell, who drew this compact biography of young British tennis prodigy Andy Murray for *GQ Sport* in 2006.

LEFT: The lives of many historical and biblical figures were chronicled on the back pages of *Eagle*, from Frank Hampson's account of St Paul to his epic swansong for the weekly, the story of Jesus in *The Road of Courage*. Frank Bellamy also painted life stories of King David, Marco Polo, General Montgomery and, most famously, Winston Churchill. This original art from *The Happy Warrior*, written by Clifford Makins, ran on 22 August 1958.

53

RIGHT: The life and works of James Joyce are made accessible in 1994's *Joyce for Beginners* by David Norris and distinctive collagist and caricaturist Carl Flint, part of the successful *Beginners* or *Introducing* educational graphic novels.

LEFT: Adapting the 1885 diaries of Sir Merton and Lady Russell-Cotes' travels in Japan, here recalling a school visit, Shaun Garner and Sean Michael Wilson collaborated with manga artist Sakura Mizuki on *The Japanese Drawing Room* for Bournemouth's Russell-Cotes Art Gallery & Museum in 2006.

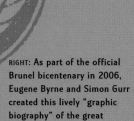

RIGHT: As part of the official Brunel bicentenary in 2006, Eugene Byrne and Simon Gurr created this lively "graphic biography" of the great Victorian engineer.

RIGHT: To compete with *Playboy*'s lavishly painted, soft-porn parody strip *Little Annie Fanny* by Harvey Kurtzman and Will Elder, *Penthouse* magazine transferred Frederic Mullally's *Wanda* text stories, started in September 1969, into the sexy, if not sexist, romp *Oh Wicked Wanda!*, illustrated by Ron Embleton. In this strip, her third story, from November 1973, Wanda von Kreesus lures Governor Reekin and Senator Bedwell Cleverly into compromising positions with Little Annie Un-Funny and Anal-Maria Schmieren on board her private jet.

ABOVE: Edward Heath adorns the cover of Edward Barker's *Edward's Heave* one-man special from 1973.

RIGHT: Steve Bell's *Maggie's Farm* started appearing in London listings magazine *Time Out* in 1979, the year Margaret Thatcher was elected. Here, her lies decimate the fairy population.

BELOW: British editions of the American *Mad* magazine added more home-grown content under editors Dez Skinn and Ron Letchford, like this Harry North cover for the 25th anniversary special in 1984.

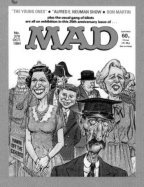

ABOVE: Based on daring model Veruschka, John Kent's pop-art *Varoomshka* exposed flesh and corruption on Mondays in the *Guardian* from 1969 to 1979. Here, in a twist on *The Emperor's New Clothes*, she plays a shivering Britannia, dismissing Harold Wilson but taken in by Edward Heath.

BELOW: Prevented from working by a court injunction slapped on him after trying to free himself from his agent, alternative comedian Alexei Sayle resorts to writing a "soppy and harmless" children's book, which then becomes part of the 1987 graphic novel *Geoffrey the Tube Train and the Fat Comedian*. Here, he has to contend with his housing estate's dehumanising architecture. Art by Oscar Zarate.

ABOVE AND LEFT: The *Spitting Image* TV series released its own *Giant Komic Book* in 1988. This political twist on the 1960s SF film *Fantastic Voyage* sends the miniaturised Jeffrey Archer, Edwina Currie, John Gummer, Cecil Parkinson and an East German agent trapped inside Margaret Thatcher's body to solve "a problem at the seat of power" and unblock "the Prime Ministerial Passage". Art by Harry North.

LEFT: Hot on the heels of his election landslide in 1997, New Labour's leader became the bionic *B.L.A.I.R. 1*, inspired by TV's *Six-Million-Dollar Man* and *2000AD*'s answer *M.A.C.H. 1* by Pat Mills and Enio Legis-amon. Art by S.B. Davis from Prog 1034, 18 March 1997.

FAR LEFT: Grant Morrison and Steve Yeowell courted controversy with their *New Adventures of Hitler* for *Crisis* in 1990. Speculating that the future Führer had visited Liverpool in 1912, they show Adolf having tea with a grotesque version of Britain's national symbol John Bull, from whom he picks up a lot of his ideas. Original blueline colouring by Nick Abadzis and Steve Whitaker.

55

ABOVE AND RIGHT: Queen Elizabeth has abdicated to let Charles succeed her, but now the truth is out: he had an older, black twin brother who was truly next in line but was hidden and raised in secret. Now dead, his son becomes the rightful heir to the throne. *King Leon* is by Peter Milligan and Jamie Hewlett with Jo Flatters, Glyn Dillon and Philip Bond and ran in *A1* in 1992.

FAR RIGHT: Malcolm X's public statements after meeting Mohammed Ali finally lose him his ministerial post for the Nation of Islam in Wayne Massop's biography in *Sphinx* 4, June 1991.

56

LEFT: In his 320-page *Alice in Sunderland*, Bryan Talbot has built a remarkable multi-layered "dream documentary" about history and storytelling centred around the lives and myths of Lewis Carroll and Alice Liddell, the "real" Alice, and their links with Talbot's home city of Sunderland.

ABOVE: After telling the stories of Kurt Cobain and Eminem in graphic novels, Barnaby Legg and Jim McCarthy and illustrator Flameboy turned to the late influential rap/hip-hop artist Tupac Shakur in 2005's *Death Rap*, shown here in a tranquil moment before he was shot on the streets of Los Angeles in 1996.

FAR LEFT: Nobody is spared in *Tozzer*, Rob Dunlop and Peter Lumby's sick, hilarious movie spoof. This page from their 2002 graphic novel *Tozzer and The Invisible Lap Dancers* savages *Harry Potter*, *The Matrix* and *Chucky*.

LEFT: Lucy Sweet updates those fanciful dream dates with pop stars from girls' comics in *Unskinny* and *Whores of Mensa*. In the Laminate Land store, she meets wood-mad Justin Timberlake ("Timber by name, Timber by nature") who offers his "free laying service".

BELOW LEFT: *McFly's Magic Bus!* continues the tradition of boy band comics for girls, this one by Kerry Wilks and Sean Longcroft appearing in the BBC monthly *It's Hot*, in the style of the 1965 *Beatles* TV cartoons.

ABOVE: In his 2003 *Guardian* strips *The Writer at Work*, Tom Gauld shows the banal daily struggle of famous authors, in this case Dylan Thomas, to write.

57

Down on Jollity Farm

"ALL THE LITTLE PIGS, THEY GRUNT AND HOWL, THE CATS MIAOW, THE DOGS BOW-WOW, EVERYBODY MAKES A ROW, DOWN ON JOLLITY FARM." THE PLAYFUL SPIRIT OF MAYHEM when animals run wild fills this 1930s song, *Down on Jollity Farm*, credited to Leslie Sarony and revived in 1967 by The Bonzo Dog Band, who took their name from cartoonist George Studdy's cheerful, cheeky pup. From farmyards and forests to country estates and suburbs, the wonderlands of walking talking animals, often behaving and misbehaving uncannily like us, have been favoured realms of Britain's illustrated literature for children since it fully blossomed in the 19th century. A worried, scurrying white rabbit with jacket and fob-watch leads Alice down a rabbit hole. Another younger rabbit named Peter slips into a tempting, fruit-filled garden. On their first meeting, a friendly mole and a nattily dressed rat take a picnic along the riverbank, while a honey-loving bear and a timid piglet are two new friends made by Christopher Robin. These and other outstanding British illustrated classics are closely related to the early comics involving animals, not only in their similar cosy settings and charming, eccentric characters and themes, but also in the very styles and practitioners of their illustrations.

The fact that Charles Folkard and Mary Tourtel were both accomplished children's book artists certainly helped them to be hired to develop *Teddy Tail* in 1915 and *Rupert* in 1920 respectively, among the first animal strips in British daily newspapers. The close association between more or less fanciful humanised animals and children's fiction also explains why such characters were few and far between among the very human players in Victorian weekly comics aimed at adults and why they only proliferated later in Edwardian weeklies and newspaper strips aimed solely at the young. One exception was *Signor McCoy*, the tales of a tempestuous circus horse and possibly comics' first recurring four-legged performer, created in 1897 for the weekly *Big Budget* by Jack B. Yeats, son of the painter and brother of the famous Irish poet W.B. Yeats.

Another unmistakeable early influence from that year was the work of American cartoonist James Swinnerton, in particular his squat little *Journal Tigers* which he started in 1897 for the *New York Journal*, modelled on the Tammany tiger, symbol of the city's Democratic party. Inspired partly by this and Swinnerton's feline philanderer *Mr Jack* in 1903, Julius Stafford Baker developed the following year a much tamer, very English junior cat, Tiger Tim, leader of a gaggle of mildly mischievous animal pupils at *Mrs Hippo's Kindergarten*. The first in a veritable zoo of comic characters, he began on 16 April 1904 as a sporadic strip for the *Daily Mirror*. By November, Tiger Tim starred in one of the earliest of many free comic supplements for the little ones, *The Playbox*, which came not with a newspaper but with a magazine, initially *Home Chat* and then *The World and*

RIGHT: Chimps enjoy an afternoon tea-party at Regent's Park Zoo, London, in 1929.

BELOW: George Studdy named his loveable dog Bonzo in *The Sketch* on 8 November 1922, adapting him into animated films from 1924 and weekly strips in *Tit-Bits* from 1926, which were syndicated to America. This tin toy dates from circa 1925.

OPPOSITE : Animals in joyful abandon are Roy Wilson's forte, as seen here in his watercolour painting for the frontispiece of the 1956 *Radio Fun Annual* entitled "Hayseed Farm prepare to go on the air!"

BELOW: With his lively loose lines and ear for the showman's banter, cartoonist Jack B. Yeats created *Signor McCoy, The Wonderful Circus Hoss* in 1897. This panel shows a naughty boarding-school boy in a boater giving the horse a trick peppered bun, from *Big Budget* 42, 2 April 1898.

McCOY AND THE SCHOLLARDS.

2. "That very evening at the show, one of them little schollards up and offered McCoy a bun—just when he was a-doing his high jumping act, a-flying over five-barred gates like a hangel (which comes before the clownd and the pig playing football act). Well, the Signor took that bun, and, would yer believe it——

RIGHT: Teddy Tail's nine-panel newspaper strips by Charles Folkard in the *Daily Mail* started being reprinted in books in September 1915. This example dates from 1920.

his Wife. Tim finally earned his stripes on Valentine's Day, 1914, when he was granted the front page in colour on the first issue of children's weekly comic *The Rainbow*. A few months later, Baker was replaced by Herbert Foxwell, who steered the feline tyke and his pals, now known as The Bruin Boys, to even greater success. The series was sold abroad, notably to Italy where Tim's elephant chum Jumbo took the lead and gave his name to the country's first weekly comic in 1932. At home, after *The Rainbow*'s end in 1956, Tiger Tim continued almost unchanged in *Playhour* and *Jack and Jill* until 1985.

By the 1920s, as the British public struggled to return to some sort of normality after the tragedies and traumas of the First World War, many found comfort and escapism in the growing number of newspaper strips for children. In a constant quest to boost circulation, national and provincial newspaper and magazine editors were eager to emulate the successs of the Folkard's smart-minded, smartly dressed, domesticated mouse *Teddy Tail* in the *Daily Mail* and of children's weekly comics like *The Rainbow*. Many added their own junior characters, especially animals, spinning some off into supplements, annuals, merchandise and clubs joined by readers in their thousands. In 1919, the *Daily Mirror* drafted in artist Austin Bowen Payne and writer Bertram Lamb, who was nicknamed "Uncle Dick" in the paper. They devised the eventual menagerie-à-trois of Pip the dog, Squeak the penguin and Wilfred, the bunny they adopted in 1920, whose baby talk

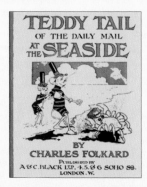

"Gug!" and "Nunc!" inspired the affectionate term for admirers of the strip. On 3 January 1927, the *Mirror* founded a club for them known as The Wilfredian League of Gugnuncs. By April the following year, the W.L.O.G. had enrolled over 340,000 members and, thanks to international editions and syndication, "warrens" and "burrows" of Gugnuncs could be found throughout the world. Uncle Dick explained the meaning of "Gugnuncliness": "A Gugnuncly boy or girl is (1) always cheery, (2) always kind to dumb animals, (3) always willing to help and 'champion' children younger than themselves. In schoolboys' language, Gugnuncliness simply means 'being decent'."

In 1919 in the *Daily News*, a bear called Happy popped up as a minor supporting player and one of the pets living in a post-biblical ark, relocated to Ararat Avenue in a London suburb. From single panels, James Horrabin expanded his *Adventures of the Noah Family* into strips which were compiled into Christmas and summer-holiday collections under the title *Japhet and Happy*. The little bear cub quickly rose to be the true star and boasted his own readers' club known as the Arkubs.

By far the longest-lived and most famous of these newspaper animals was *Rupert the Bear*, created for the *Daily Express* in 1920 by Mary Tourtel, wife of the paper's night news editor, and continued after Tourtel's eyesight began to fail by Alfred Bestall from 1935. Never would a speech balloon or sound effect disrupt the rural tranquillity and magical fantasies of this series. Though confined to two equal-sized daily panels, at times only one, Tourtel occasionally divided a panel into two images to form more of a sequence. Later, a curious rule was set to keep children's attention on the character, when it was decided that Rupert must appear in every panel, no matter what. The requirement never to lose sight of the protagonist created real narrative challenges for writer Ian Robinson, who, when forced once to leave Rupert imprisoned in a castle, had to instruct artist John Harrold, Bestall's successor from 1976, to show the bear in the far distance, straining out of a barred window.

In the 1920s, everybody was doing animal strips, from *Bobby Bear* in the *Daily Herald* to the avuncular elephant *Uncle Oojah* in the *Daily Sketch*. In May 1928, one month after eight thousand Gugnuncs packed the Albert Hall for a concert, the *Sheffield Evening Telegraph* unveiled their four-panel furry friend, a large, lisping white cat called Gloops, penned by mystery artist "Cousin Toby." Anyone who spotted a Gloops club member wearing their "Thmile" badge was expected to "thmile" back.

Another regional city paper, the *Liverpool Echo*, was home to their own critter who proved as popular with adults as with children. The elegant pig-about-town, "Count Curly Wee, so debonair and spry/ The eldest son of Lord de Swyne and heir to Porker Stye" first appeared there on 21 September 1937 with his "friend-in-chief" Gussie Goose. Their serialised exploits were told in clever rhyming couplets by two locals, Edinburgh-born authoress Maud Budden and Roland Clibborn, an artist born in Philadelphia, who illustrated 10,274 drawings until two years before his death aged 90 in 1969. Compiled and coloured like *Rupert*'s tales into hardback annuals, the *Curley Wee* cult spread to other British papers and as far away as South Africa, Madras and Australia. The pig's adventures were followed avidly by the Desert Rats in the Second World War and by President Gamal Nasser, who refused to ban the feature despite the Suez crisis.

Meanwhile by 1933, Charles Folkard's *Teddy Tail* in the *Daily Mail* had been awarded his own "League" and had

expanded to whole-page tales in the coloured *Boys and Girls Daily Mail* supplement, drawn by Charles's younger brother Harry. After seven months he was replaced by Herbert Foxwell, bought up by the *Mail* to leave his job on *Tiger Tim*. Foxwell was paid well to craft up to three pages every week of *Teddy Tail*. Without Foxwell, Tiger Tim continued to delight youngsters on *The Rainbow*'s covers.

While many artists on new family and adult strips in newspapers and their supplements had been allowed to tell their jokes entirely through hand-lettered balloons, captions and sound effects in their illustrated panels, many of those working with those tools for children were still saddled with superfluous typeset narratives or "librettos" of up to five lines beneath every panel. This Victorian tradition was related to the long-winded, laborious captions of many a cartoon in *Punch* magazine and to the priority given to the written word over pictures in children's fiction. Publishers wanted to keep the text below the panels in order to persuade parents that reading comics could be as educational an activity for their offspring as reading "proper" books. In fact, few seem to remember ever ploughing through this verbiage for themselves. The vocabulary in them, for a start, was

ABOVE: Easter egg antics with Tiger Tim and his fellow Bruin Boys in their ninth outing by Julius Stafford Baker. *The Rainbow* certainly lived up to its name with its bright colours on this cover, dated 11 April 1914.

BELOW: Herbert Foxwell drew *Teddy Tail* on the big broadsheet two-colour covers of the *Boys and Girls Daily Mail*, free every Saturday with the paper. In this relic from 16 May 1936, the youngsters put on a scarecrow's clothes to trick Mrs Whisker into getting them new clothes for the summer. To their dismay, she has bought them dungarees, work outfits worn by labourers. In an early story, when Teddy fell down a hole, his helpers tied such a tight knot in his tail to pull him out, that he had never been able to untie it.

RIGHT: Teddy Tail vanished from the *Daily Mail* in 1940 but returned after the war in more modern serial adventures by "Spot", alias Arthur Potts. Here he rides a snorting "troglopodus" with his pals Doctor Beetle and Piggy Douglas on the cover of the black-and-red 1951 reprint booklet *Teddy Tail and the Cavemen.*

sometimes much too advanced for youngsters, and in most cases children had no need to read them, because all they needed to know was clearly shown and told in the panels. Crime novelist P.D. James distinctly remembers her mother buying *The Rainbow* for her. "From a very early age, I longed for her to read me this wretched comic, but she of course was usually very busy. I can remember very clearly the moment when I discovered I could read it myself and the huge excitement and pleasure that swept over me. It wasn't very difficult, because after all there were the pictures and underneath the words just illustrated the pictures, so I wasn't being all that brilliant! But I suddenly realised I didn't have to ask her to read it to me, I could read it myself, and how wonderful that was." To give them some credit, the captions were not always redundant and could elaborate a fairly simple story by adding witty details and asides. Nevertheless, it must have been confusing at times when what the characters said in the text below did not match their dialogue balloons above—like watching a film with mistranslated subtitles.

Change was coming, however. Since *Mickey Mouse*'s 1928 film debut, Walt Disney's animated cartoons had enthused movie-goers in British picture palaces and given rise to local clubs. In America, Mickey was awarded his own newspaper strip in 1930, developed into a pacey adventure serial by Floyd Gottfredson, which was soon syndicated widely across Europe. In Britain early in 1935, an advertisement appeared in the *Daily Telegraph* seeking comic artists. On holiday at the time, Basil Reynolds was alerted to it by his father and he responded to the anonymous box number. In due course, he heard from a Mr Rosenberg of Willbank Publications, Shaftesbury Avenue, London, whose letterhead included a small head of Mickey Mouse. At his interview, Reynolds learned about the plans for *Mickey Mouse Weekly*, the first children's comic in Britain to be printed in photogravure, a costly process using thin tuolene-based inks on smooth, white paper to give the sort of rich, crisp reproduction that was impossible on the letterpress printing on newsprint.

Reynolds was told that as well as showcasing anglicised Disney strips and other imports, the new comic needed original homegrown material. He came up with *Skit, Skat and the Captain,* about "the world's smallest cabin boy and his skatty cat", as well as *Shuffled Symphonies,* variations on Disney's *Silly Symphonies* cartoons. As the artist since 1931 on the British *Mickey Mouse* annuals published by Dean & Son, Wilfred Haughton was the natural choice to illustrate all the gang on the weekly's front cover, drawing entirely with coloured inks, while his *Bobby Bear* newspaper strip ran inside. As well as reprinting the American Disney pages, the weekly featured new adventures of Donald Duck by William Ward, who added a canny Scottish canine named Mac as Donald's companion. The first issue of *Mickey Mouse Weekly* hit the stands on Saturday 8 February 1936, the

day of the week when kids flocked to morning cinema clubs. In all, out of a total of twelve pages for tuppence, no less than eight and three-quarters were created by British writers and artists. Liberated from the ballast of superfluous text, all of them used the thoroughly modern system of comics and helped the medium come into its own.

Although the staid subtext-heavy style proved surprisingly slow to fade,

persisting well into the 1950s, Mickey's immediate success showed there was now no going back. Another breath of fresh air blew in from north of the border in 1937, when D.C. Thomson in Dundee, Scotland gave kids an early Christmas present in the form of their first proper comic, as opposed to another of their almost entirely text-based boys' story papers *Adventure*, *Skipper*, *Rover* and *Wizard*. *The Dandy* was truly fine and "dandy" in its bright colours, neater half-tabloid size like the story papers, and in those livelier, less twee humour strips that jettisoned blocks of text and used balloons, or, in the case of its speechless cover star *Korky the Cat*, almost pure visual pantomime. No need to read much at all here, perhaps a sign or rhyme, but the jokes sprang to life before your eyes. Parents might not approve, but this was the sort of comic

children wanted to buy themselves. It proved so instantly popular, that another comic was hatched a mere 35 weeks later. *The Beano*, as in a festive feast or a boss's dinner for his workers, also led with animals on its front page to catch kids' eyes, first an egotistical ostrich named Big Eggo and then, from 1948 until 1974, a black bear cub in shorts and braces called Biffo. In 1953, the new *Topper*, as in top hat, followed suit, putting cheeky chimp Mickey on its tabloid-size cover.

The battle for children's pocket-money pennies was hotting up by 1938, when giant Amalgamated Press (AP) retaliated against the serious threat posed by *Mickey Mouse Weekly* and *The Dandy*. Strategies included concocting new rival weeklies, among them their first photogravure tabloid *Happy Days* and the wireless tie-in *Radio Fun*. After his apprenticeship in the 1920s under AP artist Don Newhouse, pupil Roy Wilson was soon outshining his master and was naturally assigned to the front covers of both new titles. Animal antics were one of Wilson's fortes, whether in sets featuring toothy-grinned George the Jolly Gee-Gee or the merrily chaotic Chimpo, supporting actors like Occy the Octopus in

ABOVE: From 1937 to 1941 Donald Duck enjoyed new adventures created by William A. Ward in *Mickey Mouse Weekly*. Donald was joined by his Scottish cohort Mac in foiling the dastardly plans of regular baddie Eli Squinch, trailered in the 2 July 1938 issue.

LEFT: Bursting into photogravure colour, *Mickey Mouse Weekly* transformed British comics in 1936. Its covers, such as this first issue, were drawn by Wilfred Haughton.

BELOW: Muffin the Mule had been a children's favourite on BBC TV since 1946, designed by Ann Hogarth and brought to life by story-teller and singer Annette Mills. He starred in *TV Comic* from its first issue in 1951. Here he tries to "lag" himself like a pipe to keep warm. Art by Neville Main for the 18 December 1954 issue.

Muffin was walking home one day when he overheard two ladies talking about the best way to keep the hot water pipes warm in cold weather.

"What will keep pipes warm will keep us warm too," Muffin told Peter when they met later in the garden. Peter said he would go and find some felt.

ABOVE: In secret, the British Foreign Office hired writer Don Freeman and *Jane* artist Norman Pett to adapt George Orwell's 1945 political fable *Animal Farm* into strips to be exported as anti-communist propaganda.

Pitch and Toss, or extras adding delightful sight gags on the sidelines. All of Wilson's funny wonders didn't just smile, they positively beamed with exuberance, their every frozen movement vibrating with brio.

Portrayals of wildlife in the comics, ranging from the most unnaturally humanised like Tiger Tim to the most true-to-life like Black Bob, commonly embody some aspects of human nature, perhaps because we tend to project our emotions onto animals, presuming that they feel and see life as we do. This presumption is as old as ancient myths and folk tales, nursery rhymes and farmyard and jungle fables such as the oft-told allegories of Aesop, Perrault and La Fontaine. It lives on in phrases that characterise foxes as sly, monkeys as mischievous, dogs as loyal or pigs as greedy. Working in reverse, animalistic traits could also reveal truths in humans according to theorists of physiognomy, who once seriously proposed that people's external physical resemblance to a certain creature would unfailingly indicate their inner

personality. To this day, Steve Bell in *If...*, Peter Brookes in *Nature Notes* and other political caricaturists follow the example of draughtsman extraordinaire Grandville who exposed nineteenth-century French public figures by mutating them into their beastly equivalents.

Nothing so savage would be tolerated within the tame pages of children's comics. From the post-war years, for all the zany, often anarchic humour introduced by *The Dandy*, *Beano* and their kin, they lost little of their fundamental innocence and, in the case of nursery titles, some would argue quite rightly. But that very innocence adds a disturbing resonance when the medium is used for more controversial subjects. George Orwell knew this when he adapted the barnyard fable into trenchant political commentary in *Animal Farm* in 1945. Not long after, a secret department of the Foreign Office with links to MI5 had paid Orwell for the rights to adapt his "fairy tale" into newspaper strips. Kept hush-hush at the time, this plan was revealed only fifty years later, in 1998 when the files were declassified, to be part of the British government's Cold War counteroffensive against communist propaganda. Comics could be discreetly acceptable as persuasive educational tools, especially for the barely literate abroad; as one department member enthused in 1951, "With a skilful storyteller one should have thought that it could be made into a very effective piece of propaganda down to village audience level." Sometime after, writer Don Freeman and

1924

1938

1950

1968

1989

2006

artist Norman Pett of *Jane* fame reduced Orwell's story to a 78-episode serial, intended for export and described in government departmental telegrams as "a brilliant satire on the communist regime in the USSR". Secret funds were used to pay Freeman and Pett and to assist foreign papers as far afield as Burma and Brazil to print the strips, which seem not to have been published in Britain.

Back in the press at home, one shining example of the shift from carefree fantasy to topical issues was *Flook*. With the pen of Trog, alias Wally Fawkes, writer Douglas Mount conceived this transforming dream-creature who befriends a young boy, Rufus, for the *Daily Mail* in 1949 as a counterpart to Crockett Johnson's American strip *Barnaby*, about a boy and his Irish fairy godfather. While other fanciful beings like Ken Reid's *Fudge the Elf* and Tove Jansson's *Moomin* from Finland stayed in that fairy-tale vein, successive *Flook* scripters such as jazzmen Humphrey Lyttleton and George Melly infused Trog's art with the satirical spirit emerging in the 1960s in comedy clubs and *Private Eye*.

From their beginnings to today, funny animals in comics and animation have had close ties. Early on, George Studdy and Roland Davies each filmed animated cartoons of their own strips, *Bonzo* and carthorse *Come On Steve*. Even earlier, in January 1921, Lancelot Speed had first animated *Pip, Squeak and Wilfred*. The two-way traffic between TV and strips has brought plenty of hit shows to the printed page from *Muffin the Mule* to *Wallace and Gromit*, though *Fred Bassett*, *The Perishers* and a computerised *Rupert* are among the rather fewer animal strips to cross over in the opposite direction onto the small screen. There's no denying the impact of American animators Tex Avery and Chuck Jones on John Geering, Bob Nixon and other British artists, whose comics like *Puss and Boots*, *Mowser*, *Gums* or *Kid Kong* could at their best attain a level of derangement close to

those masters. The influence of the ruder adult humour of *Viz*, which began in 1979, spread to IPC's new kids' title *Oink!* in 1986. The pig-themed fortnightly, however, seems to have over-stepped some line, as by issue eight retailers moved it from the children's racks to the top shelves for adults.

Previous adults-only comics had provoked controversy and court cases. Since the 1960s, in their quest to reject the status quo, underground artists such as Hunt Emerson, William Rankin and today's Lorenzo Etherington looked back to admired forebears such as Herbert Foxwell and Roy Wilson to subvert their traditional innocence with more radical values, exploring an altogether wilder anarchy. Some felt this had gone too far when fifteen-year-old schoolboy Vivian Berger collaged Rupert's head onto an explicit sex-romp comic by Robert Crumb in June 1970. For this, the three editors of the "School Kids' Issue" of the paper *Oz* were convicted of obscenity in 1971, though their sentences were quashed on appeal. In 2003, that same lustful Rupert stomped into Alan Moore and Kevin O'Neill's darkly satiric graphic novel *League of Extraordinary Gentlemen*, in which Rupert and all the rest turn out to have been the experiments of H.G. Wells's infamous Doctor Moreau. In one scene, when Tiger Tim crouches down to lap some water, Rupert scolds him: "Not to go on all fours, Tim!" It reveals the struggle of these humanised animals with their animal instincts, an all too human struggle that is finally also our own.

ABOVE: In the second volume of *The League of Extraordinary Gentlemen*, Alan Moore and Kevin O'Neill reveal the dark secret of Rupert, Tiger Tim and all the other turn-of-the-century humanised animals in British comics and children's books: they were all hybrids and rejects created by H.G. Wells' mad scientist Doctor Moreau.

BELOW: Looking out for Wallace, the silent, long-suffering Gromit has to be prepared for all kinds of weather. Aardman Animation's Oscar-winning duo have been enjoying new adventures in their monthly comic since October 2005. Art by Jimmy Hansen.

The big day, Saturday 14 April 1928, has arrived and Pip, Squeak and Wilfred join the eight thousand ticket-winners and members of the Wilfredian League of Gugnuncs who will convene that afternoon on London's Royal Albert Hall for an unforgettable afternoon concert. This whole page from the *Daily Mirror* includes a letter from Uncle Dick and other news from W.L.O.G. members and their "burrows" and "warrens" far and wide.

ABOVE: Packed to the rafters in the Albert Hall, W.L.O.G. members held their biggest party yet. One highlight was the half-hour live broadcast on BBC radio, which featured comedian Will Hay being inducted into the League and the singing of *The Gugnunc Chortle*. In the programme introduction, Uncle Dick wrote, "Sing your loudest—remember that your voices will be heard by listeners in all parts of Great Britain. At the same time, Gramophone records are to be made of our efforts so that, years hence, we may hear once again the songs we shall be singing today." The lyrics were:

Gug! Gug! Nunc! Nunc!
Gugnuncs merry are we!
We sing this song, for we all belong
To the W.L.O.G.

Stand by—friends all—
Members merry and free!
For hand-in-hand goes the gugly band
Of the W.L.O.G.

Nunc! Nunc! Wilf! Wilf!
To Wilf we bend the knee,
To Wilf we sing, to the gugly king
Of the W.L.O.G.

Gug! Gug! Nunc! Nunc!
To friends of all degree!
Give gugly hugs to the nuncly gugs
Of the W.L.O.G.

RIGHT AND FAR RIGHT: The trio's grand home, Mirror Grange, was made into an impressive doll's house, on which all kinds of craftsmen and artists laboured. Exhibited around the country, each room could be opened up to allow visitors to peer inside.

LEFT: Eight thousand members of the Wilfredian League of Gugnuncs converged on the Royal Albert Hall, London at 3pm on Saturday 14 April 1928 for a Grand Gugnunc Party.

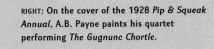

RIGHT: On the cover of the 1928 *Pip & Squeak Annual*, A.B. Payne paints his quartet performing *The Gugnunc Chortle*.

"GUG, GUG! NUNC, NUNC! GUGNUNCS MERRY ARE WE!"

BELOW: More Gugnuncs gather round Wilfred the rabbit kneeling in the front row.

A "GHOSTLY" FIGURE IN THE "HAUNTED" TOWER

Although it is rumoured that the Tower of Mirror Grange is haunted, there is little that is ghostly about the weird yet familiar figure of Auntie, whom we see waving a welcome to the incoming tenants.

"Giving a good idea of the solid rock on which Mirror Grange is built"

Rupert in Mysteryland

RUPERT IS STARTLED

The Chinese says, "Please follow me,"
And soon his conjuring room they see.

"Now first," he cries, "a cloth I'll take";
He spreads it, flicks it—there's a snake!

When Rupert several tricks can do,
The boy says, "Watch this egg, you two!"

He gently waves a wand about;
"It's disappeared!" the youngsters shout.

The Chinese boy takes Rupert and Pong-Ping into a room filled with a strange assortment of tables and cards and boxes and goldfish. "What about this trick?" says the boy as he lays a cloth over a little table. Then, speaking some strange words, he flicks the cloth up and reveals a fearsome snake, which wriggles off and darts into a hole in the wall. Rupert is very startled.

After teaching Rupert some simple little tricks the Chinese boy picks up a wand and puts an egg on a little table. Then he gives the wand some flourishes and, to Rupert's amazement, the egg is no longer there. "Oh, do let me have that little stick," he cries. "It is exactly what I need for my party. Won't the others be puzzled to know how it's done!" In his excitement he quite forgets to ask how to bring the egg back again.

RIGHT: The magic show was another childhood wonder of the earlier part of the 20th century, particularly if the magician was the legendary oriental conjurer Chung Ling Soo, shown above with his wife and a young assistant. Part of the great illusion was that he was in fact William Robinson, a New Yorker. Even offstage, when the press wanted to interview him, he claimed not to speak English and used an interpreter.

LEFT: Oriental conjuring and origami are important motifs in the *Rupert* stories serialised in the *Daily Express*, as seen in the Chinese girl Tiger Lilly and the pekinese dog Pong Ping. This page comes from the two-colour 1938 *New Rupert Book* by Alfred Bestall.

BELOW LEFT: Three artistic reigns maintained the highest quality of illustration on *Rupert*. In 85 stories starting in 1920, his creator Mary Tourtel established the refined linework and gentle fantasy identified with the strip. Her stories also revealed an enthusiasm for the Pre-Raphaelite and the medievalist.

BELOW MIDDLE: Many of Tourtel's fairytale elements were developed further by Alfred Bestall from 1935, who also added new characters and settings. His panels were beautifully watercoloured for the annuals. Avoiding speech balloons and sound effects, every story is told both in rhyming couplets beneath each panel and in a storybook libretto on each page.

BELOW RIGHT: Bestall's greatest successor, John Harrold, maintained that tradition for many years after him, starting in 1976.

ABOVE: Mary Tourtel introduced other members of the bear's loving family, including Rupert's younger sister Joan and Beppo, his pet monkey, shown here in a seaside panel reprinted in the 1949 *Monster Rupert* hardback collection.

Rupert and Pong Ping

RUPERT IS GIVEN A WARNING

At supper Rupert's in a fix;
He finds he has to use chopsticks.

A hissing startles Rupert Bear.
He turns. "A dragon's lurking there!

The dragon shouts, "It is a shame!
I've been neglected since you came!"

"My dreaded uncle flying there
Will carry off your friend, young bear."

"My old favourite's son! Welcome, welcome!" cries the Emperor. And Rupert is delighted to hear the kindly ruler speak a language that he understands. "Well, you must be hungry after your long journey," the Emperor goes on, and almost at once the friends find themselves at a table with a wonderful meal in front of them. Rupert, though, does have a bit of trouble with his chopsticks at first. Later when they set out to tour the palace, Rupert, who is lagging behind, hears a hiss from a corner and turns to find the Emperor's pet dragon. To his horror a grate by the scruff of the neck and drags him out on to a wide terrace. "Listen," it hisses. "I was the Emperor's favourite till your friend came. Tell him to go back at once or my uncle, the Flying Dragon, will put an end to him—understand?" He points towards the sky and there Rupert sees the sinister form of the great Flying Dragon.

Rupert, Beppo and the Kite

RUPERT FINDS THE STONES

They're dragged towards the forest trees,
And then the kite drops with the breeze.

It's caught up in a giant oak.
To get it down will be no joke!

"There's Beppo, Podgy! And just see!
The stones he's on! Why, there are three!"

The pals feel sure beyond a doubt,
These are the stones the note's about.

The kite moves so fast that Podgy has to let go and Rupert is dragged even faster after it. Then when it is well over the wood the wind drops ... and so on the kite and Beppo. The pals plunge into the trees heading for where the kite came down. They find it caught up in a big oak. "It's going to be no joke getting this free," Rupert groans. "But first things first. We've got to find Beppo." And, indeed, of the little monkey there isn't a sign.

In fact, the kite isn't hard to free, as a sharp tug by Podgy reveals, and the pals take it with them when they search for Beppo. It is quite a while later that Rupert climbs a tree to search a clearing and spies Beppo. He is playing on a group of stones ... three stones! Rupert yells to Podgy and they race to the stones. Yes, three of them. And big. The pals exchange looks. "Oh, Beppo!" Rupert laughs. "I think you've just led us to a fortune!"

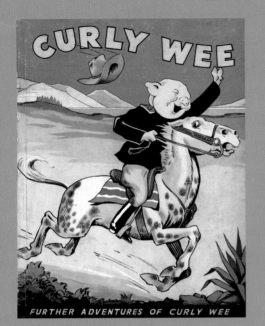

ABOVE AND ABOVE CENTRE: Our heroic pig Curly Wee gallops through the Wild West in this 1952 annual.

ABOVE: "Thmile" was the motto of Sheffield's cheery pussycat Gloops. He raises one here in his 1936 annual, when his fish-shop sign gets misread as that of a shoe repairer.

BELOW AND RIGHT: Horrabin's sweet little bear Happy nearly always stole the show from his young master Japhet. This episode ran in the 1936 summer book.

ABOVE AND LEFT: Identical, apart from Snuff's white-tipped tail, these three silent pups charmed mothers and their children in *Woman* magazine starting in 1947. They were created by "Tim", alias William Timyn, who went on to produce *Bengo* and *Bleep and Booster* for BBC TV's *Blue Peter*. Here they scare a bully with a magnifying lens used to watch early televisions.

ABOVE: Ostrich Big Eggo was *The Beano's* first cover star from 1938 to 1948. Here, using a helicopter backpack, he has dropped an exploding egg on Hitler and Mussolini on 19 July 1941, drawn by Reg Carter.

RIGHT: Resourceful Korky the Cat finds a clever substitute for his broken signage for New Year 1941 on this *Dandy* cover drawn by James Crichton.

FAR RIGHT: More silent comedy on *The Beano* cover for 24 January 1948, with Biffo the Bear drawn by Dudley D. Watkins. On 10 September 1949, he too suddenly got the gift of speech.

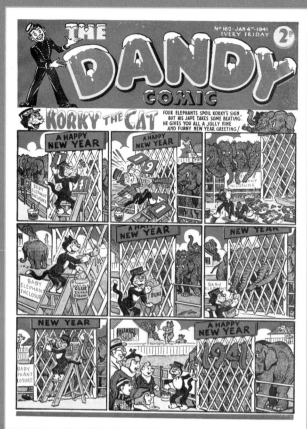

RIGHT: Black Bob began as a text serial in *The Dandy* in 1944, a year after the first *Lassie* film. "The wisest sheepdog in Scotland" became a picture strip starting in 1956, drawn by Jack Prout.

FAR RIGHT: A dog could also be a girl's best friend, as in this tale of the courageous Alsatian Solak in the Canadian north entitled *A Dog Under Suspicion* from the 1956 *School Friend Annual*. Wrongly accused of being a savage brute, Solak proves himself by rescuing pet pup Frisky, who is stranded among logs floating down the rapids. The artist is unknown.

ABOVE: *Crackers the Pup* featured in the weekly comic *Crackers*, from which the kindly pooch got his name. Original art by Don Newhouse, who drew the strip from 1932 to 1941.

LEFT: Skinny, starving *Skit the Kat* by Harry Banger (rhymes with danger) comes from Gerald Swan's 1949 *Funnies Album*.

BELOW: Mrs Hulme-Beaman's loveable *Larry the Lamb* proved popular on the 1930s BBC radio show *Toytown* and on telly from 1947. George Moreno drew this *TV Mini-Book* in 1955.

BOTTOM: A fine undersea panel of original art by Basil Reynolds for *Skit, Skat and The Captain* in *Mickey Mouse Weekly*, 1939.

71

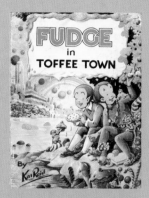

ABOVE: British newspaper strips have also accommodated some delightfully strange fantasy creatures. Ken Reid's lusciously imaginative *Fudge the Elf* began in the *Manchester Evening News* in 1938 and returned after the war for a sixteen-year run and numerous annuals, this one from 1950.

RIGHT: The work of Raymond Briggs is not always categorised as comics, but his deliciously revolting portrayals of life in Bogeydom could not be anything else. *Fungus the Bogeyman* was a hit from the day it was published in 1977.

ABOVE FAR RIGHT: In 1954, partly to compete with the *Daily Mail*'s *Flook*, the London *Evening News* hired Finland's Tove Jansson to put the cast of her illustrated *Moomin* books into strip form for the first time. She was assisted from 1958 by her brother Lars, who took over completely from 1961 until the final episode in 1974. There was only this one collection in English in 1957.

RIGHT: Blond boy Rufus began in 1949 as the title character of this *Daily Mail* strip drawn by Wally "Trog" Fawkes, but his furry changeling pal took over and changed the strip's name to *Flook*. In *The S.S. Tapioca Cruise* from a 1958 collection, Flook's shape-shifting nose came in handy.

RIGHT: Writer George Melly brought his sharp wit and topicality to *Flook*, as in this episode from *Flook For A Neighbour* in 1965, which mocks politicians' pretences at accepting immigrants.

LEFT: Although Harry Smith's *Billy the Bee* might have looked like a slight children's fantasy, in fact it made clever, oblique comments on issues of the day, like an insect version of the American satirical funny animal strip *Pogo* by Walt Kelly. It began in 1966 in the London *Evening Standard* and this episode comes from the 1967 story *The Day The Worms Turned*. Smith built up an extensive research library on all aspects of insect life.

LEFT: In 1968, former animator Harry Hargreaves created *Hayseeds* for the London *Evening News*. While he was inspired by *Pogo*, he played with a larger ensemble and tried lighter, less political humour. No single character dominated the strip, but among his regulars was the bemused badger Toby, shown here. In 1974, the strip was dropped but was soon restored by public demand and lasted until 1980, shortly before the paper closed.

LEFT: *The Perishers*, a gang of street kids and an Old English sheepdog, entertained *Daily Mirror* readers for nearly fifty years. After a faltering start in 1958 in the paper's Manchester edition, Maurice Dodd began writing the strip and a year later it went national. Dodd worked with artist Dennis Collins until 1983, when Collins retired. Dodd then took on the whole job until 1992, when new artist Bill Mevin joined him; he continued to write the strip until his death in 2005. In this daily from the 1972 *Perishers Book*, Boot justifies not sharing his bone with his Bloodhound chum, BH 9 (Calcutta) Failed.

LEFT: Following complaints from dog fanciers about Alex Graham's inaccurate drawings, the *Daily Mail* bought him a basset called Freda, who became his life model for the *Fred Basset* strip, shown here from the first year, 1963. Among his fans was P.G. Wodehouse who was fond of this breed, calling Wooster's simpering admirer Madeleine Basset, or simply "the basset".

73

ABOVE: The endless war between cat and dog could reach surreal levels in the pages of *Puss and Boots* for *Sparky* from 1969 to 1977 and then in *Topper* until 1979, drawn by John Geering.

LEFT: Leo Baxendale uprooted The Three Bears from the *Goldilocks* fairy tale to America's wild Wild West. Insatiably hungry, they first appeared in an earlier Western strip by Baxendale, *Little Plum, Your Redskin Chum*, before getting their own *Beano* strip from 1959.

ABOVE: *Mickey the Monkey* by Dudley Watkins was the front-page attraction on Thomson's oversized weekly *The Topper* from its start in 1953 until 1986. This extract is from the 1958 *Topper Book* which appeared in a full-colour, landscape format.

RIGHT: From the same annual comes the chicken-chasing *Foxy* drawn by Charles Grigg. Here Foxy uses a big bass drum in another of his elaborate ploys that always backfire on him.

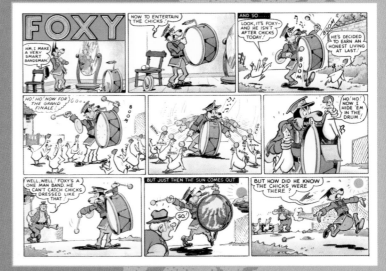

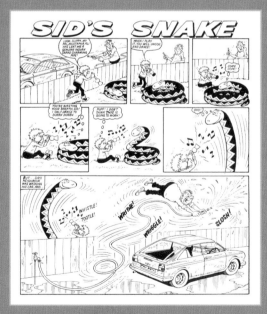

LEFT: Spoiled rotten, his Lordship's wily moggy Mowser always got the better of butler James in Reg Parlett's stately-home farce for *Valiant*, this episode from 23 November 1974.

BELOW: In his teeny bow tie, *Mighty Moth* outwits Dad yet again in this page by Dick Millington from the 1970 *TV Comic Annual*.

ABOVE: Drawing snakes in funny comics had been forbidden by editors of Amalgamated Press who did not want to frighten young readers, but when IPC took the weeklies over, the cover star of their new two-in-one *Whizzer and Chips* in 1969 was *Sid's Snake*, named Slippy. This page by Mike Lacey ran in the 1991 annual.

LEFT: Also in *Valiant*, Reg Parlett drew the inventive half-pager *The Crows*, this one from 14 December 1967.

LEFT: *Basil Brush, The Herbs, The Clangers, The Wombles* and other animal favourites from children's television were all adapted into comics. Here is the Cosgrove Hall-animated series *Dangermouse* from *Look-in*, 2 April 1983, drawn by Arthur Ranson. Here, our rodent hero and his assistant Penfold escape from the past in their time-travelling grandfather clock.

BELOW: Dougal, the shaggy dog from *The Magic Roundabout* TV series, dreams of winning Dylan the rabbit's disco contest, in a strip written by Jane Carruth and drawn by Gordon Hutchings for the 1973 *Dougal's Annual*.

After *Jaws* in 1976 came *Gums*, a toothless shark who kept losing his dentures. John Geering drew this page for *Buster*.

A logical, ecological answer to power cuts by Gus Gorilla, drawn by Alf Saporito in *Cor!! Annual*, 1981.

This ape is a huge kid who causes havoc for Granny Smith. Robert Nixon drew this in *Monster Fun*, 14 August 1972.

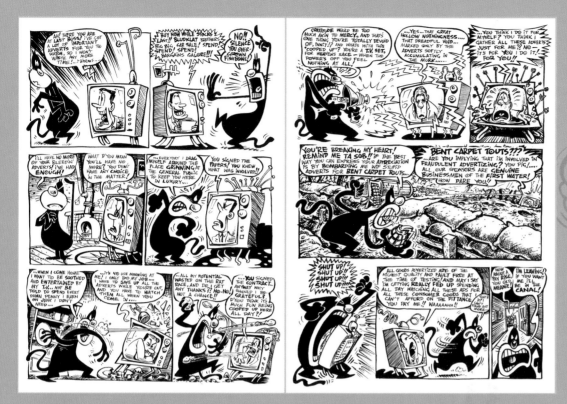

ABOVE: Home after a harrying day of constant smirking, *Calculus Cat* finally turns on his TV, which proceeds to bombard him with adverts and drive him out of his own house. Hunt Emerson pinpoints our love-hate relationship with the telly in *Escape* 5, 1984.

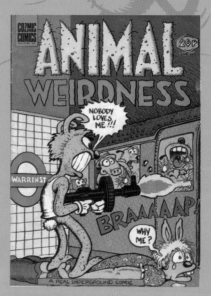

ABOVE: Written by Tym Manley, Hunt Emerson's lascivious *Firkin the Cat* has been reporting on human sexuality in the men's magazine *Fiesta* for 25 years since 1981.

RIGHT: Deranged *Dumb Bun* guns down tube commuters—appropriately at Warren Street station—in this 1974 themed anthology *Animal Weirdness*. The influence of American Robert Crumb, father of Fritz the Cat, is clear on Malcolm Livingstone's cover.

LEFT: The distinctive William Rankin took the styles of more innocent, old-fashioned British comics and suffused them with the dope culture of America's West Coast. His laid-back bumblebee *Buzz* took flight in *Serious Comics*, Rankin's solo one-shot from 1975.

ABOVE: Savage Pencil's bilious scrawls for *Rock'n'Roll Zoo* captured the anger of punk in the weekly paper *Sounds* starting in 1977. This strip from 1981 mocks vacuous music industry execs desperate for the next big thing.

LEFT: The pig-themed *Oink!*, conceived in 1986 by Patrick Gallagher, Tony Husband and Mark Rodgers, injected some fresh, gross-out humour into kids' comics. Ian Jackson drew this 1987 holiday special cover.

FAR RIGHT: Pooches don't come more disgusting than *Pete's Pup* in *Oink!*, 1987, by Jim Needle.

BELOW: Editor Uncle Pigg foils his prudish nemesis Mary Lighthouse, a parody of morality campaigner Mary Whitehouse, in *The Oink! Book 1988*. Written by Mark Rodgers and drawn by Ian Jackson.

RIGHT: In *Jim*, Steven Appleby's 2003 graphic novel, a once typical family cat returns after his first death and decides to live the rest of his nine lives differently. Here, he copes with lust and neutering.

BELOW: Alan Grant and Simon Bisley's poop-obsessed *Shit the Dog* sniffs the air in his 1997 poster magazine.

BELOW: There are always strange goings-on down on the farm with Gary Northfield's *Derek the Sheep*, like being shrunk to a tiny size in this 10 September 2005 tale. Derek has been one of *The Beano*'s most popular new stars since 2004 and even has his own blog.

ABOVE: It's a typical British summer for Wallace and Gromit in *A Pier Too Far*, written in 2005 for their monthly comic by Dan Abnett and drawn by Jimmy Hansen.

LEFT: Be careful what you tell Fluffy, a baby rabbit who is sure it is human, seen here on holiday with its supposed daddy in Paris. Simone Lia self-published her quirky graphic novel in four parts from 2003.

RIGHT: In Robin and Lorenzo Etherington's serial *Malcolm Magic*, starting in 2003, life for their boozy bunny changes forever when he winds up in the wacky land of Nod-Suf and has to pilot a plummeting dragon to escape an avalanche.

Wheezes in the Tuck Shop

"THE ONLY GOOD THINGS ABOUT SKOOL ARE THE BOYS WIZZ WHO ARE NOBLE BRAVE FEARLESS ETC. ALTHOUGH YOU HAV VARIOUS SWOTS, BULLIES, CISSIES, MILKSOPS, GREEDY GUTS AND OIKS with whom i am forced to mingle hem-hem. In fact any skool is a bit of a shambles AS YOU WILL SEE." With these misspelt yet pithy remarks, young Nigel Molesworth ushers us into the secrets of St Custard's School in the 1953 bestseller *Down With Skool*, in which *Punch* writer George Willans drew on his teaching experiences, conspiring with cartoonist Ronald Searle. It may be coincidence, but J.K. Rowling named the school attended by Harry Potter "Hogwarts", which was also the title of a Latin play by Molesworth in Willans' sequel *How To Be Topp*.

In fact, Rowling's School of Witchcraft and Wizardry seems to have revived the rather soured fantasy world of the traditional exclusive British boarding school. Not every "old boy" or "old girl" looked back fondly on their years packed away at an early age from their parents for months at a time. Once strictly single-sex, overwhelmingly white and for the offspring of the well-to-do, this institution could be rife with indignities and cruelties by teachers and between pupils. Liberal reformer Thomas Arnold exposed some of these issues as early as 1857 in *Tom Brown's Schooldays*, one of the earliest books specifically written for boys, while more than a century later in 1968 Lindsay Anderson directed the film *if....* as a radical indictment of the education system, and of British society in microcosm, that ended in violent revolution by the pupils. In the past, your class could often be decided by where you were taught: the

question, "What school did you go to?" used to be a deciding factor in your opportunities and status. Greater flexibility and equality mean that this is probably less true now, but where and how you were educated will determine most people's lives as long as John Major's 1990 vision, or pipedream, of "a classless society" fails to materialise. If anything, the boarding school is appealing once more via Rowling's novels, because, though problems persist, she shows Hogwarts as "classless", inclusive and open to all with magical ability, regardless of sex, class, race or nationality.

In a sense, the Harry Potter saga can be seen as the latest in the long and peculiarly British tradition of school stories. George Orwell, a former public school pupil and then a teacher himself, explained this genre's fascination in an essay for the magazine *Horizon* in March 1940: "The most definite dividing line between the petite-bourgeoisie and the working class is that the former pay for their education, and within the bourgeoisie there is another unbridgeable gulf between the 'public' school and the 'private' school. It is quite clear that there are tens and scores of thousands of people to whom every detail of life at a 'posh' public school is wildly thrilling and romantic. They happen to be outside that mystic world of quadrangles and house colours, but they can yearn after it, daydream about it, live mentally in it for hours at a stretch." However unrealistic and anachronistic these school stories could be, even when the boys' story papers *The Gem* and *The Magnet* began

RIGHT: Nothing goes better with your weekly comic than a bag of penny sweets from the tuck shop. No, it's not Honeydukes from *Harry Potter* but one seen in the 1960s educational weekly *Look and Learn*.

BELOW: Extra strong itching powder from mail-order emporium Zonko's Joke Shop.

OPPOSITE: On the cover of *Wham!*'s Fireworks' Day special in 1964, Leo Baxendale draws The Tiddlers and their teacher Super Sir, *Dan Dare's* biggest fan Danny Dare, Frankie Stein and others in glorious colour.

DOINGS AT WHACKINGTON SCHOOL
BY A SKOLLAR

1. "WE did a fine lark on the 5th. We had a half-holiday, and me an' the other fellars rigged up a guy in the shed. It looked a proper treat.

3. "After we had knocked off evenin' prep., and had lighted the bonfire, Basher (that's the bully) shouts, 'Four of you kids go to the shed and fetch the guy!'

ABOVE: More bad spelling by "a skollar" at an upper-class boarding school, where boys make a guy for 5 November 1897, by Tom Browne in *Big Budget*.

RIGHT: Billy Bunter scoffs a cream tea in the BBC TV series, played by Gerald Campion at the age of 29.

BELOW: The *Casey Court* street kids get into another mess running their own comic. Allan Morley drew this joke-packed crowd scene for *Chips* in 1925.

in 1907 and 1908, they provided wish-fulfilment via a spectrum of schoolboy types, offering "a model for nearly everybody".

Much as we might admire the sterling if rather bland "goodies" in comics as models, we tend to enjoy their less perfect, fallible cohorts far more, like *Tintin*'s blustery, whisky-loving Captain Haddock or Mickey Mouse's irascible foil Donald Duck. So too with the cult that grew up around Billy Bunter, an overweight, cunning, squealing glutton of a schoolboy at Greyfriars, a supposed former monastery near the south coast of Kent. Tapping furiously for forty years on the same Remington typewriter, Charles Hamilton wrote almost all the *Bunter* prose fiction under the name Frank Richards, one of more than a dozen of his pseudonyms, clocking up 72 million words in 7,000 tales. From Richards's description, Bunter and company's stories were first illustrated in *The Magnet* in 1908 by Arthur Clarke, but after his death in 1911, Charles Chapman took over until the school story paper fell victim to wartime paper shortages in 1940. Chapman later told the *Reading and*

Berkshire Review that the Fat Owl of the Remove had "… started off as an ordinary fat boy as you'd find in any group of schoolboys. Then we made him short-sighted and put glasses on him. Later we parted his hair in the middle and put him in check trousers". This was a device "to make Billy all the more conspicuous and emphasise the tightness of his trousers". Like a later prize moocher, J. Wellington Wimpy in the American strip *Popeye*, who would "gladly pay you Tuesday for a hamburger today", Bunter was forever swindling half crowns for some "grub" on the promise of a five-pound postal order which never arrived. For references, Chapman consulted Reverend Hubert Nind, the local vicar of St Leonards who had kept a preparatory school for Eton-bound boys. "What he didn't know about running a school for boys would go on the tip of my pencil," said Chapman. He immortalised Reverend Nind as Dr Locke, while a younger version became Bunter's master and nemesis, Mr Quelch.

The Magnet might have closed in 1940, but Bunter had started a new life the year before in comics. Chapman drew him first in *Knockout* in his "straight" story paper style, until issue twelve when Frank Minnit took over and his rounded cartooning turned it into a humorous feature. Minnit's version of "The Fattest Schoolboy on Earth" grew so popular that Bunter moved to the front page and top billing in the renamed *Billy Bunter's Knockout*, boosted by Hamilton's new line of books from 1947 and by seven television series and three specials. The shows in 1953 were broadcast twice-nightly, at 5.40pm for kids and 8pm for grown-ups, no doubt many of them former *Magnet* readers. In the past, British comics had an abiding obsession with "the slap-up feed" of jelly and ice cream, buns and cakes, towers of mashed potato

BILLY BAGGS, OF CASEY COURT, STARTS A COMIC.

Don't smile, but last week Billy Baggs decided to publish a rival comic paper to CHIPS, the Champion comic, and on top of these few remarks you will see how he tried to do it. Having collected a large staff from near and far, he set to work, and after a terrific struggle which caused all his artists and printers and typists and whatnot to collapse, he got out his first number. But it wasn't quite a success—at least we we suppose that it wasn't, because nobody would by it. We told Billy Baggs yesterday that he had better stick to CHIPS and be satisfied.

with sausages or bangers sticking out, the reward in many a final panel and the reader's fantasy when food was short or rationed. Other "fatties" would fill British funnies, but, despite attempts to revive Bunter since his final feast in *Valiant* in 1976, including the first of a short-lived restaurant chain named after him, his bulk and greed no longer seem so funny amid today's concerns about junk food and childhood obesity.

Another toff, in his Eton collar, bow tie and silk top hat was young Lord Marmaduke, Earl of Bunkerton, who debuted in *The Beano* on 30 July 1938. Nicknamed Lord Snooty, he was never "snooty" as in aloof and superior. Rather, he would do all he could to avoid his "softy" upper-class playmates and boring duties for his matronly Aunt Matilda. Although Snooty didn't go to school, he had to put up with private tutors. He much preferred to shin down a drainpipe to a small garden shed, where he would change into a cap, worn-out clothes and trousers with braces and sneak off to play with his lower-class pals down in Ash Can Alley. What readers found intriguing about Snooty was the idea of a plucky real-life young lord, like *Little Lord Fauntleroy* filmed in 1936, mixing easily with ordinary poor kids, akin to those in Hal Roach's *Our Gang* movies from 1922 onwards. Incidentally, the *Our Gang* urchins themselves starred in new picture stories in the early *Beano* issues. This friendship across the divides of class and money rarely emphasised Snooty's wealth, as in the later American comic books about boy billionaire *Richie Rich*, nor was the other kids' poverty played for laughs. Sometimes, Snooty would seek social justice for his less well-off chums, in one story making the owners of a gasworks reduce the pollution that was damaging the nearby residents' health. Snooty's quick change and double life were shortly dropped and he stuck to wearing his smart Lordship's outfit. Gradually, the street kids became welcome guests at Bunkerton Castle and his auntie's disapproval of them

lessened. After a year or so, Snooty and his pals (presumably with no home or parents of their own) wound up living together in the castle under the eye of Auntie "Mat".

From the start, Snooty's playmates never questioned his innate right to lead them, no matter how foolishly or how frequently he led them into scrapes with the mean Gasworks Gang. *Snooty* artist Dudley Watkins had some experience drawing street kids, as he had been illustrating a whole page in *The Sunday Post Fun Section* since 1936 featuring a spiky-haired tyke who sat on a bucket named Oor Wullie, Scottish for "Our Willie". Watkins drew the changing roster of Snooty's pals over almost thirty years, as they lost their winking, cart-pulling goat Gertie and gained the impish Snitchy, originally one of the Ash Can Babies. He was soon joined by twin brother Snatchy, both with big chins and all-in-one romper suits. The pals' antics were suspended exactly eleven years after they began, on 30 July 1949. Back for Christmas 1950, Snooty felt gloomy because four of his gang had left: "Hairpin [Huggins has] gone to America, [Skinny] Lizzie's gone to boarding school, and Happy Hutton and Gertie the Goat have gone to live in the country." By advertising for new members, Snooty recruited several homeless *Beano* starlets who had lost their strips: *Big Fat Joe* and *Contrary Mary the Moke*, a bright little donkey, who had both been in *The Beano* when it began; *Doubting Thomas*, last seen in 1942; and the girls

ABOVE: Scotland's cherished little scamp Oor Wullie sat on his bucket in the first panel of nearly every front page of *The Sunday Post Fun Section* since he began on 8 March 1936. Here, in 1938, Wullie gets into trouble following George Washington's example of never telling a lie. It should be read in a Scots accent, and to help, here's a glossary of some words: "dinna" is don't; "falsers" are false teeth; a "piler" is a cart; and a "tanner" is sixpence. Clarity and cleverness combined in Dudley Watkins' art and timing. The wee kid still appears every Sunday, skilfully illustrated in Watkins' style by Ken Harrison.

ABOVE: Nipper never spoke his first word, arriving in the *Daily Mail* on 30 August 1933. Brian White's silent toddler and his baby brother rescue some of the comics recycled in wartime paper drives. On 24 November 1940, to coincide with the publication of the new *Nipper* annual, the *Mail* published a knitting pattern for a Nipper doll with the suggestion, "You can knit him in time to take him to the children on Sunday week". On that day, parents could take advantage of special pre-Christmas reduced fares on the trains to visit their much missed children evacuated to the country.

Polly Wolly Doodle and her Great Big Poodle and *Swanky Lanky Liz*, a beanpole with her nose in the air. Except for the animals, the gang was all there until the axe fell in 1992. Some in the press suggested that Snooty had become politically incorrect, a symbol of old-style Tory paternalism no longer in favour under John Major; *Beano* editor Euan Kerr put it more simply: "Snooty is quite out of date and baffling to today's generation."

Those who attended school in the decades after the Second World War, however, would probably have recognised or understood the anachronistic trappings in their comics, because, despite improved standards and investment, many British classrooms in the 1950s remained rooted in the Victorian public school traditions of strict discipline, corporal punishment and for many the compulsory uniform of cap, tie and blazer. Post-war reforms might have extended the leaving age to fifteen and guaranteed extended education for all, but from 1944, a child's future could almost be decided by the eleven-plus exam. This selection process put youngsters under great pressure. Pass and they got a superior grammar school education that could lead to university and a profession. Fail—and four out of five did, most of them working-class —and they were sent to a frequently inferior secondary modern school with diminished prospects. No wonder some kids classified as failures at this tender age saw little point in their lessons and wound up as trouble-makers and truants headed for expulsion.

Still, any potential *enfant terrible* who felt the urge to rebel could find some outlet in the period's fiction and films. They could choose from Anthony Buckeridge's *Jennings* novels starting in 1950 or Richmal Crompton's *Just William* books, begun in 1922 and filmed by Val Guest in 1947 and 1948, while Ronald Searle's first drawings of Molesworth in 1953 had been preceded by the craze for his *St Trinian's* girls, made into movies from 1954. They could turn to comics too, especially once D.C. Thomson introduced *Dennis the Menace*, drawn by David Law, into *The Beano* on 17 March 1951. Uncannily, in the same week, another *Dennis the Menace* was dreamt up by American Hank Ketcham, proof that great cartooning minds think alike. The two never met, but that cute, blond, freckled namesake would never have stood a chance against the slings and catapults of "the world's wildest boy". True, kids had been outrageously naughty in British comics for ages, as far back as Frank Holland's *Those Terrible Twins* in *The Halfpenny Comic* in 1898, one of many variations on Wilhelm Busch's *Max*

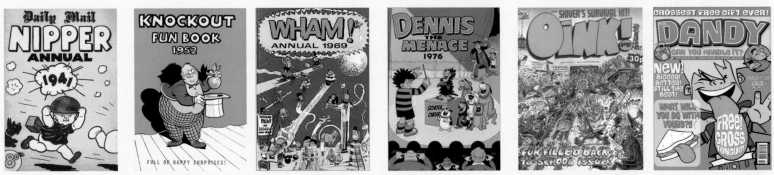

| 1940 | 1951 | 1968 | 1975 | 1986 | 2004 |

and Moritz from Germany, or the single-panel chaos of *Casey Court* invented by Julius Stafford Baker in 1902 and inspired by the shenanigans of *The Yellow Kid* by New Yorker Richard Outcault. And yet the untameable Dennis would out-menace them all, including his numerous successors, from Roger the Dodger to Sweeny Toddler.

In the late summer of 1952, *The Beano*'s Dennis made a life-changing impression on novice Leo Baxendale, who would become Britain's most influential post-war children's comic artist: "I was struck by its portent: I thought, 'I could do something like this'." The problems faced by Baxendale, aged 21, after first approaching D.C. Thomson were both stylistic and ideological. They wanted more in their same traditional style, not Baxendale's progressive approach to portraying characters also in close-up and long-shot, rather than as only their standard full- or half-figures, nor his flouting their "rules" that retribution must be deserved and bad conduct punished. Eventually, Baxendale would mostly get his way. When his Bash Street Kids first stormed into *The Beano* on 13 February 1954, they filled one large image to bursting, recalling the tumult of children and babies in some of Baxendale's favourite 1950s Carl Giles panel cartoons for the *Daily Express*, as well as one of his childhood joys, *Casey Court*. But his new series marked a significant advance in kids' comics. "Before *Bash Street*, the dominant presentation of schoolchildren had been as characters at public schools. I intended something very different: to present 'ordinary' secondary-school children ... so that *Bash Street* would appear near to the everyday life of the greater number of children in the country." To that end, Baxendale adopted the antiquated symbols of the gown and mortarboard for his nameless "Teacher", not only because their black shapes caught the eye and added weight to the page, but also because they suggested a grander grammar school, whereas the kids' lack of uniform or Latin

homework implied a typical secondary modern. By consciously making Bash Street School's status neither one nor the other but giving it a reality of its own, he maximised its appeal and its potential for comedy.

Baxendale and his brilliant *Beano* peer Ken Reid together forged most of the templates for the breed of idiosyncratic, wilful or sublimely gormless jokers who populated comics for decades after. In 1964 both artists quit Thomson for better pay and more freedom at London publishers Odhams, where Baxendale helmed *Wham!*, his bold but finally overambitious photogravure "Super *Beano*". Here and in its successors, he and Reid raised their inventive lunacy to still greater heights and inspired many in the next wave of cartoonists including Tom Paterson, Trevor Metcalfe, Robert Nixon, Graham Exton and Baxendale's son Martin.

After the state system changed again to non-selective comprehensive schools, comics took on grittier kids' dramas, such as *Grange Hill*, based on the TV series, or *Kids Rule O.K.!*, a *Lord of the Flies*-style dystopia. *Look Out For Lefty*, another shocker appearing in *Action*, caused such media outrage in 1976 when its football star praised a teenage girl fan for hurling a bottle at a rival player that IPC cancelled their strong-selling weekly. Humour also got tougher and ruder when the adults-only *Viz* flaunted children's comics conventions and dressed their flatulent Johnny Fartpants in a striped jersey and short trousers, to show him doing what *The Beano* would never allow. In 2000, Dennis's IPC rival Buster acknowledged his debt to him in his last panel by doffing the flat cap he had worn since 1960 to reveal that his unruly black hair underneath looked exactly like Dennis's. Impervious to major change, Dennis remains today's archetypal naughty kid, grazed knobbly knees and all.

ABOVE: "There's always a commotion going on in his trousers!" Simon Donald created and drew Johnny Fartpants as "very much like a British comic and yet it was about schoolboy humour which had never been in print". The flatulent frolics began in the twelfth issue of the adult comic *Viz* in November 1984.

BELOW: Dennis the Menace and his menacing mutt Gnasher run over Dad in their "one-pig open sleigh" pulled by Dennis's other pet, Rasher, customised here into a reindeer. Art by David Sutherland for the Christmas 1993 *Beano*. Gnasher was the idea of writer Ian Gray in 1968, who asked David Law to draw him as if Dennis's hairdo had sprouted eyes, legs and fangs.

LEFT: In Frank Minnit's snow-covered, holly-bedecked Christmas episode from *Knockout* in 1951, a series of Billy Bunter's trades reduces Master Quelch's big turkey to a raffle ticket, which, true to the season, comes up trumps. The weak-willed Jones Minor, introduced for the comics, could usually be manipulated by Bunter into joining in his schemes. Earlier in 1951, on 12 July, the author of the *Bunter* stories, Frank Richards alias Charles Hamilton, wrote to Minnit about his comics: "Though no artist, I also draw something in connection with that page!" Richards was referring to the £5 concession he was paid each week for the use of his creation, the same sum as Minnit was paid for drawing the comic—and the sum of the fictitious postal order that deceptive Bunter was always promising was on its way.

ABOVE: Gathered outside Rowland's, the school tuck shop, older Eton schoolboys wear the school uniform of a black tailcoat, waistcoat, false shirt collar and top hat, while younger boys wear 'bum-freezer' jackets. Eton boys wore top hats with their Eton suits until the Second World War when shortages caused the hat to be phased out. The Eton suit was widely adopted during the Edwardian era by private schools as the everyday dress of younger boys.

LEFT: Bunter surprises Quelch on the cover of *The Magnet*, Saturday 12 June 1937, drawn by Leonard Shields, perhaps from a layout by Charles Chapman.

RIGHT: Charles Chapman, who illustrated the *Bunter* stories in *The Magnet*, also drew him in comics. These two opening panels come from a two-page instalment he drew in *Comet*, Saturday 14 September 1957, adapted from one of Richards' stories.

FROM A STORY BY THE FAMOUS AUTHOR, FRANK RICHARDS

BILLY BUNTER of Greyfriars

Harry Wharton, Bob Cherry, Frank Nugent, Johnny Bull and Hurree Singh, the Indian boy, were known as the Famous Five of Greyfriars. As they made their way to the school gates one half-holiday, the fat figure of Billy Bunter hurried towards them.

His round face brimming with wrath, the fat owl of the Remove form glared after the Famous Five as they strolled out through the gates. In the lane outside was a poorly dressed man with a tray of matches and a label attached to the front of his jacket.

Lord Marmaduke—"Snooty" to you—and his streetwise pals come to the aid of the local bootless urchins with a fund-raising campaign.
When this flops, they round up some dogs and get them trained to steal shoes, so the uncaring public can experience being poor and barefoot.
Beano artist Dudley Watkins adds jokes, like the dog with a dunce's hat, into almost every panel in this social-conscience episode from 1939.

ABOVE: "Smile please!" The official photograph from 1926 of Class 1 of a middle-class all-boys school, most of them in their best grey flannel uniforms or jerkins.

LEFT: It's the war of the tuck shops when plucky fourth-former Sandy Dean deduces that dodgy competitor Skinflint Blayde is behind a mysterious fire that has damaged the school's shop. Barry Nelson's serial ran for nearly thirteen years in *Lion* and was drawn here by an unknown artist through the agent Gwen Wooley on 24 July 1954.

BELOW: Before *The Flintstones*, there was *Stonehenge Kit, The Ancient Brit*, caveboy comedy drawn by Reg Parlett from *Knockout*, 23 December 1951. In this inventive parody of the Festival of Britain that year, Kit sees "three dimensional pitchers", a nod to the Festival's innovation of 3D Cinema, and visits the science exhibits in the "Dome of Discovery".

BELOW: To compete with *The Dandy* and *The Beano*, Amalgamated Press launched *The Knockout* in 1939. Two of its junior stars were *Our Ernie*, the Entwhistle lad from Wigan, and overeager boy scout *Deed-A-Day Danny*, both penned by Hugh McNeill. He drew this episode in 1942 at the same size as it would appear in the weekly on a blue airmail letter which he sent from North Africa where he was stationed in the army.

88

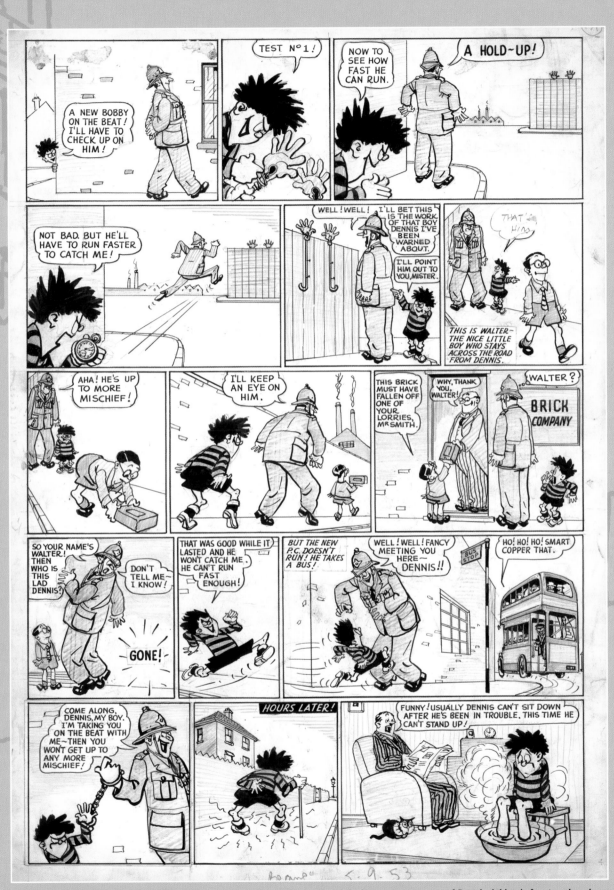

Anarchy in UK comics storms into *The Beano* in 1951. Dennis the Menace is the catalyst to dispel the lingering quaintness soaf of British children's funnies, though not quite overnight. David Law's lines bristle with a barely contained energy that belies his perfectionist draughtsmanship. As Molesworth had his "weedy wet" opposite number Fotherington-Thomas, so here Dennis comes up against Walter with his glasses and neatly combed hair, from Saturday 14 November 1953. Boys are expected to be naughty and there are no soft options.

Beano readers enjoyed twist after twist in only twelve panels as the Bash Street Kids persuade Teacher to get them ringside seats at the circus.
When they pass Teacher's home, you can spot his identical wife, a dustbin full of homework and a front gate made of canes and mortarboards.
To achieve such details Leo Baxendale drew this original artwork in two halves for The Beano of 29 July 1961.

LEFT: Crazy-paving was once all the rage on patios and here Roger devises a cunning dodge with a fishing rod and fly to save him from having to wield a heavy one-hundred-weight hammer, but it inevitably backfires on him. Ken Reid drew this page for the 1962 *Beano Book*.

ABOVE: Never seen without his working-class flat cap, Buster began in his own weekly in 1960 as the supposed "son of Andy Capp", much to the surprise of Reg Smythe, creator of the childless Andy and Flo in the *Daily Mirror*. Andy was never seen (he was probably off down the pub), though Buster's mum looked a lot like Flo. Hitting conkers or horse-chestnuts threaded onto string was once a common game, but recent worries about safety have led to it being banned in many schools. Drawn by the Spanish artist Angel Nadal for the first *Buster Holiday Fun Special* in 1969.

ABOVE: More caps and blazers in *The Dandy*'s boarding-school comedies starring keen-witted Winker Watson. When form master Mr Creep cancels the half-term holiday, Winker and his brother Wally compete to find ways to escape the school grounds. Eric Roberts began drawing this series in 1961.

ABOVE: Bully Beef lived up to his name, tormenting Chips, but usually ends up the worse for it. Jimmy Hughes drew this for the 1972 *Dandy Annual*.

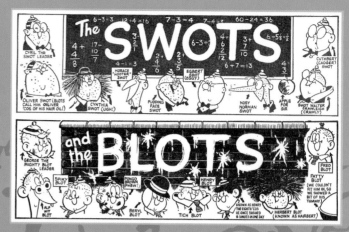

ABOVE: In Leo Baxendale's follow-up for *Smash!* in 1966, gang warfare across the divides of class and IQ pits the creepy, clever upper-class kids against their messy lower-class rivals.

LEFT: After *Bash Street*, Baxendale went back into the classroom to invent *The Tiddlers* for *Wham!* Corporal punishment and wooden desks with inkwells might now be things of the past, but canes and water pistols full of ink were perfect props for slapstick. This ran on the cover on 30 October 1965.

BELOW: Baxendale's potty boy inventor Clever Dick joined *Buster* from 1970. His "invenshuns" are the modern counterparts of the sublimely complex mechanical solutions by cartoonist William Heath Robinson (1872–1944) to the most mundane of tasks, in this case, how to deliver piping hot chips to his dad before they go cold.

BELOW: Whereas Lord Snooty is pals with the poor, the spoilt rich kid Ivor Lott looks down on "riffraff" like Tony Broke, a pun on "stony broke" or penniless. Reg Parlett drew their first day at school in *Cor!*, 6 June 1970.

LEFT: Ever since Brian White's *Nipper*, "Babies Rule OK!" in kids' comics. One of the wackiest developers of Baxendale's later style is Tom Paterson, the brain behind the terrorising baby Sweeny Toddler. This deranged tale from the 1978 *Shiver and Shake Annual* involves Sweeny rescuing his pet frogs from a drooling French chef. The pages are sprinkled with extra sight gags starring that little black cat, as well as Sweeny's ghastly frog impersonation and lots of Baxendale's signature signs, floating words and arrows. Don't miss the small thundercloud of gloom over the doomed frogs.

BELOW: Two totally out-of-control tots for the price of one when Barrie Appleby's Cuddles, born in 1981 in *Nutty*, teamed with the disastrous Dimples in *The Dandy*. "Daddums" never stood a chance.

ABOVE: *The Beano*'s happy brood included Baby Face Finlayson, drawn by Ron Spence from 1972. Here, the pram-riding miniature bandit escapes the law by turning his "Wanted" posters upside down, handily forming a different face, but he is recognised in the end when he does some handstands.

LEFT: Meet sweet-toothed Baby Crockett, a play on Davy Crockett, who thinks and speaks in his own intelligible "baby-speak". Bill Ritchie drew this dental health warning in the 1962 *Beezer Annual*.

ABOVE: In *The Nervs*, Ken Reid takes us inside the body of Fatty to see all its grotesque inner workings and the different departments struggling to maintain it. These are Reid's original artworks for the final episode in *Smash!* 162, 8 March 1969.

RIGHT: Among the numerous kids with exceptional gifts in comics, Faceache must be about the weirdest, able to "scrunge" or transform the "excess molecules" in his face, and his whole body if need be, into all manner of hideous shapes. Here, Ken Reid's body humour shows Faceache's X-ray session freaking out a doctor, from *Buster*, 26 March 1977.

To win one pound, Dare-A-Day Davy invited "Powsters" (readers of *Pow!*) to set him a challenge, in this case "Let a frog loose in a posh café", which Ken Reid elaborates into stomach-churning mayhem. Reid refers to censorship in his penultimate panel; in fact, one *Davy* episode was banned as entirely unsuitable for publication. This is his original art, drawn in two halves, for *Pow!* 106, 25 January 1969.

BELOW: Several edgier real-life dramas for children's TV in the 1980s were adapted into comics. Phil Redmond's *Grange Hill* for the BBC became the serial *Grange Hill Juniors* in *School Fun*, the first weekly devoted to school funnies. Here Zammo is feeling guilty about his faulty bike causing Jonah to be hospitalised in a coma, but then he writes to Jonah's favourite pop star to ask him to try and wake the injured boy with his songs. Art by Brian Delaney for 24 March 1984.

ABOVE: In *Look Out For Lefty* by Tom Tully and Tony Harding in *Action*, 18 September 1976, left-footed school-leaver Kenny "Lefty" Lampton is taken on by local third-division football club Wigford Rovers for their reserves. He has a chance of joining the first team as a substitute if he plays well in this game, but treacherous rival Jarvis Jenkins sets him up to fail. Furious at this, Kenny's girlfriend Angie Roberts chucks a Coke bottle at Jarvis and she not only shifts the blame to thugs from the other team's supporters, but is silently praised as "Good ole Angel!" by Kenny. This apparent endorsement of hooliganism and *Action*'s violence in general prompted fierce criticism by the media, parents, the Football League and others and IPC's decision to halt the title five weeks later. Three weeks later, after Kenny himself was nearly hit by a flying bottle, he tried lobbing it back at a gang of enemy fans called The Rotherfield Rippers, but he is stopped in time by the captain: "Us professionals are supposed to set an example!" This moral lesson came too late, however, to save the weekly from suspension after the following issue.

LEFT: The violent near-future serial *Kids Rule O.K.!* appears on the controversial cover by Carlos Ezquerra of *Action*, 18 September 1976. What upset many is that the helmet, bottom right, suggests that it is a policeman being attacked by the chain-wielding youth.

RIGHT: Brian Finch's *Murphy's Mob* for Central TV revolves around the members of Dunmore United's youth club, run by Mac Murphy. Here a "tartan 'orror" from Glasgow causes trouble on the housing estate. Drawn by Barrie Mitchell in *Look-in*, 16 April 1983.

ABOVE: In his quest for creative freedom, Baxendale quit IPC in 1975 to create the first of three solo annuals for publishers Duckworth, which introduced Willy the Kid the following year. Liberated from editorial and format constraints, he cuts loose in this 1976 carol-singing scene.

LEFT: Baxendale admirer Steve Bell, the *Guardian*'s political and strip cartoonist, imagines how the lives of The Bash Street Kids and Minnie the Minx might have worked out thirty years later in 1984. Oblivious to his ugliness, Plug always knew he was destined for greatness.

ABOVE: Chris Donald took Bully Beef's knockabout violence in *The Dandy* to absurd extremes in his foul-mouthed Scottish psychopath Biffa Bacon, who first "biffed" a total stranger in glasses in *Viz* 7, 1981. In this later opening scene, Biffa is stunned to find his stubble-chinned parents trying to be middle-class by playing "crur-kay" (croquet) and eating "canopies" (canapés). This episode was concocted by Chris and Simon Donald, Simon Thorp, Graham Dury and David Jones for *Viz* 94, February 1999.

RIGHT: Flatulent Johnny Fartpants promises to be on his best bottom behaviour on his first holiday on his own to meet his French and German counterparts. Disaster strikes while he is crossing the English Channel when the hovercraft's engine fails, but Johnny's gigantic pumps save the day. Simon Donald and Graham Dury devised this tale for the 1988 *Viz Holiday Special*.

LEFT: Taking a cue from Sue Townsend's 1982 novel *The Secret Diary of Adrian Mole, aged 13¾*, Hadrian Vile was another bespectacled "clever dick" whose "Kung-Foo" scares off the school bully. His spelling is as hopeless as Molesworth's in this entry from his diary, zanily drawn by Ian Jackson for *Oink!*, 20 September 1986.

ABOVE RIGHT: Caricatured skinheads also caused "aggro" in 1980s humour comics. In his boots and braces, Tom Thug, a reference to Tom Thumb, is finally caught by the truancy officer. Tough but thick, he is so far behind at school that he is relegated to the first-year class who are even better at bullying than he is. Lew Stringer created this for *Oink!*, 4 October 1986.

RIGHT: More trouble breaks out near the football terraces with Chris Long's label-conscious "bovverboy" Trogga, from *Escape* 5, 1984.

FAR RIGHT: Contrary to the more up-to-date, realistic comics of the 1970s, *Just William* harked back to the more innocent 1920s era of Richmal Crompton's original books, adapted into a 1977 TV series and spin-off annual. Here, after his explosives experiments and pocket-money are stopped, the scruffy dreamer plots to run away from home. Artist uncredited.

BELOW: New kids on the *Beano* and *Dandy* blocks include skateboarder Ollie Fliptrick, determined to stop developers building houses on his skatepark. Art by Karl Dixon in *The Dandy*, 14 February 2004.

BELOW: Getting into the spooky spirit of Halloween, black boy detective Dreadlock Holmes dresses up as Frankenstein and goes trick-or-treating with his sister in *The Dandy*, 30 October 2004, by Stephen White.

ABOVE: In *A Trip to Twinsanity* in 2005, Brian Wood's *Cramp Twins* spun off from their TV cartoons into comic albums. Because Wayne Cramp forced Lucien to use his toothbrush, DNA tests using both unlikely twins' brushes mistakenly reveal that they are identical.

ABOVE: "From the mouth of babes ..." Faceless baby seer Leviathan, Levi for short, is more interested in the big questions than acquiring "social skills", but the big kids can't understand his baby talk "Dep!" and force him to conform. Peter Blegvad addresses the dark and droll in his 1990s *Independent* strips.

99

Holiday Playtime with 'GIRL'!

RACES! GAMES! COMPETITIONS!

Have you seen our holiday playground at:—

BRIDLINGTON • CANVEY ISLAND • LITTLEHAMPTON
LLANDUDNO • LOWESTOFT • MARGATE • BOGNOR
BARRY • MORECAMBE • NEWQUAY • SANDOWN • SKEGNESS
SHANKLIN • PORTHCAWL • RAMSGATE • AYR

And next week we shall be in
Paignton, too!
Come along and join in the fun!

Don't forget your current
copy of GIRL

It is all FREE!

Watch out for local news of our Treasure Hunt in many other seaside towns

HOLIDAY PLAYTIME!

It's high summer at the seaside at Worthing in August 1955 and the kids all scream with glee, frantically waving their comics, as this photograph is snapped. They are brandishing the current issues of *Eagle*, published on the glorious 12th, or *Girl*, published two days before (and one or two copies of *Swift*, too), which entitled you to a free afternoon of fun and games on the beach. As the advertisement in *Girl* that week, shown ABOVE LEFT, proclaimed: "Races! Games! Competitions! It is all free!" On the cover of *Eagle*, Dan Dare is in underwater peril, produced by Frank Hampson and his studio, while on the cover of *Girl* Wendy sets off on a rescue mission to save her best friend Jinx, held by smugglers, in a story by Stephen James, illustrated by Ray Bailey and Philip Townsend.

Things to Come

"ON AUGUST FOURTH, EARTH YEAR NINETEEN HUNDRED SIXTY-NINE, THE FIRST BEING SET FOOT ON THE MOON AT THIS POINT ... HIS NAME WAS HOMO SAPIENS."

SO READ THE TEXT engraved on a metal plaque screwed onto a sculpted pillar of rock standing on the lunar surface. Amazingly, this striking image appeared in 1959 in the newspaper strip *Jeff Hawke* by Sydney Jordan, whose prediction of the actual date of the first moon landing a decade later, on 21 July 1969, was out by only two weeks. Jordan later recalled, "To come within fourteen days of the event from ten years previously was a happy chance, but my choice of the year 1969 was based on my knowledge and understanding of the potential of American and German spaceflight engineering." This is one example of how the worlds of science fiction and science fact can be more closely connected than we sometimes realise, feeding off and informing each other.

Harsh critics tended to dismiss the popular writings of Jules Verne, H.G. Wells and other pioneers of the genre as the stuff of daydreams or, worse, as irresponsible fantasies. They forgot that, before we can construct and live in the future, we need to imagine it. What better way to do this than in the words and pictures of science fiction in books, films and comics? From the man-made monster reanimated by Doctor Frankenstein, to the malfunctioning inventions of Wallace in *Wallace and*

RIGHT: Alexander Korda's 1936 adaptation of H.G. Wells' 1933 book *The Shape of Things To Come* was a landmark in British science fiction film-making.

BELOW: Children were instantly attracted to this 1950s *Magic Robot* magnetic game made by Merit Toys and so was artist Denis McLoughlin, who used the robot to draw from in his comics.

Gromit, these speculative stories enable us to explore the varied relationships between men and machines, society and science. Whether dire warnings such as Wells' *The Shapes of Things to Come* in 1933 or amusing spoofs, they help us predict and prepare for the unstoppable march of progress and the benefits and dangers it brings.

By the dawn of the 20th century, many of Verne's novels had been translated into English and serialised in the weekly *Boy's Own Paper*, while Wells had built a huge readership since his debut, *The Time Machine*, in 1895. Their success would encourage other British authors to try tales of fantastic science, some of them rather rudimentary, in the pages of boys' story papers. Several of these dramatic adventures would eventually be recycled and adapted into comics, but for the moment comics were essentially comical and so new technology was at first treated as a subject for comedy. Prime examples include *Professor Radium* by Tom Wilkinson. While Radium began simply as a know-it-all and busybody, he soon became one of the archetypal nutty professors, devising a novel notion each week in *Puck* from 1904 to 1916, which inevitably ended in disaster. The Machine Age would prove ripe for satire in the work of the American Rube Goldberg and the Dane Storm Petersen, as well as the almost practical contraptions, held together by knotted string, of Britain's William Heath Robinson. H.G. Wells admired him for "his deliberate, cold-blooded absurdity".

OPPOSITE: Denis McLoughlin paints the front cover of this *Adventure Annual*, published by T.V. Boardman c. 1953, showing his intrepid spaceman Swift Morgan firing a ray gun at a familiar-looking robot.

BELOW: In *Puck* on 18 August 1906, Tom Wilkinson has his Professor Radium invent "an automatic policeman. They are made of wood and wheels and are lifelong teetotallers. You simply press a button and get all the information you please." But hitting the wrong button, as short-sighted Mrs Hayseed has done here, causes chaos.

5. "Ah, that's better now! Wunnerful what a difrince glarses make, isn't it, sir? She's living with her aunt, at 21, Belmont or Belmint, or p'raps it's Nelinont Road, London, and we've just come——" By the bye, old Hayseed has fairly dislocated its old neck, hasn't he? Talk about fright. Even Radium has it,

Any absurdity was not intentional in the first science fiction serial in British comics in 1936, though there was a quaint Englishness and clunky Jules Vernean charm to the story and designs of *Ian on Mu*. It was created for children by Hugh Stanley White in the revolutionary *Mickey Mouse Weekly*. White brought alien creatures into British comics with the Hexpod, which fellow artist Basil Reynolds recalled as "an endearing celestial being ... with six seaweed-type arms and six seaweed-type legs sprouting from it. In spite of its paucity of language (it confined itself to strange remarks like 'Ig!' and 'Ca!'), it was extremely popular". White's rendering was ornate, old-fashioned and similar to that of artist Dick Calkins, whose *Buck Rogers* strip introduced science fiction into American newspapers in 1929 and later ran in the British magazine *Everybody's*.

Another American export, *Flash Gordon*, lush with the glamour of Alex Raymond's illustrations, streamlined the look of science fiction wherever it went. In Britain, his Sunday page strips from 1934 began to be reprinted in colour in the story paper *Modern Wonder* in 1939, supported by the *Flash Gordon* movie serials shown from 1936. Their influence is clear on Denis McLoughlin, who gave his blond space hero the almost identical name of *Swift Morgan* in 1948 in the first of a series of American-size comic books printed as orange-and-green photogravure. After three issues, Denis was joined by his scriptwriting brother Colin. Denis's spacecraft, guns and robots may look familiar, because he drew them from toys he bought in Woolworths, where his comics were mainly sold. As for the sleek white outfits of Swift Morgan and his female companion Silver, they recall costumes in the 1936 film of Wells's *Things To Come*. Sometimes the McLoughlins overstepped the line. In one adventure set in ancient Rome, Silver is pinned down by a lecherous emperor who leers, "As a servant you are no use, but ..." This suggestive panel led to the issue being banned by Woolworths.

RIGHT: Tweed three-piece suits are the Jules Vernean fashions in Hugh Stanley White's charming serial *Flashing Through*. Here, botanist Wade and crew are saved by his young daughter Sheila from a "half-mad scientist" and the side effects of a passing comet, only to hurtle towards the planet Que. This cliffhanger appeared in *Mickey Mouse Weekly*, 2 July 1938.

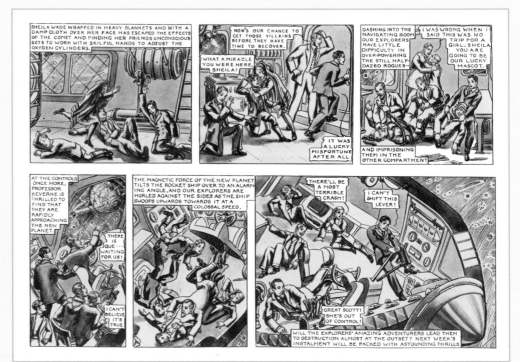

Far more suggestive scenes would become the norm for the beefy mystery man Garth, washed ashore in 1943 in the *Daily Mirror*, reduced in wartime to only eight pages. While newspaper strips had caught on in Britain later than in America and were initially aimed more at children, strips like *Garth* would take a surprisingly relaxed attitude towards near-nudity and innuendo. The puritan restraint between Flash Gordon and his ardent girlfriend Dale Arden was not for Garth. Built like Charles Atlas, he was the object of virtually every female character's desire and obliged many of them, though mostly off-panel. The *Mirror*'s female readers could fancy him too, while the men could fantasise about being him.

A young officer in the Royal Army Service Corps had another fantasy in 1944, as he gazed up in horror at the vapour trails of the Nazis' "rocketbombs" pounding the port of Antwerp, Belgium. He wished he could be up there, flying in the Royal Air Force; the RAF board had accepted him, but the Army would not let him transfer. Years later, thinking back to that ravaged sky, Frank Hampson realised that "space travel was born in those neat cottonwool lines. The lines were, alas, the first realisation of the dreams of the scientists and inventors who had been working for years with little two- and three-foot models. Hitler warped their dreams into ends that were foul and repulsive. But dreamers have a habit of not giving up. And now the world is on the threshold of the greatest step in its history. Very soon man is going to cross space and explore the planets around him." Demobbed in 1946, Lieutenant Hampson would live his dream of flight in 1950 by creating an alter ego for a "new national strip cartoon weekly", *Eagle*. Dan Dare's debut showed him as a tall, lean, heroic version of Hampson, right down to his pipe and his distinctive eyebrows scarred during the war. Dare's stout batman Digby from

Wigan showed another side of Hampson, the solid, no-nonsense Lancastrian family man.

The unlikely co-founder of *Eagle* was Marcus Morris, a clergyman who with Hampson's help had modernised his local parish magazine and went on to form The Society of Christian Publicity in 1948. After Hitler's brutalising effect on much of Germany's youth, Britain's children were seen more than ever as in need of protection and sound guidance. In response to his concerns that a minority of American comics available as imports or British reprints were exposing children to gore and sadism, Morris teamed up with Hampson to offer a thoroughly wholesome alternative. When their first proposal, a newspaper strip, appropriately a Sunday page, about Lex Christian, an East End chaplain, was scuppered by the death of the *Sunday Empire News*'s editor, they resolved to go all out and create a whole weekly comic. In the dummy, they sent their padre into space as *Dan Dare*; luckily, by *Eagle*'s first issue, he had lost his dog collar and been re-named "Pilot of the Future".

The future would land in the heart of London, on the South Bank of the Thames, on Friday, 4 May 1951, when the public first filed through the gates of the Festival of Britain. Located diagonally opposite the Houses of

ABOVE: No fears of radiation poisoning when you're Captain Conquest. You can grab an engine's uranium to disable the Martian invaders' ship, then speak the magic word "Karagan" and revert to reporter Flash Dale. The name of Captain Conquest's alter ego and his winged helmet like the god Mercury's show the undoubted influence of *Flash Gordon* on Michael Hubbard, who drew this for the 1952 *Knockout Annual*.

LEFT: Flying saucers became so much part of the culture that they appeared as sherbet-filled sweets.

ABOVE: In the 1949 dummy of *Eagle*, Dan Dare was a rather smug interplanetary vicar, whose original name had been Lex Christian. This might have been closer to the fantasies of editor Reverend Marcus Morris than those of Frank Hampson. Fortunately, Dare was soon changed to a "Pilot of the Future" for the *Eagle*'s first issue on 14 April 1950.

RIGHT: This model of Dan Dare's arch enemy The Mekon was created in 1977 to Frank Hampson's instructions by Terry Reed, a sculptress who worked on the *Eagle* staff, and was shown in London's Science Museum until 1984. It was 104 cm (41 inches) tall.

BELOW: It looked as if the aliens had landed. The centrepiece of the 1951 Festival of Britain was the Dome of Discovery, shown here lit up at night.

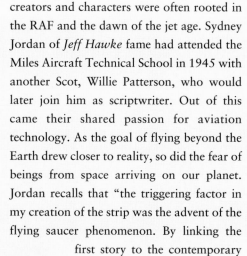

Parliament, the former 27-acre bombsite was dominated by the 365-foot diameter science exhibit, the Dome of Discovery, which looked as if a flying saucer had landed next to the river, and by the Skylon, a sculpture soaring 300 feet high like a sleek space rocket poised for lift-off. The Festival was a time machine that transported eight million visitors to a visible, tangible future "made in Britain". As designer Hugh Casson wrote in 1976 in *A Tonic to the Nation*, "The real achievement ... was that it made people want things to be better, and to believe that they could be." The new spirit of national optimism after Elizabeth II's coronation per-vaded Hampson's picture of a very British future, although not everything in it was rosy. Dare's first urgent mission took him to Venus in search of the right conditions to grow food for a starving, overpopulated Earth. This scenario would have struck a chord with British readers who had to put up with rationing that was even stricter than during the Second World War right up until 1954.

Dan Dare was the first of several "Pilots of the Future", whose creators and characters were often rooted in the RAF and the dawn of the jet age. Sydney Jordan of *Jeff Hawke* fame had attended the Miles Aircraft Technical School in 1945 with another Scot, Willie Patterson, who would later join him as scriptwriter. Out of this came their shared passion for aviation technology. As the goal of flying beyond the Earth drew closer to reality, so did the fear of beings from space arriving on our planet. Jordan recalls that "the triggering factor in my creation of the strip was the advent of the flying saucer phenomenon. By linking the first story to the contemporary newsworthy nature of the 'sightings', it was possible to make a 'space' connection [in the strip], at a time when rocket science was still in its teething stage." Jordan made Jeff Hawke an RAF fighter pilot, which also helped sell the concept in 1954 to Max Aitken, son of *Daily Express* publisher Lord Beaverbrook. Aitken had flown in the Battle of Britain and worked with several of his RAF mates on the paper's editorial board. In the opening story, Hawke is rescued from his stricken plane in the upper atmosphere by a flying saucer and resuscitated from the brink of death. Telepathic aliens offer him a choice: either to return to Earth and forget all he has seen, or "to go among the peoples of the galaxy, to see a hundred suns, to breathe the air of a thousand planets, and finally to dwell with us between the stars". Without hesitation, Hawke decides: "I choose the stars ... the black spaceways ... and the shining silence".

The spaceways were soon buzzing with other airmen who had chosen the stars, in comics and on the air. *Dan Dare* was adapted into a Radio Luxembourg serial from 1951, of which sadly no episodes survive, and was followed in 1953 by Charles Chilton's *Journey into Space* on the BBC, which starred Jet Morgan and his

Dare, Digby, Sir Hubert and Peabody are on their *Voyage to Venus* to find the right conditions to grow food for a hungry Earth. In the lush alien jungle, Dare blasts a giant python and saves Treen defector Sondar. Original art by Frank Hampson with his studio in fine form from *Eagle* 24, 29 September 1950.

crew. This was adapted into comics but only in 1956, after the radio series had ended. Less clean-cut space pilots included Captain Condor, unjustly imprisoned and on the run to clear his name, Jet-Ace Logan, a hot-headed rebel, and smooth investigator Rick Random, who solved cases set centuries ahead. *Rick Random* artist Ron Turner showed him smoking, typical of detectives of the 1950s, though, as he said, "somewhat anachronistic, as it's highly unlikely that the physical act of inhaling large quantities of smoke for pleasure will exist 300 years from now". Using his exuberant imagination, Turner crafted towering Art Deco-inspired architecture and sleek spacecraft that were all shiny metal and sharp fins.

Still recovering from the devastating effects of the war, people needed to look forward to a brighter, better world and found tales of technological wonders appealing and even spiritually uplifting. As households filled with the latest labour-saving devices and transport and communications advanced, comics reflected the prospect of living with all kinds of marvels, from mechanical pals Brassneck, Big Klanky or Robot Archie to boys' toys like General Jumbo's remote control army and Flip McCoy The Floating Boy's backpack helicopter. The time-travelling Tardis was as much of a character in the BBC TV series as all the Doctor Whos and their assistants. Joining them in the comics came Terry Nation's exterminating Daleks, the chilling outcome of living creatures fusing themselves with technology to survive.

Other ever more wonderful machines became the real stars of Gerry Anderson's 1960s science fiction television puppet series. It was not long before the idea of a comic devoted to them found a publisher. Anderson brought in as editor Alan Fennell, a writer whose adaptations of *Supercar* and *Fireball XL5* in *TV Comic* had won him the job of writing for the shows themselves, to

adapt them to the page. Anderson suggested that he model the new weekly on a futuristic newspaper, something Hampson had already done on the cover of *Eagle* 25 in 1950. Fennell applied this design idea to the front cover of the new comic, entitled *TV Century 21,* by using bold headlines and large colour photos, a format not seen in actual British newspapers until years later, and dating the issue one hundred years in advance. Fennell's aim was to create the equivalent of *Eagle* for the 1960s, so to draw the comics inside, he wanted to hire the cream of *Eagle*'s artists. He asked Frank Bellamy, artist on *Heros* in *Eagle*, to draw *Stingray,* about a nuclear-powered submarine and its crew, fighting the Aquaphibians, for the first issue of *TV*

Century 21 due out on 23 January 1965. Bellamy felt committed to *Eagle* and so declined, but once *Heros* was over, he joined the new comic, where he took on Anderson's next series, *Thunderbirds.* Transferring their unnaturally proportioned puppets into comics posed a problem. According to Bellamy, "I had to decide whether to make them look like the puppets they were, or the people they were supposed to be. I went for forgetting they were puppets, other than simplifying the heads, which had to be recognisable from the established versions on the television." Another difference for British audiences, used to watching the colour shows in black and white on the box, was that the photogravure comics were painted in dazzling widescreen colour, years before colour television would begin in Britain.

Millions watched the moon landing in 1969, a momentous event that might seem to make science fiction redundant. Some three months earlier, *Eagle* had folded its wings, only a year or so from its 20th anniversary. In the 1970s, Anderson's following series, as well as successive *Doctor Whos* and other shows, would continue to appear in comics. In 1975, however, when Kelvin Gosnell, an office junior, suggested an SF comic to the head and deputy of IPC's boys' comic department, he recalls, "They told me science fiction was dead and it would never sell." What they had not read was a newspaper feature by film critic Alexander Walker. Writing about director George Lucas's *Star Wars* hit that was in production, he predicted that science fiction

1947   1953   1966   1981   1992   2005

would be the next big thing in Hollywood. Gosnell put his proposal in a memo to his colleague, writer and editor Pat Mills, noting "even if it planned to run only as long as the boom lasts, it must make money while riding the crest and could be used for a merge when [note when, rather than if] it becomes uneconomic. Although, given the right mix, I am certain that it would stand a good chance of surviving much longer than the movie boom." How right he would be. Mills sent the proposal up to the top and got the green light to develop a science-fiction comic. Never expecting a lengthy run, IPC managing editor John Sanders would later come up with its title: "Normally, a successful comics lasts for up to twelve years, so I joked at the time we should call it *2000AD*, because it would be dead and buried by then." In fact, the "Galaxy's Greatest Comic" would outlast the date it was never meant to see. When the millennium neared, speculation was rife that *2000AD* would have to change name, perhaps to *3000AD*, but as one lifetime reader, "SNB" from Nottingham, put it in 1999, "I don't care what they call it next year. The content has seldom had anything to do with that date anyway, it's just semantics. What matters is that it was, is and always will be part of what makes me me." *2000AD*'s title stayed unchanged; more than a date, it had become a brand, an attitude, an identity.

Disturbingly, the closer we get to the future, the closer *2000AD*'s sardonic extrapolations of ourselves and our world come to resemble real life. In the sprawling Mega-City One, formerly America's Eastern seaboard, its inhabitants are subject to all the pressures of overcrowded city life, crammed into termite-mound-shaped apartment blocks named after unlikely celebrities, like Britain's high-rise sink estates, and seduced into eccentric fads like Fatties' competitive overeating or Otto Sump's cult of ugliness. *2000AD*'s most original character was the strong-arm future cop Judge Dredd. Garbed in punk accessories like the large zip, heavy chains and massive boots, he was a nightmarish response to the British establishment's fears about the social and industrial rest of the period and a warning as to how policing might evolve after the riot police that quelled the miners' strike and poll tax riots. Academic Martin Barker researched *2000AD*'s readers and found that while some enjoyed the irony and critique, others took Dredd at face value, admiring his incorruptibility and endorsing his methods as the only way to stop crime. Dredd's double-edged sword of satire cuts both ways.

In contrast, after assorted revamps of the clean-cut Dan Dare, in *2000AD* (1977), *Eagle* (Version 2, 1982), *Revolver* (1990), the *Planet on Sunday* newspaper (which ran for only one issue on 16 June 1996), in *The Times* as Peter Brookes's strip *Dan Blair*, and in a CGI-animated TV series, his fans have sent him back to the 1950s where he began in new retro tales for *Spaceship Away* magazine by Keith Watson, Don Harley and other original artists. As for the eagle that adorned *Eagle*'s covers—flying high, looking forward—it lives on in Dredd as a more sinister symbol, worn on every Judge's right shoulder, belt and badge, perched on the front of their Lawmaster bikes and over the Chief Judge's chair. This eagle is not the inkwell or church lectern that inspired Hampson; it is a symbol of the agents of justice—brutal, faceless, concealed within their helmets.

But comics since the 1970s have bred new heroes, like Luther Arkwright in *Near Myths* and *pssst!,* who liberates the British from Cromwellian tyranny to restore the monarchy, or V, a terrorist or a freedom-fighter dressed in a Guy Fawkes mask, who wrests control of the country from an Orwellian dictator. Messianic or anarchist, these and other figures for the new millennium help us to see that we don't have to face the future with Dredd.

FAR LEFT: In 2004, Brighton Police in riot gear look on uneasily while they protect the Labour party conference from a pro-hunting demonstration outside.

BELOW: Could Judge Dredd, illustrated below by his original designer Carlos Ezquerra, become the face of British policing in the 21st century?

RIGHT: Versatile daily strip cartoonist Steve Dowling came up with the concept of *Garth* with BBC producer Gordon Boshell in 1943 for the *Daily Mirror*, but it was with writers Don Freeman, Peter O'Donnell and Jim Edgar that Dowling chronicled the first 25 years of the hero's multiple past and future lives, ably assisted by John Allard. Dowling drew this strip in 1964; it is from the *Garth* episode entitled "The Rebels" by O'Donnell, about an alternative history in which Hitler has won the war.

RIGHT: By 1971, the *Mirror* felt that *Garth* was in need of updating, so they hired Frank Bellamy as illustrator, who replaced the bulky strong-man look with a more dashing, thin-waisted leading man. This strip comes from the close of the episode "The Women of Galba", written by Jim Edgar in 1973.

RIGHT: After Bellamy's death in 1976, Martin Asbury took over and drew Jim Edgar's script "Mr Rubio Calls" in 1977. Garth kept his mystery to the end in 1997, when Martin Asbury's last cliffhanger sent him hurtling back to his origins, as if the 44-year saga had finally come full circle.

BELOW RIGHT: Frank Bellamy's cover for the 1975 *Daily Mirror Book of Garth*.

BELOW: Male readers who wanted a body like Garth's could order muscle-building courses from the Body Sculpture Club.

LEFT: Few daily newspaper strip artists had rendered such believable alien creatures and their other-worldly surroundings before Sydney Jordan on *Jeff Hawke*. His skilful control of chiaroscuro and feathering combined with an innovative use of dot and textured screentones to pull each drawing together. This example, taken from original artwork, comes from the 1957 story *Out of Touch* written by American SF author and former comic artist, Harry Harrison.

ABOVE: The cover by Brian Bolland for the second and final book of *Jeff Hawke* strips in 1987. This compiled the story "Counsel for the Defence", an outer-space satire of cumbersome courtroom procedure, written by Willie Patterson in 1961.

LEFT: In this three-strip sequence from "Counsel for the Defense", Hawke and his crew seem powerless as arch-villain Chalcedon hijacks his trial proceedings and manages to hoodwink the judge into pardoning him for all his crimes. Another signature approach by Jordan is his regular use of a single-panel strip to give widescreen vistas of his cast and settings, as in the third strip here.

111

LEFT AND ABOVE: Before the microchip was the valve, the idea of miniaturising computers was barely the stuff of science fiction. So artist Ron Turner based his futuristic building-sized brain, Big-Jumbo, on the first bulky post-war computers such as the Univac 1, Universal Automatic Computer, ABOVE. It was 50 feet long and 25 feet wide, and used 5,600 valves, 18,000 crystal diodes and 300 relays. It was the first commercially available computer in America in 1951. Turner's original art was drawn for *Sabotage from Space* in *Super Detective Library* 111, September 1957, one of Rick Random's 27 cases in the series.

BELOW: These three pages come from Random's last case, *The Kidnapped Planet*, written by Bob Keston in *Super Detective Library* 163, December 1959. They demonstrate Turner's daring ideas and execution of technical design: Rick's cockpit control panel crammed with buttons, dials and TV communications screen; the complex "Astro-Graph" for projecting planetary data; and elegant one-person rockets, one of them piloted by Rick's very capable and attractive colleague.

ABOVE: *Express Super Colour Weekly* devoted most of its colour centre spread to this strip based on the popular BBC radio series *Journey into Space*. It was written by creator Charles Chilton and drawn by Italy's Ferdinando Tacconi, who came to live with the Chiltons for a time to draw the strip. This first episode appeared on 28 April 1956.

RIGHT: Michael Butterworth and Geoff Campion created the impulsive Jet-Ace Logan for *Comet*. In this page by their successors, David Morton and John Gillat, for *Comet*, 16 November 1957, Logan and co-pilot Plum-Duff Charteris are forced to retreat in the face of enemy ships on Saturn's moon, Titan. Logan's run came to 413 episodes from 1956 to 1964.

ABOVE: In 1952, Battle of Britain pilot Roland Beamont was the first test pilot to make a double Atlantic crossing by jet, inspiring a squadron of jet aces in 1950s comics.

ABOVE: Thanks to their trusty transmitter, cadets Jason and Mike can master intergalactic communications across "millions of miles" and alert Captain Condor. Frank S. Pepper's *Condor*, drawn here by Ronald Forbes on 3 May 1958, was *Lion's* rival to *Dan Dare* in *Eagle*.

113

ABOVE AND RIGHT: Nicknamed "Tin-Bonce" and riveted like a red cast-iron boiler, Robot Archie surprises his masters Ted Ritchie and Ken Dale with his super-strength feats. The 1976 *Lion Annual* cover is by Geoff Campion. The comic page by George Cowan ran in *Lion*, 13 August 1966.

FAR RIGHT: The only man able to control the British secret weapon known as *The Steel Commando* is barefoot Lance Corporal Ernie "Excused Boots" Bates, except here when a short circuit gives the robot soldier a shock. Alan Henderson drew this for the 1976 *Lion Annual*.

RIGHT: The crazes for model soldiers and remote-control cars inspired General Jumbo, below left, alias chubby Alfie Johnson in naval cap and droopy socks. Directing his own tiny army with the control and flashing aerial on his wrist, Jumbo keeps order and sorts out smart alecs and ruffians. Drawn by Paddy Brennan in the 1957 *Beano Book*.

FAR RIGHT: Charley Brand's tin pal *Brassneck*, below right, helps him get his own back on mean teacher "Fatso" Snodgrass, who is forced by the headmaster to play the rear of the school pantomime's horse. From the 1971 *Dandy Book*, art by Bill Holroyd.

114

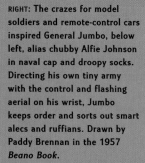

LEFT: Long before E.T., friendly, sometimes furry, aliens were landing in the comics, deliberately or stranded by fate, and were usually befriended by Earthlings. *The Whizzers of Ozz* zoomed in on their space car to the large pages of *Topper* in 1966. They were two twin boys with pudding-bowl haircuts, called Krik (the dark-haired one) and Krak from the country of Whizz on the planet Ozz. They had come to Earth on a school geography project to study the planet and bring back a list of articles. They join up with Willie Walker to complete their special assignment together. Drawn by Paddy Brennan from *Topper* 722, 3 December 1966.

BELOW: Marooned on Earth, speechless and harmless, the ape-like alien Galaxus is rescued by brothers Jim and Danny Jones. They have their hands full, though, trying to save the creature from harm, as it can only exist either at King Kong-size or shrunk down to the palm of your hand. This arctic tale drawn by Solano Lopez was in the first *Buster Holiday Fun Special* in 1969.

115

RIGHT: Penny's space pets Pogo and Ponda travel with her on the Astraquest rocket to investigate a strange craft orbiting our planet, but Ponda gets underfoot and causes a malfunction. Penny's uncle got top billing in the *Don Conquest* serial written by Kelman Frost and drawn by Harry Winslade for *Mickey's Weekly*, 3 November 1955.

ABOVE LEFT: Rocket ship Fireball XL5 is part of World Space Fleet and is shown here hunting down space pirates on a page painted by Mike Noble in *TV Century 21*, dateline 28 May 2066—always one century ahead. In the 1960s era of the United Nations and other global institutions, Gerry Anderson's various TV series envisioned an advanced but embattled 21st century kept safe only by technologies run by security organisations and one World Government.

ABOVE RIGHT: In *Stingray*, a sleek submarine sails under the flag of the World Aquatic Security Patrol and blows up the terror fish of deep-sea terrorist Titan in *TV Century 21*, 28 May 1966, drawn by Ron Embleton.

RIGHT: The shapes of buildings to come are prescient in this architectural feature from the 1966 *TV Century 21 Summer Extra*, art by Eric Eden, a former *Dan Dare* artist.

FAR RIGHT: In *Captain Scarlet*, the lofty World Fair Tower is under threat from a Mysteron assassin. Art by Ron Turner in the first *Captain Scarlet Annual* in 1967.

Scott Tracy's mission in Thunderbird One to rescue two trapped marathon runners takes an unexpected twist in this cliffhanger ending.
Frank Bellamy heightens the impact with his vibrant colours, dynamic compositions and distinctive jagged and serrated panel borders.
This second page of the *Thunderbirds* spread is from *TV Century 21* 173, 11 May 1968 and is shot from Bellamy's art.

117

KEREN STARED DOWN INTO THE UNCONSCIOUS FACE OF HIS FORMER FAITHFUL COMRADE.

BUT AT LAST WE HAVE A CLUE... A LIVING CLUE!

IT SEEMS POSSIBLE THAT THE WHITE-MASKED RAIDERS ARE RECRUITED BY FORCE AND MADE TO SERVE THE WILL OF SOME EVIL PERSON OR PERSONS. I HAVE A PLAN... TO DELIBERATELY ALLOW A TRUSTED OFFICER OF THE TRIGAN FORCES TO BE RECRUITED BY THESE FIENDS...

SOME DAYS LATER, THE EMPEROR TRIGO AND OTHERS GATHERED IN PERIC'S LABORATORY. THE GREAT SCIENTIST POINTED TO THE STILL-UNCONSCIOUS ROFFA.

HYPNOSIS! I HAVE SUBJECTED HIS BRAIN TO EXHAUSTIVE TESTS AND FIND IT TO BE ENTIRELY DOMINATED BY HYPNOTIC SUGGESTIONS IMPLANTED BY A PERSON OR PERSONS UNKNOWN. HOWEVER, THE BRAIN RETAINS A STRONG IMAGE OF AN EVENT IMMEDIATELY PRECEDING THE HYPNOSIS... LISTEN...

LOST... LOST IN THE MIST... THE LONELY INN IN THE HILLS...

THE EMPEROR INTERRUPTED.

BUT WHAT USE WOULD THAT SERVE? YOUNG ROFFA WAS SUCH A TRUSTED OFFICER... AND LOOK WHAT HAPPENED TO HIM!

QUITE SO, IMPERIAL MAJESTY. BUT MY PLAN IS TO HYPNOTISE THE OFFICER MYSELF SO THAT HE DOES NOT FALL UNDER THE EVIL WILL!

KEREN LEAPT TO HIS FEET.

I'LL GO!

SO IT WAS THAT KEREN'S MIND WAS SUBJECTED TO CERTAIN HYPNOTIC SUGGESTIONS FROM PERIC.

YOU WILL DISREGARD ALL OTHER SUGGESTIONS AND REMAIN TRUE TO YOUR TASK, WHICH IS TO LEARN ALL THERE IS TO KNOW ABOUT THE WHITE-MASKED RAIDERS AND WHOEVER CONTROLS THEM. DO YOU UNDERSTAND?

I... UNDERSTAND.

LATE ONE EVENING, KEREN RODE UP TO THE HILLS AND LOOKED ABOUT HIM IN THE GATHERING MIST.

NOW TO FIND THE LONELY INN...

In a unique blend of classical Roman epic and futuristic science fiction, *The Rise and Fall of the Trigan Empire* was based on the records recovered from a spaceship that crashed on Earth. Here Emperor Trigo and scientific advisor Peric attempt to foil another threat to his rule. Two lavish pages appeared each week in *Look and Learn*, most written by Michael Butterworth and drawn by Don Lawrence. This original art was printed in issue 510, dated 23 October 1971.

119

ABOVE: The Saturday-night ritual of hiding behind the sofa began in 1963 when Doctor Who travelled through time in his Tardis disguised as a police telephone box. Jon Pertwee, the third to play the time lord from 1970, is captured here by the Daleks who plan to turn him into one of their own through surgery. Art by Gerry Haylock from the centre of *Countdown* 57, 18 March 1972.

LEFT: Dalek history was told in their own comics and annuals. As their Emperor Dalek is rebuilt, his memory cells project a past indignity. Richard Jennings painted this for the 1966 *Dalek Outer Space Book*.

RIGHT: Fourth Doctor Tom Baker finds a scrapheap Cyberman in Steve Moore's tale, drawn by Mike McMahon and Adolfo Buylla for *Doctor Who Monthly*, November 1981.

RIGHT: In "Burger Law!", Judge Dredd has to cross the Cursed Earth, the radioactive wasteland of Middle America, to deliver a life-saving vaccine to Mega-City Two on the West coast. En route, he and his punk charge, Spikes Harvey Rotten, are caught by one of two feuding rival gangs devoted to their favourite brand of hamburger. The publishers' jittery lawyers prevented this pre-*Super Size Me* fast-food satire, by T.B. Grover, alias John Wagner, and Mike McMahon, from ever being reprinted since it first appeared in *2000AD* Prog 72, 8 July 1978. This suppression was unnecessary as neither chain complained.

120

RIGHT: Another definitive Dredd artist is Brian Bolland, who shows how far "The Lawman of the Future" will go to get his man, even going down the neck of a dinosaur to arrest him in its stomach. Written by Wagner for the 1982 *2000AD Annual*, this is Bolland's only full-colour Dredd story.

FAR RIGHT: In the controversial "Soul Food", drawn by Bolland, Dredd is captured by a familiar-looking mad Colonel and is saved by the sacrifice of a creature that resembles a famous advertising mascot. This story, written by Jack Adrian, alias Chris Lowder, was in *2000AD* Prog 78, 19 August 1978.

In Mega-City One, the gargantuan conurbation on America's east coast, it's another ordinary day of space-born threats and mass urban panic, quelled by the lethally effective Judges. John Wagner's new stories for the 1982 *Judge Dredd Annual* marked Mike McMahon's first opportunity to work in fully painted colour and resulted in some of his best-ever pages, shown here from his original artwork.

ABOVE: *2000AD* unleashed several other bizarre SF stars. With his horns, claws, hooves and steaming nostrils, Nemesis the Warlock looked demonic, except that he and his race are victims of the true monsters here, ourselves. Earth, or Terra, has elevated xenophobic genocide to a galactic scale, gripped by Torquemada's bigoted doctrine known as Termight. It gave Pat Mills and Kevin O'Neill the chance to purge their childhood religious dogma and assault the evils of racism and religious bigotry. In this colour centre spread above from Prog 335, 24 September 1983, Nemesis is reminded by his familiar, Grobbendonk, of the ritual combat between two weird centaur creatures. These turn out to be his wife and a rival, in which Nemesis is the prize: "For in the race of Warlocks, the female of the species is deadlier than the male."

ABOVE: Rogue Trooper is a cloned G.I. with blue bullet-proof skin and the bio-chips of three dead buddies in his backpack, helmet and gun. From Prog 319, 4 June 1983, by Gerry Finley-Day and Cam Kennedy.

ABOVE: John Wagner and Ian Gibson came up with their Chandleresque Sam Slade Robo-Hunter, a P.I. in a future London called Brit-Cit, overrun with robots. Alan Grant wrote this case in Prog 275, 31 July 1982.

123

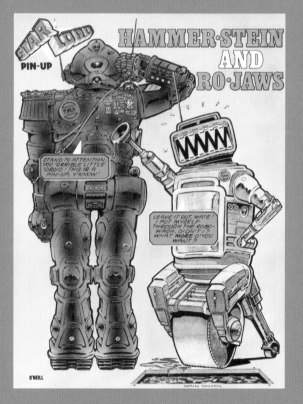

ABOVE: Kelvin Gosnell helmed a new *2000AD* offshoot, *Starlord*, in 1978. Planned as a 64-page, all-colour monthly like European magazines, it was scaled back to a 32-page bi-weekly. One hit character in *Starlord* was Strontium Dog, a mutant bounty-hunter, teamed with red-bearded Viking descendent Wulf. This spread from 15 July 1978 was written by John Wagner and drawn by Carlos Ezquerra.

RIGHT: *Starlord*'s other stars were war droids Ro-Jaws and Hammer-Stein, drawn here by Kevin O'Neil for the 16 September 1978 issue.

LEFT: Student delinquency goes thermonuclear in *D.R. and Quinch* by Alans Moore and Davis from *2000AD* Prog 351, 14 January 1984. Here, Waldo "Diminished Responsibility" Dobbs goes on a date to a youth club where Ernie Quinch's shocking reputation precedes him.

RIGHT: Early attempts at more sophisticated SF comics were limited in the mostly juvenile weeklies, although *Countdown*, a successor to *TV21*, did run an ambitious serial, also entitled *Countdown*. Illustrated with John Burns's multi-coloured panache from 1971 until 1974, it may be one of Britain's first uncollected graphic novels, with designs based on the film *2001: A Space Odyssey*.

FAR RIGHT: The real arena for more adult comics was the British underground scene, inspired by 1970s American comix and French magazines and albums. *Wurtham View 2000* was Dave Huxley's dig in 1982 at Dr Fredric Wertham, U.S. psychiatrist campaigner against comic books in the 1950s and loathed by their fans. Here, his namesake looks on aghast as his viewing system of the past catches a prime minister in flagrante. With his intense colouring inspired by Richard Corben's techniques, artist Angus McKie was picked up by *Métal Hurlant* in Paris and *Heavy Metal* in New York.

ABOVE AND RIGHT: From the pages of *Nasty Tales* came Ogoth the Wasted, caught between gangs of lesbians and gays in a lawless dystopia. Mick Farren and Chris Welch tried to offend almost everybody in 1972 and succeeded. Ian Rakoff wrote an *Ogoth* screenplay but copyright disputes halted the project.

FAR RIGHT: Writer Grant Morrison began his career as both writer and artist, here on cool mystic Gideon Stargrave with his flares, shades and rock-star style for *Near Myths* 4, 1979.

ABOVE: In writer Alan Hemus's last tale of his recurring hero in Thomson's fantasy picture library series *Starblazer* from 1979 to 1991, *Skald* is saved from the Verod tribe's flaming torture by a floating iron-clad trophy-hunter from space. Feverish imagery by Argentina's Enrique Alcatena in *Starblazer* 274, 1990.

LEFT: The first truly adult SF graphic novel in Britain began in 1978 in *Near Myths*. Bryan Talbot's *Adventures of Luther Arkwright* drew on such influences as Michael Moorcock's multiversal heroes and Nic Roeg's innovative film-making, here to show the regicide of a parallel England's Charles I. Talbot completed his trilogy in 1989 through the patronage of Serge Boissevain, publisher of *Pssst!*.

BELOW LEFT: *Mauretania Comics* by Chris Reynolds and Paul Harvey began as their self-published showcase. In this page from *The Golden Age* in *Mauretania Comics* 6, 1989, Reynolds' lyrical writing and bold graphics convey the transcendent within a seemingly mundane urban environment, as the narrator describes being driven through a golden arch and past a copper policeman.

BELOW RIGHT: Raymond Briggs dealt with the trusting optimism and sad fate of two elderly survivors of a nuclear attack on Britain in *When The Wind Blows*. His landmark graphic novel published in 1982 sparked heated debate about the government's inadequate precautions should the bomb ever be dropped.

125

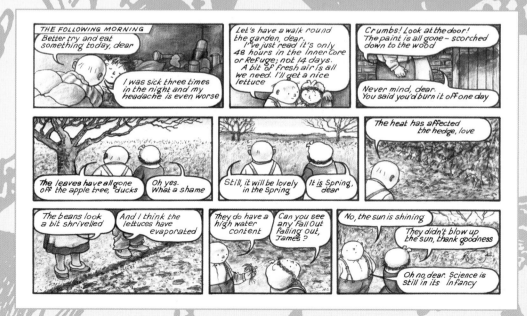

ABOVE: As with previous competitors—films, radio and television—comics in the 1980s adapted to the threats of computers, video games and fantasy gaming. Claiming to be the first computer comic, *Load Runner* ran *Invasion of the Arcadians*, which exaggerated fears that too much gaming was bad for children's health. Peter Dennis drew this cover for the first issue on 23 June 1983.

ABOVE RIGHT: Games offer many stories and endings instead of only one, so comics competed with role-playing comics. Judge Dredd featured in *Diceman* in 1986 by Pat Mills and Bryan Talbot. The choice of panel you read next and whether you survive are decided by two dice.

ABOVE FAR RIGHT: Another tactic was the photo-strip, tried in the new-look *Eagle* in 1982, but it proved unpopular and costly. Writer Alan Grant continued *Doomlord*, about a turncoat alien invader in disguise, as a traditional comic drawn by Heinzl, alias Alberto Giolitti. This page ran on 7 April 1984.

RIGHT: Terry Pratchett's *Discworld* tales are Britain's best-selling fantasy series. His *Guards! Guards!* was adapted into a graphic novel in 2000 by Stephen Briggs and Graham Higgins.

FAR RIGHT: Warhammer adapted their role-playing worlds into comics like *Daemonifuge* from 1999, written by Kev Walker and drawn by Jim Campbell. In 2000, another gaming company, Rebellion, bought *2000AD*'s characters to turn them into popular games.

126

127

ABOVE: George Orwell's Big Brother is now reduced to a reality TV phenomenon, but in 1949, his dystopia *1984* was a coldly logical projection of Stalin's Soviet Union and other dehumanising regimes. In *V for Vendetta*, starting in *Warrior* in 1982, Alan Moore and David Lloyd applied a similar logic to Margaret Thatcher's government and envisioned the rise to power and suppression of liberties by a corrupt right-wing extreme. Here, Evey, rescued from rapists, discloses to the masked V, a so-called terrorist bent on vengeance, how she and her family became victims of the Fascists.

TOP RIGHT: Of all the media during eighteen years of Thatcherism, comics were among the most politically outspoken. An older Dan Dare becomes a willing pawn controlled by the Thatcher-like Prime Minister Gloria Monday, written by Grant Morrison and drawn by Rian Hughes in *Revolver* in 1990. CENTRE RIGHT: Warren Ellis and Chris Weston gave Dan Dare another dark spin in 2004 by imagining how one ruthless man from a post-war *Ministry of Space* ensures that Britain can conquer the stars. BELOW RIGHT: In the radical *2000AD* offshoot *Crisis* in 1987, black teen Eve is drafted into the *Third World War*, "a global Vietnam with multinational corporations playing the part of the USA", by Pat Mills and Carlos Ezquerra.

Time Warp

ABOVE: However fantastically, graphic novels are responding to Britain's multicultural richness. Nail-spitting Anglo-Indian beauty Tippoo and her marginalised friends create their own future amid pre-millennial tensions in graphic novelist Ilya's *Time Warp*, like a minimum-wage *This Life* as written by Philip K. Dick.

RIGHT: In the radiant *Rogan Gosh* from 1990, Pete Milligan and Brendan McCarthy concocted a tale of "Time Travel, Rudyard Kipling, Enlightenment for Yobs, the Corridors of Uncertainty, Sitar Ray-guns and the whole vexed question of Indian science fiction ... written in the succulent, over-descriptive style of an Indian restaurant menu".

TOP RIGHT: In Grant Morrison and Philip Bond's 2006 Anglo-Asian SF rom-com *Vimanarama*, Muslim teen Sofia's arranged marriage to Ali gets derailed by ancient Indian heroes and demons revived from beneath Ali's family corner shop in Bradford, one of whom here tries proposing to her.

RIGHT: Devlin Waugh (a play on Evelyn Waugh) is a vampire, Vatican exorcist and bored eccentric who combines wit and fisticuffs with 22nd-century martial arts in *Judge Dredd Megazine*, here by John Smith and Colin MacNeil in 2005.

FAR RIGHT: Dave Gibbons based his 2004 graphic novel *The Originals* on his teen years in a gang of Mods, transposing to the future their anti-racist attitude and embracing of black music as well as their war with rival gang, the Rockers.

128

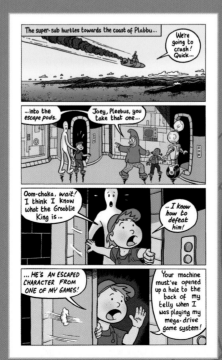

ABOVE: The Internet may not be the future of comics but it offers possibilities that print cannot match. In the original web incarnation of their 2003 graphic novel *Scarlet Traces*, Ian Edgington and D'Israeli devised special effects and limited animation on many pages. They speculate how Wells's *The War of the Worlds* might have turned out differently if the British Empire had been able to acquire the Red Planet's technology from one survivor and use it to retaliate against the enemy.

FAR LEFT: The prospects look good for comics on the Internet, mobile phones, iPods and whatever comes next. Could this be Paul Rainey's "Ultranet", a way to access content from the future? Since 2005, in his SF kitchen-sink serial *There's No Time Like The Present*, Rainey asks how having "tomorrow's jam" today might disrupt people's lives. Like that of Barry here, spongeing off his parents and downloading future porn all day.

LEFT: Print comics can still captivate kids glued to their TVs and computers. Nick Abadzis' 2001 graphic novel turned two kids' everyday worlds upside down when *The Amazing Mr Pleebus* steps out of their TV screen and takes them back inside it to experience some exciting exploits themselves.

Jolly Hockey Sticks to Sheroes

"RIGHT OUT OF THE BLUE AND WITH NO ONE EVEN THREATENING HER, JANE PEELED A WEEK AGO. THE BRITISH 36TH DIVISION IMMEDIATELY GAINED SIX MILES AND THE BRITISH ATTACKED THE Arakan. Maybe we Americans ought to have Jane, too." Under the headline "Jane Gives All", the American forces newspaper *Round-Up* did not exaggerate the inspirational impact the *Daily Mirror*'s comic-strip heroine had on the Tommies. It was no coincidence that, after years of teasing and lingerie, artist Norman Pett had finally caught his character in one panel in the altogether, drying herself with a towel the morning after 6 June 1944. That day was D-Day, when a great armed armada had swept across the Channel to take the Normandy beaches. What better way for Jane to congratulate the troops following that historic day and boost their morale further. Her naked, immobile pose may have reminded some of the "artistic" tableaus they had ogled at London's Windmill Theatre, in which the Home Secretary had allowed pretty girls to be seen on stage without clothes, provided that they represented a painting or sculpture and did not move an inch. Jane truly was "The Forces' Sweetheart", read by the armed services everywhere, even on board ships and subs, in special editions of the paper which the *Mirror* supplied in batches sometimes weeks or months in advance and issued one a day. As Leslie Thomas, author of *The Virgin Soldiers*, later reflected, "Today it may seem unreal that such a small and innocent pastime kept men sane in destructive days. But it *was* the small smile that kept people going on."

RIGHT: Christabel Leighton-Porter was Norman Pett's life model for Jane and performed as Jane on stage in musical revues, though not in the nude.

BELOW: Fritzi the dachshund takes part in his mistress's balancing act from the second *Jane's Journal* by Pett in 1945.

The *Mirror* agreed with *Round-Up* and thought that Americans should "have Jane, too". Despite the paper's efforts to export the strip via America's powerful syndicate King Features, editors there felt that readers of the family-friendly funny pages would be far less tolerant than their supposedly reserved British counterparts of daring glimpses of nipples, breasts, bottoms and states of undress, let alone total (though never full-frontal) nudity. Much of Jane's risqué charm was lost when artist Norman Pett was forced to cover her exposed flesh with more clothes and remove all arousing suspenders and stockings for the American version. Little wonder the strip bombed. At the time, America was enduring one of its periodic repressive phases, which saw the postal authorities try to ban the mailing in *Esquire* magazine of Alberto Vargas's pin-ups, far milder than *Jane*, on the grounds of obscenity. In contrast, in Britain, when Pett fell behind in production and the strip was suspended, Jane explained her disappearance in a small cartoon, covering her modesty with some curtains and exclaiming, "Give me a break. I can't find my panties!" The next day, the first of many mail-bags from readers arrived at the *Mirror*'s Fleet Street offices filled with pairs of undies, coveted articles in that time of clothes shortages. Not long after, her Nazi-foiling exploits resumed.

Jane had not always been an undercover adventuress prone to losing her underwear. Norman Pett had created her in 1932 for *Jane's Journal*, subtitled

OPPOSITE: Recalling Milton Caniff's sultry Dragon Lady from *Terry and the Pirates*, Modesty Blaise goes Oriental with her partner Willie Garvin in this 1984 painting by John Burns for a reprint book cover.

130

THE MODERN MAIDEN AND HER WAYS.—No. 1.

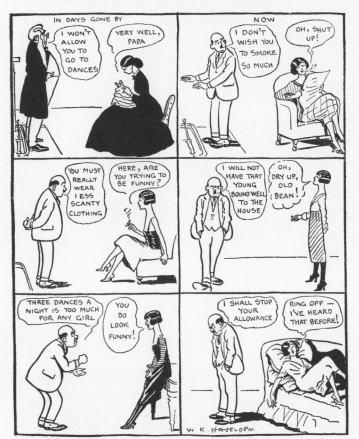

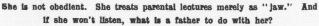
She is not obedient. She treats parental lectures merely as "jaw." And if she won't listen, what is a father to do with her?

ABOVE: Father of the British newspaper strip, William Kerridge Haselden commented on news and society in his *Reflections* for the *Daily Mirror* from 1904, collected into annuals from 1908. In this sample, the first of six about *The Modern Maiden and Her Ways* in the 1921 annual, he contrasts a daughter's meek obedience to her father in the past with a rebellious, cigarette-smoking daughter of the day. In the book's introduction, Haselden comes out in favour of "this extraordinary, this freakish, this absolutely incomprehensible younger generation. ... You may condemn her frivolity if you like, but her cheeriness may pull you out of the gloom!"

RIGHT: Lethal hockey stick at the ready— one of Ronald Searle's *St Trinian's Girls*.

The Diary of a Bright Young Thing, an ironic sobriquet used by Noel Coward, Evelyn Waugh and others to describe the often vain and vacuous upper-class hedonists of the period. Pett's original Jane could be a slightly dizzy, if not dumb, blonde, not unlike the unmarried American strip star Blondie invented by Chic Young in 1930. Jane's gag-a-day antics with her little dachshund Fritzi served as a fashion catalogue for female readers and mild titillation for the males. In many ways, she was the newspaper successor to earlier flappers like Alexander Akerbladh's 1920s twins Flossie and Fluffie in *Merry & Bright*, and before them the party girl Eve, bubbly wife of Adam and darling of the high-society magazine *Tatler*. Eve's illustrator, Fish, was a strange fish indeed, one of the few female strip cartoonists in this period. Anne Harriet Fish illustrated this flapper with Beardsley-esque delicacy to accompany the satirical column *The Letters of Eve* from 1914 to 1920 and in three *Eve* books "by Fish and Fowl"—the latter referring to Edward Huskinson, *Tatler*'s editor. Further down the social scale, in the cheap weekly comics for all the family, few women landed leading parts before the Second World War. Those who did tended to be far from young and glamorous,

such as chubby char ladies Mrs Sudds by Oliver Veal and Big-Hearted Martha by Cyril Price, Veal's battle-axe Aunt Tozer or Bertie Brown's bun-burning cook Pansy Pancake. One 1930s exception was Peggy, Pride of the Force, a pert, leggy policewoman in *Larks* weekly by brothers Reg and George Parlett.

As for junior comics heroines before the War, *Mirror* readers met the bright, bubbly moppet Belinda in 1935, while early learners might start reading about adorable little angels in sugary-sweet nursery comics and children's books. Older girls looking for bolder, heartier role models, however, turned to the girls' story-papers, densely typeset prose with the odd illustration, starting with the *School Friend* from 1919. Based on *The Gem* and *The Magnet* for boys, these elaborated on the mystique of the girls' public school, including Billy Bunter's equally fat and wily sister Bessie, written by Bunter scribe Charles Hamilton under the pseudonym Hilda Richards. It was the genre's overly hearty, games-playing pupils who helped give rise to the description "jolly hockey sticks", apparently coined in the 1950s BBC radio show *Educating Archie* by the actress Beryl Reid, who played the ventriloquist dummy Archie Andrews's girlfriend, Monica.

Modernisation of the girls' story papers into comics began in May 1950 when Amalgamated Press (AP) brought back *School Friend*, cancelled in 1940, as the first post-war comic aimed at girls. Its fanciful thrillers, especially the cases of the masked, robed investigators *The Silent Three at St Kit's*, made *School Friend* such a hit, outselling *Eagle* at a million copies each week, that its editor Reverend Marcus Morris countered with a "sister paper to *Eagle*" called simply *Girl* in November 1951. When sales quickly plummeted, Morris had his theories: "We had made *Girl* too masculine. We therefore made it more romantic in its approach, more feminine. The adventure and danger can be there but the reason for it must be the search for a long-lost uncle or father. If you can add a fair amount of personal rivalry, jealousy and a very close friendship, so much the better." His addition of these ingredients, for example in *Wendy and Jinx*, best friends at Manor School, on the cover, and *Belle of the Ballet*, orphaned at a dancing school, inside lifted *Girl*'s sales in 1952 to a steady 650,000. In response, AP redesigned their surviving story paper *Girls' Crystal* into the strip format in March 1953 and eventually D.C. Thomson joined in, first with *Bunty* in January 1958, home of *The Four Marys*.

Before this, tomboys, tearaways and obsessives had been the usual heroines in Thomson's unisex children's funnies. From their inception, nosey snoop *Keyhole Kate* was sticking her protruding nose in at *The Dandy*, while *Pansy Potter* was proving her strength in *The Beano*. In 1941, Ronald Searle drew the first cartoon for *Lilliput* about a school of suspender-wearing miniature she-devils, resuming after the war. The *St Trinian's Girls'* macabre wickedness provided an unlikely outlet for some of Searle's grim memories of his time as a Japanese prisoner-of-war. These "girls behaving badly" going unpunished by their blasé, debauched teachers gave a topsy-turvy spin to the goody-goody swots in *School Friend* or *Girl*. It also gave a free rein to that secret demoness lurking within many female readers stifled by propriety. Searle grew to loathe his creations and stopped drawing them, but the public loved their outrageous naughtiness, and they were brought to the big screen in 1954 in the first of five films. In 1953, Thomson developed a feminine equivalent to Dennis the Menace in Beryl the Peril, also drawn by Davey Law for their new large-format *Topper*, and followed this in *The Beano* with Leo Baxendale's Minnie the Minx, in his mind less a female Dennis, more "an Amazonian warrior". "I wouldn't

have her just thumping a boy in the face. It's too crude. I'd have Minnie with her scything punch that went round three boys' jaws in turn and she'd be standing on somebody's hoof with one foot, kicking somebody else up the bum with her other foot, and she'd still be left free to bite somebody with her teeth! And she probably had her pet frog up her jumper, too, blasting Minnie's victims with a peashooter!" From then on, girls could always be the equals, and often the betters, of boys when it came to menacing.

Strikingly different portrayals of adult femininity blossomed during and after

the war in the newspapers, when the curvaceous glamour and docile availability of Jane's assorted sisters sent men's pulses racing. Emphasising beauty over brains, Arthur Ferrier hired top models of the day to pose for *Our Dumb Blonde*, *Film Fannie*, *Spotlight on Sally*, and chorus girl *Eve*. Despite fresh competition from these and other lovelies, Jane remained popular long after the war. If anything, she became even more of a pin-up when Pett handed over to his gifted assistant Michael Hubbard in 1948, until she finally sailed off into the sunset in 1959 with her lifelong beau

ABOVE: His use of extra tall panels enabled pin-up king Arthur Ferrier to show Sally and friends from their hairdos down to their stilettos in his weekly strip *Spotlight on Sally* in the *News of the World*. In this example from 1945, the strip's first year, he employs "squeens" or spiral lines around the head to symbolise Dizzie's confusion. Such "dizzy dames" and "dumb blondes" appealed to men but were hardly inspiring to women, who had tasted responsiblity during the war and were now being expected to return to the home.

RIGHT: A clever ruse to show pop stars' photos and plug their new records in romance comics was to base stories loosely on the titles of their latest releases. The Ricky Nelson song "Someday" featured in *Valentine*, 10 January 1959, art by Gaty (Christian Catignol).

BELOW: Bunty, "the girl just like you", hides her ice cream from greedy Hannah Hood. "Too bad our smart lass hasn't seen/that four-legged scrounger on the scene!" The ending of this cover story, told in rhyme and without balloons, opened the 2 August 1958 issue of *Bunty*, reportedly drawn by Peem Walker.

Georgie Porgie. Strips became closely associated with striptease in much of the populist British press, who would take an even more relaxed attitude about the increasingly bared flesh of science-fiction beauties from the late 1960s like Scarth, Axa or Danielle than that of their photographed "Page Three" starlets. While such exposure was not palatable to more middle-class, respectable papers, several added a touch of feminine class as well, notably the *Daily Mail*, which introduced cool sophisticate Carol Day, created in 1956 by David Wright. In 1962, the *Daily Express* responded by asking Peter O'Donnell and Jim Holdaway, who were co-creating the *Mirror*'s Romeo Brown and his abundant girlfriends at the time, to invent a female adventurer for them. Their proposal was accepted and ready to roll, when at the eleventh hour the *Express* baulked at the prospect of a "woman of the underworld" running around in a family-oriented paper. Luckily, Charles Wintour, editor of the London *Evening Standard*, understood how Modesty Blaise could appeal as much to women as to men and the *Standard* became her home in 1963 for 38 years.

The 1960s had begun to swing and the tough, independent, intelligent Modesty heralded the seismic social and sexual shifts to come. So too did the thoroughly modern *Tiffany Jones* in the *Daily Sketch* in 1964, a milestone as the first newspaper strip in history written by an all-female partnership, writer

Jenny Butterworth and artist Pat Tourret. Comics, like the other mass media, had long been male dominated, especially at the top, Marie Duval, Anne Harriet Fish and Mary Tourtel being rare early exceptions. As elsewhere in the workplace, it had taken far too long for women to win more opportunities. Often when they did, their work was anonymous, as was the general rule, or if they were granted a credit, several adopted masculine pseudonyms, such as "Chris Garvey" (June Mendoza) or "Barry Ford" (Joan Whitford). From 1950, the plethora of titles aimed at female readers from AP and Thomson, 54 in total over the next thirty years, including their new romance lines, gave more opportunities for women to contribute. As well as Butterworth and Tourret, these included artists Evelyn

1945   1952   1964   1978   1990   2004

Flinders and Shirley Bellwood. Several rose to the rank of editor, such as Nina Myskow on *Jackie*, and yet much of what British girls and women read in their comics was still ultimately dictated by male publishers.

By the early 1970s plummeting sales proved that the old blokes at magazine publisher IPC were out of touch with their female readers, so Pat Mills and other male writers were allowed to pump up the dramatic tension for a new girls' weekly in 1971. "The spirit of *Tammy* was terrific," says Mills. "It was a revolution because it didn't have the flowery language, or stories about girls who were secret agents or cat girls, or pony stories. This was because John Purdie, who came from D.C. Thomson, had picked up the right way of doing girls' comics from *Bunty*, a very solid story book." Darkness gathered over the pages of girls' comics as never before. A prime example, and perhaps *Tammy*'s most cruel tale, is *Slaves of "War Orphan Farm"*, in which a callous Ma Thatcher (this was

before Maggie) forced wretched waifs to slave in a quarry. Probably the ultimate waif tragedy, though, was *Nothing Ever Goes Right*, told in jarringly misshapen panels in Thomson's *Judy* in 1981. At its climax, Heather Morgan's rescue of two children trapped in a demolished house makes her weak heart finally give out and she is buried, unknown, in an unmarked grave. According to *Judy* artist Ron Tiner, this tale "remained an all-time favourite among the readers". Some might wonder how the men behind these almost Victorian weepies felt about subjecting young heroines to frequently harrowing ordeals, but, as Mills pointed out, "[*Tammy*] was very evil and powerful. It never had censorship problems because mental cruelty isn't visual on the page."

To explode the limiting clichés perpetuated in the girls' and teenage comics

and present their own images of themselves in all their variety and uniqueness, women cartoonists turned to other outlets such as feminist magazine *Spare Rib* or the *Guardian*'s women's pages where Posy Simmonds, Ros Asquith and others were published. Sisters were also doing it for themselves by taking inspiration from the American *Wimmen's Comix* from 1972 and French *Ah Nana!* from 1976. They also set up their own magazines and imprints, from Suzy Varty's *Heröine* in 1978, the *Sour Cream* collective in 1980 and Erica Smith's *Girl Frenzy* in 1991 to Carol Bennett's *Fanny* range and today's *Whores of Mensa*. These female voices bring fresh, diverse ways to see women and conceive comics. Without them, would male creators have come up with *Halo Jones*, determined to carve her own life out of a bleak dystopia? Or *Tank Girl*, the prototype "shero", a skinhead St Trinian's terror, though still prone, like Jane, to losing her clothes? The fact remains that few publishers' doors were flung open to women; barely a handful have ever worked for *The Beano* or *2000AD*. Any openings for them in the illustrated girls' comics vanished when they were all but wiped out by costlier photo-love stories in the early 1980s. Something precious was lost, as Arthur Ferrier warned decades before: "[A photo's] mechanical fraction of a second is not as near life as the synthesis of moments every drawing represents." Also, girls were growing up more quickly and *Jackie*, *Bunty* and the like, even with photo stories, were no match for the racier, boy-obsessed *Bliss*, *Sugar* and *Just 17*. But today, British girls are reading comics again: translated manga from Japan, where young female artists have founded a whole genre, *shojo*. The signs are positive that manga are inspiring a generation of British women to do the same.

ABOVE: Risks and rewards of seeking a boyfriend online are explored by Sweatdrop Studios' Joanna Zhou in 2005's *Cybercrush*, a manga-influenced mini-comic printed out from the artist's computer in full colour.

LEFT: Raised on rebels Beryl and Minnie and unmoved by *Bunty*'s sensible heroines, Lorna Miller learnt from America's 1990s alternative comics, *Hate* and *Eightball*, that her own comic, *Witch*, was a perfect way to channel her anger and subversive humour.

135

BELOW: Both lampooning and pandering to the male breast fetish, Alan Martin and Jamie Hewlett outdo Madonna's late-1980s post-feminist image by equipping *Tank Girl* with deadly missile-sized mammaries.

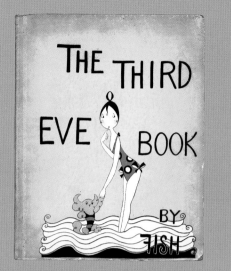

¶ Eve thinks that the scarcity of dancing men at the little hops which were recently rife has swollen the heads and shrunk the manners of youthful warriors to an alarming extent

¶ The queue of would-be dancing fairies is assuming alarming proportions

¶ And it looked at one time as if the coupon system would have to be extended to the situation

¶ But gallant America has stepped into the breach, and the situation is relieved once more

ABOVE: With her kiss curl, bobbed hair and skimpy bathing costume, *Tatler*'s Eve and her Pekinese Tou-Tou are caught on the 1919 cover of *The Third Eve Book* by Anne Harriet Fish and writer Edward Huskinson.

RIGHT: The *Eve* strips in *Tatler* touched lightly on the social impact of the First World War. Here, Eve bemoans the shortage of male dance partners. "The coupon system" refers to wartime rationing. Luckily, American troops stationed in Britain solve the problem.

LEFT: With the cute curls and constant cheer of Shirley Temple and Little Orphan Annie, homeless waif Belinda Blue-Eyes charmed her way into the *Daily Mirror* in 1935. She was drawn by "Gloria", alias Steve Dowling, until 1943 when Tony Royle took over until her final bow in 1959. In *Shooting Star* by Royle from 1948, she auditions for producer Ivor Tallant and gets her first break into moving pictures.

BELOW: The *Shooting Star* booklet shows a sculpted 3D portrait of Belinda on the cover by an uncredited artist.

ABOVE: The Windmill was famous as the only theatre in London where nudity was permitted. Even then, it was only allowed if the girls didn't move. This gave rise to the saying, "If it moves, it's rude." The only nudes who did move were the fan dancers, and the skill of their dance was to keep themselves covered by huge ostrich-feather fans as they danced. From its opening night on 4 February 1932, the Windmill was a roaring success.

ABOVE: Jane started life as a flapper in *Jane's Journal, The Diary of a Bright Young Thing*. Created by Norman Pett, the newspaper strip began on 5 December 1932 in the *Daily Mirror*, but had none of its later raciness. In 1938, Pett discovered model Christabel Leighton-Porter and, along with writer Don Freeman, revamped the strip. Jane began losing her clothes, becoming a nubile reminder of what the lads were fighting for. Here, her bird act tricks the Nazis in Pett's *Jane's Journal* booklet from 1945.

ABOVE: "We never closed": the Windmill Theatre, London, pictured on a rainy day in around 1940, prided itself on staying open throughout the Second World War.

LEFT: This 1937 Coronation Day special, later watercoloured by Norman Pett, is one of only a handful of his originals drawn during his sixteen years on *Jane* to have survived. It sold at the first auction of the late Denis Gifford's collection in 2001 for £1,800.

ABOVE: From her initial outing in the first issue of *The Dandy* in 1937, gangly *Keyhole Kate* was always peering through her glasses, sticking her pointy nose where it wasn't wanted. This early set was drawn by Allan Morley in 1938.

ABOVE: *Pansy Potter, The Strong Man's Daughter* (this rhymes only in Scotland) never knew her own strength. Hugh McNeill first drew her in *The Beano* in 1938.

ABOVE: Master of mayhem Leo Baxendale reprised Minnie the Minx for publishers Odhams in *Smash!* with the fiendish proto-feminist Bad Penny shown on the cover of the 19 February 1966 issue.

LEFT: Artist Davey Law was chosen to come up with a female version of his character *Dennis the Menace* in 1953 for *The Topper* and the equally formidable *Beryl the Peril* was the result, this page from 9 January 1954.

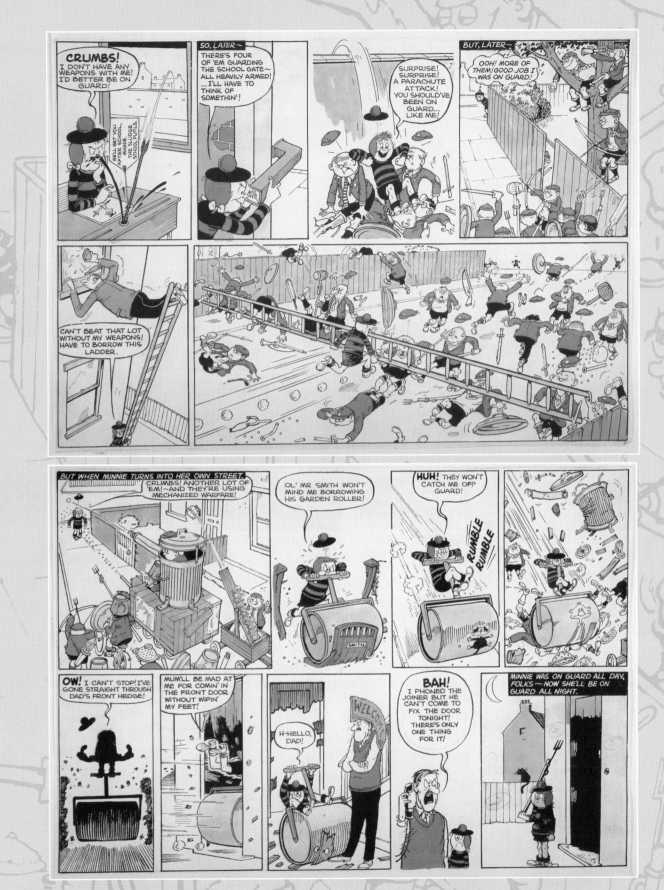

Minnie the Minx never bothers to marmalise one schoolboy when she can mow down loads of them with a ladder gripped in her teeth or a garden roller. Leo Baxendale's joke-filled panels always reward close attention, from one boy's ear caught on the ladder to the devilish horns that sprout on Minnie's hat. And wait until you spot what Minnie has doodled in the first panel! Original art for *The Beano*, 7 June 1958.

140

ABOVE: Fairground owner Mr Belton has sent his unruly daughter Rosa for one term to St Elmo's boarding school "to be taught how to be a young lady". Put under the charge of *The Four Marys*, she smokes, wears make-up and seems determined to get expelled. Here, in her first game of hockey, she is sent off due to a foul. Rosa's rebellious streak causes chaos but is eventually calmed in this fifteen-page story drawn by Bill Holroyd for the 1980 *Bunty Book for Girls*.

ABOVE: "If someone is the victim of injustice, then The Silent Three will strike!" So speaks Betty Roland (1), leader of this secret society formed at St Kit's boarding school with Joan Derwood (2) and Peggy West (3), each with their number on their cowl and dressed in long green robes and black masks, which they hid under loose floorboards in their study. This eight-page colour tale featured in the 1960 *School Friend Annual* illustrated by Evelyn Flinders.

LEFT: Jill Crusoe, shipwrecked like Daniel Defoe's Robinson Crusoe, found a "girl Friday" named M'Lani. This adventure ends with Jill saving M'Lani from fierce warriors who Jill frightens off by projecting magic-lantern slides she found among the wreckage washed up on the beach. Drawn by Roland Davies for the 1959 *School Friend Annual*.

ABOVE: Michael Hubbard drew the story *Fourth Form Newsgirls* for *Schoolgirls Picture Library* 255, 1964, in which the pupils discover an old printing press and start their own newspaper, exposing a visiting pop singer as a robber in disguise.

LEFT: The climax of *Circus Ballerina*, lead story for the 1963 *Princess Gift Book for Girls* painted by Bill Lacey. Sally Doyle, a dancer in her parents' circus, which was touring America's Midwest, comes to the rescue of an injured and jilted Russian ballerina by replacing her as the Snow Maiden and luring gruff ranch-manager Bob Gray through the winter night to her side. Ballet, circus, western and romance all rolled into one.

BELOW: Acclaimed painter June Mendoza took over the job of drawing *Belle of the Ballet* for *Girl* from John Worsley but used a unisex pseudonym—Chris Garvey.

RIGHT: In *Bella at the Bar*, Bella Barlow's prowess at gymnastics helps her endure her difficult home life as virtually a slave to her uncle and aunt and an unpaid helper in her uncle's window-cleaning business. In this *Billy Elliot*-like scene, Bella comes to the aid of Gerry, a boy learning ballet, who is bullied as a "cissy" by his classmates. John Armstrong based Bella on his niece and drew this for the 1977 *Tammy Annual*, written by Primrose Cummings.

ABOVE: In response to the success of Gavin Maxwell's 1960 novel *Ring of Bright Water*, the 1962 *Princess Gift Book for Girls* also featured *Bonny the Otter*, beautifully illustrated by Ron Embleton.

141

LEFT: Sunny Sue Day narrated her own and her suburban family's everyday experiences in *The Happy Days*. Serialised for thirteen years after starting in *Princess* in 1960, it was drawn by Andrew Wilson and written by mother-of-five Jenny Butterworth. Sue was awarded her own solo annual in 1962, for which the opening episode was rerun in colour.

ABOVE: Sue's father, a keen modernist painter, was persuaded by bearded bohemian Mr Strickland to try being a full-time artist, at least for two days, much to his family's consternation. This was reprised in the 1970 *Princess Gift Book for Girls*.

TOP RIGHT: *June and School Friend Library* 455, 6 May 1968, reprinted a 1963 tale of Sue Day's transatlantic TV broadcast via the Telstar communications satellite, launched in 1962.

BOTTOM RIGHT: The cover of the first and only *Sue Day Annual* was by Bill Lacey.

LEFT: The annual's endpapers, showing a detailed map of Sue's home town.

LEFT: As featured in Gerry Anderson's *Thunderbirds* puppet series and modelled on and voiced by his wife Sylvia, Lady Penelope Creighton-Ward was International Rescue's London agent, assisted by "The Nose" Parker, ex-burglar supreme. Here she's operating solo to uncover a plot to trick young supporters of women's rights into stealing industrial secrets to help the hostile "Bereznik" government. Frank Langford drew this centre spread for *Lady Penelope* 14, 23 April 1966.

BELOW: The over 200-year-old Valda, the Norse name for a spirited warrior, is rejuvenated once more by the Fire of Life for her second serialised adventure and resumes her mission to protect nature and wildlife. This opening page from *Mandy* in 1970 was drawn by Dudley Wynn.

ABOVE: French actress Avril Claire is secretly fearless French Liberation agent Mam'selle X, evading the Gestapo in the Occupied Zone. In *The Mystery Parachutist* in *June and Schoolfriend Library* 408, 1967, she takes the lead in an assault with two British agents on a Nazi-held chateau. Art by Giorgio Giorgetti.

LEFT: Being an underwater stunt double on a Caribbean film shoot is Alona the Wild One's latest assignment in the 1970 *Princess Gift Book for Girls*. Leslie Ottway's deft washes enrich the sunny surface scenes and the later watery depths.

RIGHT: Movies were a big influence on the "picture serials" in *Roxy*, a common name for local cinemas. English belle Ruth is a *Prisoner in a Palace* of a powerful Arabian prince, who is determined to marry her. His spiteful sister vows to seduce Ruth's true love on this striking splash page from *Roxy* 50, 21 February 1959, drawn by Dudley Wynn.

BELOW: Thwarted pop songwriter Gay Marne can't get her compositions considered by supergroup "The Beatsters". But in this scene she discovers that her new mystery boyfriend manages the band and she hears them play her song. Drawn by Luis Garcia, *Sweet Santa* ran in *Love Story Library* 507 in 1964.

LEFT AND FAR LEFT: Lorna has landed the lead in a new musical but falls for Alan, an admirer who comes every night and sits in the front row. Breaking her contract, she abandons the stage and sacrifices *All for Love*. *All for Love* appeared in *Love Story Library* 195, April 1958. The cover and interior artists are unknown. Notice how the writer took the eccentric approach of ending thought balloons with phrases such as "thought Alan, humbly".

RIGHT: A 1976 *Star Library* cover by Spain's Jordi Penalva.

BELOW: A few love comics were narrated by men. In *A Taste of Honey* Mike relates how he fell for Annette, only to find that, after he goes away for two weeks, she has already switched to another man, Harry. In this finale, Harry finds he too has been replaced and Mike walks away, offering himself to any chicks reading *Cherie* 128, 9 March 1963. Art by Jorge Badia Galvez.

ABOVE AND LEFT: Photo Love comics were not a 1970s innovation but date back at least to the 1950s. In *Love or Fame* from the January 1960 issue of *Photo Romances*, a woman is once more forced to choose between romance and a career. The uncredited story included a cameo by popular black pianist Winifred Atwell.

RIGHT: Young, three and single, Sherry, Karen and Bett were *Three Girls in a Flat*, enjoying their freedoms and often at loggerheads over a man. Sherry's breezy first-person narration and the lively lingo and modern styling show the 1960s about to go into full swing. Drawn by Italian Guido Buzzelli, this ran in *Cherie* 98, August 1962.

ABOVE: In *It Started With A Kiss* from the 1984 *Blue Jeans Annual*, Clare's unworn wedding dress reminds her of husband-to-be Paul who died in a fire. She ends up marrying his sexist mate Danny instead.

145

ABOVE: The cases of newspaper strip investigator Lesley Shane by Conrad Frost and Oliver Passingham were adapted into the small-format *Super Detective Libraries*. *Dream Crimes* ran in issue 98, February 1957.

RIGHT: Early in her tense debut story in 1956, Carol Day visits her wealthy ailing uncle and senses that he is in danger from opportunist relatives and rogues, and perhaps from his butler, and his doctor, too. The *Daily Mail* strip was initially written by Peter Meriton and later by David Wright's brother-in-law, Raymond Little. Wright's wife was his model for Carol.

RIGHT: Strong-willed model Tiffany Jones shocks her stuffy Welsh Aunt Blodmen by altering her dress for church and giving it a plunging neckline. From 1964, Jenny Butterworth and Pat Tourret charted Tiffany's career for thirteen years, first in the *Daily Sketch* and then in the *Daily Mail*.

MODESTY BLAISE by Peter O'Donnell

WE WERE IN LOVE, AND WE PLANNED TO MARRY... BUT THEN CAME THE REVOLT IN HUNGARY, AND I WAS AMONG THE THOUSANDS WHO ESCAPED

BUT NOT THE WOMAN?

NO...ANNA HAD GONE TO HER HOME IN MISKOLC... I THOUGHT SHE WOULD FOLLOW ME, BUT THE RISING WAS CRUSHED TOO QUICKLY

I GIVE YOU THE TRUTH — I LOVED MY FREEDOM MORE THAN I LOVED ANNA ...BUT IF I HAD KNOWN SHE WAS TO BEAR MY CHILD, I WOULD HAVE STAYED...

188

ABOVE: Honor Blackman played Cathy Gail in the television hit *The Avengers* from September 1962. Athletic, self-assured, an expert in judo and dressed in a body-hugging black outfit, she was another new icon—like *Modesty Blaise* from May 1963 —of female empowerment.

LEFT: In this touching sequence from *Modesty Blaise*'s second *Evening Standard* serial, "The Long Lever", Peter O'Donnell and Jim Holdaway reveal more about her traumatic childhood raised in a refugee camp. To Willie Garvin, her cohort but never a romantic interest, she will always be "The Princess".

MODESTY BLAISE by Peter O'Donnell

MY DAUGHTER IS SIX YEARS OLD NOW... AND ANNA, HER MOTHER, DIED WHEN SHE WAS BORN

WHEN DID YOU LEARN ALL THIS?

ONLY WHEN DE S'A MADE CONTACT WITH ME IN RIO DE JANEIRO... SHOWED ME DOCUMENTS, PHOTOGRAPHS, RECORDS... A LETTER FROM ANNA'S SISTER CONFIRMED BY A SPANISH DIPLOMAT WHOM I TRUST COMPLETELY

OH, THE PROOF IS POSITIVE ENOUGH... I WOULD DOUBT IT IF I COULD, BELIEVE ME

STREWTH, THIS'LL RIP THE PRINCESS APART...

189

MODESTY BLAISE by Peter O'Donnell

SO I HAVE NEVER SEEN THIS CHILD OF MINE... BUT HER SAFETY AND HAPPINESS MEAN MORE TO ME THAN POWER-GROUPS OR MILITARY SECRETS... THAT IS WHY I WAS GOING BACK

WHERE IS SHE NOW?

IT IS POLITE OF YOU TO ASK... BUT I HARDLY THINK YOU CAN IMAGINE WHAT IT IS TO BE A SMALL GIRL, QUITE ALONE, IN A PRISON CAMP —

I DON'T HAVE TO IMAGINE— I KNOW, DAMN YOU!

SURE, PRINCESS... EASY NOW

190

MODESTY BLAISE by Peter O'Donnell

STRANGE... I DID NOT THINK THAT YOUNG WOMAN COULD BE MOVED BY THE PLIGHT OF A SMALL CHILD

NO?... REMEMBER THE PRISON-CAMP AT KALYROS? YOU WERE THERE TWENTY YEARS BACK...

WHAT D'YOU RECKON THAT WAS LIKE FOR A SIX-YEAR-OLD GIRL... ON 'ER OWN?

KALYROS? MY GOD, IT WAS LIKE A CORNER OF HELL... BUT I RECALL NO CHILDREN, THEY COULD NOT HAVE SURVIVED IT

THERE'S ONE WHO DID, MATEY... AN' HALF-A-DOZEN REFUGEE AN' D.P. CAMPS AFTER THAT... YOU'VE LIFTED THE LID ON EVERYTHING THAT HAPPENED TO HER IN THOSE YEARS

191

147

BELOW: Patty invites her best friend Sharon to go on holiday with her family, but this angers Sharon's out-of-work father who insists on contributing towards his daughter's keep. The pressures of unemployment are explored in this episode of *Patty's World* in *Girl* from 28 July 1984.

BELOW: Patty visits her big sister Carol who is recovering in hospital after a fall and learns that Carol has lost the baby she was carrying and may not be able to have any more children. *Patty's World* from *Girl*, 27 December 1986.

ABOVE: *Patty's World* was a family soap opera narrated by the daughter. Unlike Sue Day, Patty Lucas was less middle-class, a bit older if not wiser at nearly thirteen, and her life was typically not like *Happy Days*. Over the course of its seventeen-year run from 1971, writer Steve Douglas and female Spanish artist Purita Campos tackled some sensitive topics for a girls' comic, while keeping up with changing fashions and social attitudes. Here, short of money and unsure about the future, Patty would prefer to get a paying job as soon as she finishes her "sentence" at the local comprehensive school rather than go on to college. This ran in *Pink* on 22 May 1976.

LEFT: In 1968, *Clive*, a moody teenage son, was the star and title of writer Angus McGill's and artist Dominic Poelsma's new strip for the *Evening Standard*, but he was soon ousted by his inquisitive little sister, Augusta. Influenced by Charles Schulz's *Peanuts*, Poelsma's signature style is to let figures and fixtures break up the outlines of his panels.

148

ABOVE: *Slaves of "War Orphan Farm"* may be the most sadistic serial in British girls' comics, showing kids being forced to labour in a quarry. Here Kate and the sickly Jill are left outside at night in the animal cage. From *Tammy*, 6 June 1971, drawn by Colin Merritt and possibly written by Gerry Finlay-Day.

149

ABOVE: *Nikola, Polish Refugee* is a surprisingly grim wartime drama for a girls' comic. It concerns a young Pole who is in search of her parents. In episode 17, she volunteers like "a true patriot" to rescue a man trapped beneath a collapsed building who turns out to be her father. Guido Buzzelli uses dark-grey washes on his original artwork for *Princess*, 15 October 1960.

ABOVE: Shirley Bellwood, a girls' comic artist since the 1950s, based Misty, ghostly hostess of this spooky weekly and eight annuals, on her elegant self.

RIGHT: The 1983 *Misty Annual* compiled the 53-page serial *Moonchild* by Pat Mills and John Armstrong. It was a *Carrie*-like chiller about Rosemary Black, whose witch's powers inherited from her grandmother awaken when bullies torment her.

BELOW: Suzy Varty edited Britain's first "women's comik" *Heröine* in 1978 and drew the one and only cover.

TOP RIGHT: In 1981, in *True Love*, her first original graphic novel, Posy Simmonds cleverly satirised the fantasies, idealised artwork, and even the pink second colour found in romance picture library comics. She contrasts these dreams with the drab reality of Janice, an avid reader, who mistakenly believes that her boss fancies her. Here, plain Janice daydreams of being the life of the party and snubbing him.

ABOVE RIGHT: Julie Hollings came up with Beryl the Bitch in college, "out of frustration at the general uselessness of men combined with the fun of being single again after ending my engagement to a pompous young curate". As a newspaper strip, Beryl bitched in the *Sunday Correspondent* in 1990.

RIGHT: Kate Charlesworth created a modern lesbian icon in Auntie Studs, star of *Naughty Little Monkeys*. This instalment appeared in the *Pink Paper* in 1994.

LEFT: In Myra Hancock's *Holiday Snaps* in 1984's *Escape* 5, punkettes Sharon and Maureen get into a cat-fight over their holiday flings. Myra used to peddle her self-published wares, like a cinema ice-cream girl, at Camden Lock Market.

LEFT: Jeremy Dennis instils her slice-of-life strips with a seemingly spontaneous brio, as in *Kate's on the Piss* from *Super State Funnies*, produced for the 1997 Caption convention in Oxford.

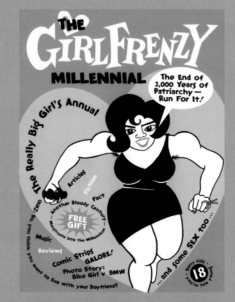

ABOVE: Erica Smith started *Girl Frenzy* in 1991. Her 1998 100-page *Millennial* was the old-fashioned girl's annual gone bad, with strips by over 30 British and international female cartoonists.

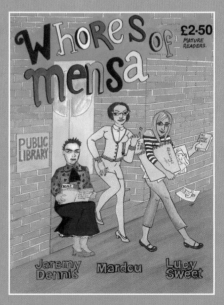

ABOVE: *Whores of Mensa* showcases Jeremy Dennis, Sacha Mardou and Lucy Sweet, a trio of contemporary British female comics creators, in this first issue from 2004.

151

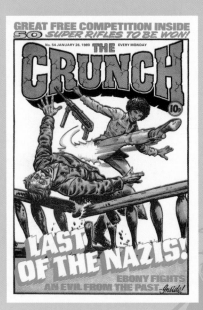

LEFT: Ebony Jones, a black martial arts secret agent, kicked her way into *The Crunch* in late 1979 as a British answer to blaxploitation movie heroine Cleopatra Jones. Ebony was the first action shero in a boys' weekly, nearly five years before Halo Jones (no relation) in *2000AD*. Cover for 26 January 1980 by Carlos Magallanes.

RIGHT: "I'm getting out of here." To escape The Hoop, a soul-destroying quarantine for the unemployed in the future, Halo Jones gets the one hostess vacancy on board a space liner thanks to her being able to speak Cetacean. Alan Moore and Ian Gibson introduced *2000AD*'s first female lead in 1984 but left her life story unfinished after three books.

BELOW: It's a weird, wild *Wired World* when you're with bleach blonde Pippa, who sports freckles and thick eyebrows, and her bosom buddy Liz. Their fears about food additives spiral into Liz being kidnapped by a child-catching ice-cream van. Created by Philip Bond for *Deadline* 12, October 1989.

ABOVE: Telepathic *Judge Anderson* and PsiKop Amisov pool their skills to read the messages from corpses, "remote-viewing" a sinister underworld beneath a Tibetan city called Shamballa. Alan Grant and Arthur Ranson created this *2000AD* series in 1990.

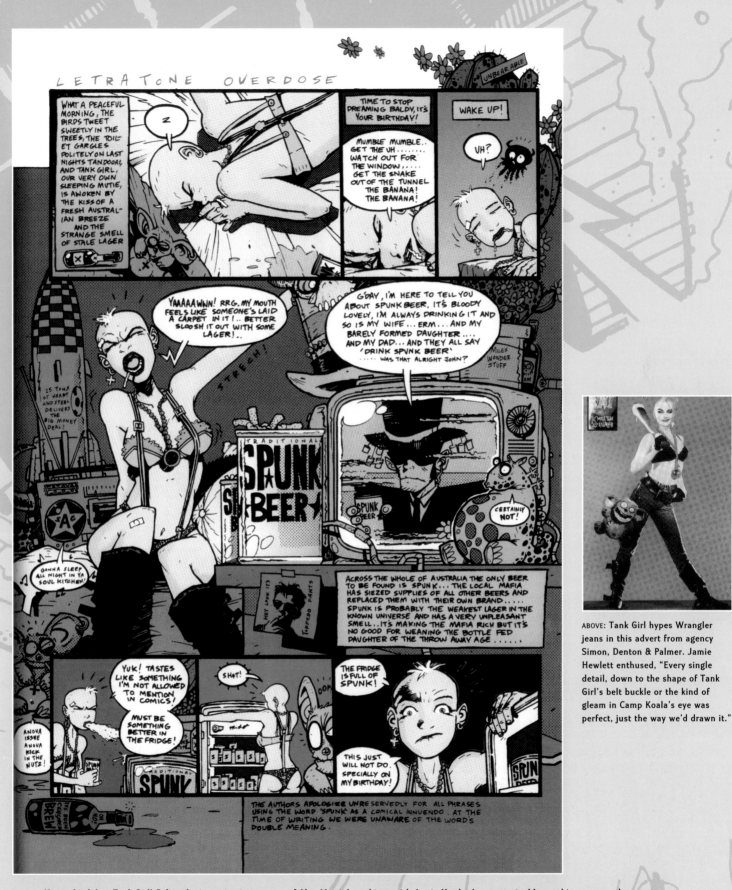

ABOVE: Tank Girl hypes Wrangler jeans in this advert from agency Simon, Denton & Palmer. Jamie Hewlett enthused, "Every single detail, down to the shape of Tank Girl's belt buckle or the kind of gleam in Camp Koala's eye was perfect, just the way we'd drawn it."

153

Happy birthday, Tank Girl! Splice the inventive irreverence of Alan Martin's verbiage with Jamie Hewlett's unrestrainable graphic energy and you get, in the words of Graham Coxon from Blur, "a loin-shattering, 125,000-miles-per-hour, knickers-on-head, hands-down-pants chick". This opener from "The Australian Job", an episode riffing on *The Italian Job*, saw her strip gatecrashed by Jet Girl and Sub Girl. Originally in *Deadline* 7, 1989, it was "colorized" for the 1993 US edition.

On 17 September 2005, Posy Simmonds began serialising her graphic novel *Tamara Drewe* in the Saturday edition of the *Guardian*. In an updated variation on the themes of Thomas Hardy's 1874 novel *Far From The Madding Crowd*, Tamara Drewe settles into her inherited family home deep in the English countryside. The new, post-nose-job Tamara soon gets noticed and arouses the desire of three male rivals: loud ex-rock star Ben Sergeant, strong, silent handyman Andy Cobb and stalled novelist Nicholas Hardiman. The whole village soon knows everybody's business, or so they think.

RIGHT: Here, in the episode of 21 January 2006, her lover and fiancé Ben expresses his city-boy loathing for the "backside of beyond" and his potentially violent possessiveness. Through multiple narrators' viewpoints, including bored teenager Casey Shaw and Tamara's *Away From It All* newspaper columns, Posy Simmonds methodically builds her characters and their interconnected tensions into a compelling and truly adult graphic novel, rich in her crystal-clear insights into modern British mores.

TOP AND BELOW: Posy Simmonds' sketchbooks spill over with preparatory drawings to pin down each member of her ensemble. Tamara and Andy appear at the top of the page and below is Nicholas's wife, Beth Hardiman, who runs a farmhouse writers' retreat.

154

LEFT: Avoiding the preachiness and fake hipness of some health-education comics, Steve Marchant talked with real-life teenage single mother Davine about her experiences and issues which he fictionalised in her own words in *Teenage Romance*, published in 2004 by the London Borough of Lewisham.

RIGHT: Sacha Mardou sensitively describes one woman's rush of conflicting emotions when a snail-mail romance between her and another budding author leads them both to cheat on their partners. She self-published *King of It* in 2006 in the second issue of *Manhole*.

ABOVE: *Looks, Brains & Everything* sums up zombiefied Shelley, kneeing the devil in the balls for what she has been put through. The 2003 book collects the first six months of John Allison's *Scarygoround* webcomics.

LEFT: When Stacey Slater eggs Ruby Allen on to sue café owner Ian Beale for personal injury after slipping on a baked-bean can, Ian foils their money-making scam by sending his customers to Stacey's for their breakfasts. Kelly Wilks and Paul Cemmick turn BBC TV soap *EastEnders* into a monthly "cartoon" for *It's Hot!* 51, May 2006.

Ripping Yarns

"A GOOD READ FOR BUDDING DELINQUENTS!" "TWO FOR A TANNER, EVERY RACE-DAY!" "VULTURE, THE MAG FOR KIDS OF CULTURE!" THESE COVER LINES MAKE THIS WEEKLY SOUND like every parent's worst nightmare, and perhaps some kids' dream. Don't go looking for rare back issues of *Vulture*, though, because it never made it into the newsagents. Only six pages of it ever saw print inside the racy little adult magazine *Lilliput* in September 1953 as a deliberately extreme parody of that far nobler bird of prey *Eagle*, Hulton Press's new title launched in 1950 under the morally unquestionable editorship of a vicar, Reverend Marcus Morris. Instead of clean-cut Dan Dare, *Vulture*'s front page starred May Fair, Queen of Venus, a glamorous showgirl villainess who seduces our hero SuperBoy. The back cover's usual biographical comic took readers back to *A Beano with the Borgias*, the Italian poisoners. The regular cut-away diagram across the middle pages was devoted to torture, *How to Make your own Rack*, while one advert offered a complete banknote forgery outfit. *Vulture*'s editor promised, "Next week, Mr Whitfield, who spent some years in the East, will tell us about Chinese tortures, and there will be a grand feature by Doctor Boddington on our digestive systems, with an attractive coloured diagram."

Because *Lilliput* and *Eagle* were both published by Hulton Press, this sly spoof could serve as a thinly disguised promotion to show by stark contrast how superior and respectable their "strip cartoon weekly" (never to be called a lowly "comic") really was. It also doubled as a barbed critique of the sleaze and violence associated with certain American comic books imported and imitated in Britain during and after the war. Branded as "horror comics", these had been attacked by Marcus Morris in the *Sunday Dispatch* of 13 February 1949: "Horror has crept into the British nursery. Morals of little girls in plaits and boys with marbles bulging in their pockets are being corrupted by a torrent of indecent coloured magazines that are flooding bookstalls and newsagents." Morris took the opportunity to publicise his still embryonic idea of what would become *Eagle*, "a genuinely popular 'Children's Comic' where adventure is once more the clean and exciting business I remember in my own schooldays—not abysmally long ago."

The moral panic over American comic books united British teachers, librarians and church leaders with unlikely, discreet allies in the Communist Party, who were strongly opposed to this ideological invasion of the nation but failed to realise that some of the very comics they condemned in fact carried anti-McCarthyite or anti-discriminatory messages. The various factions' erratic joint campaign and lobbying of MPs eventually resulted in an act of Parliament in 1955 which tarred comics with another negative blanket label of "harmful publications". This was not the first nor the last time that such mass entertainments, especially those popular among the supposedly vulnerable and potentially volatile youth and lower classes, would stir up controversy, complaints and crackdowns from the great

RIGHT: Barry Ono was a music-hall turn who saved his vast collection of "penny dreadfuls" for the nation and bequested it to the British Museum.

BELOW: A title-page illustration from a "penny dreadful" version of *Sweeney Todd*, the demon barber, whose murder spree and human meat pies seduced a generation into believing that it was all true.

OPPOSITE: Before Mr Spock, there was the pointy-eared "King of Crime", The Spider in 1965, shown brandishing his all-purpose gun on the cover of *Super Library* 4, 1967, painted by Alessandro Biffignandi.

5. One of the mystery men ever so softly opened a secret door in front of them. It led into the treasure chamber in which Rob and Dick were taking stock of the glittering objects that were piled up before them, and never dreaming there was any danger to guard against.

6. Neither of the chums heard the door open behind them, and they were filled with dismay when suddenly they heard a sound, and turned to find the two rascals they had recently befriended stealing upon them. "You are our prisoners," cried the foremost.

158

ABOVE: Rob the Rover and his pal Dick fall victim to treacherous foreign friends when they discover a treasure chamber in these two panels by Walter Booth from *Puck*, 11 December 1926.

RIGHT: Dick Turpin on his horse Black Bess fends off an attacker, illustrated by Derek Eyles on the cover of *Thriller Picture Library* 223 in May 1958.

BELOW: Colin Merritt's Chinese scoundrel *Chang the Yellow Pirate* outwitted the authorities in *Joker* from 1936 to 1939.

and the good. Many of the same arguments against them are still trotted out today as each new unchecked phenomenon takes hold, as in more recent scares about "video nasties", computer games and the internet. Their use goes right back to the precursors of so many of the non-comical comics, namely the boys' story papers and before them the Victorian novels serialised for one penny a part. Condemned en masse as "penny dreadfuls", these became the first targets of a concerted campaign to accuse a mass medium of corrupting the young.

By taking a broader perspective, it becomes clear how much the adventure genres in modern British comics owe to this earlier literature for the masses, in its sensationalist subjects, larger-than-life protagonists, addictive cheapness and often far from illustrious reputation. The *Sun* newspaper acknowledged this in 1976 when they wryly nicknamed the provocative comic *Action* a "Sevenpenny Dreadful"; perhaps the threat to civil obedience posed by its tales of out-of-control kid gangs or football hooligans was not so far removed from that posed a century or so before by the sewer-dwelling *Wild Boys of London*, considered so subversive on its reissue in

1873 that the police suppressed it. British adventure comics are part of this unbroken lineage of cheap thrills which feeds the same fundamental appetite for excitement and shocks as movies or games. It's all part of the appeal for "ripping yarns" that can lift you from the mundane into a state of heightened emotion and imagination.

In their day, the penny dreadfuls were the comics of new generations of Victorian working-class youngsters, who by the mid-19th century were becoming literate and hungry for an affordable, thrilling read. It was all very well improving children's literacy by providing all with elementary education in the 1870 Education Act, but what was then provided for them to read? Hardback children's books were beyond the price range of most and not yet available for free from lending libraries, so clever publishers took to selling them novels sliced into multiple parts with woodcut illustrations, coloured on the cover, at one penny each. Those who could not afford even this could club together, chipping in a farthing or quarter of a penny each, or made do with tatty hand-me-down copies, read until they fell to bits. The more "dreadful" of these continued the best-selling formula of the "Newgate novels", named after the prison gallows where convicted killers were strung up before crowds of thousands. On the justification that they were moralistic warnings that "crime does not pay", these spared no gory detail in their re-tellings of the misdeeds, trial and punishment of the guilty, and were as fascinated with "true crime" as today's tabloid exposés and TV docudramas.

Notorious real-life rogues gained a second life after their execution, when the penny-a-part scribes embellished them into champions of the oppressed, who then lived on through the story papers into comics and other mass media. For example, after Dick Turpin had been hanged in 1739, aged 34, his legend began to be embroidered later in the 18th century in illustrated chapbooks and broadsheets sold at travelling fairgrounds, markets and public hangings. To these were added William Ainsworth's novel *Rookwood* in 1843, which further romanticised the squat, balding robber and former butcher's assistant Turpin into a dashing gentleman of the road, and Edward Viles's 1863–68 penny-a-part novel *Black Bess*, named after Turpin's trusty steed, which was issued in no fewer than 254 episodes totalling 2,028 pages. Similarly, Turpin's French-born predecessor Claude Duval, hanged in 1670, was turned from a murderous highwayman into a Royalist freedom-fighter pitted against Midas Mould and the roundheads of a tyrannical Cromwell for his strip debut in *Comet* in 1953. When Charlie Peace eventually arrived as a strip in *Buster* in 1964, he was billed as "the most daring and notorious criminal in Victorian London", sweetened for kids into a colourful rogue who foils the police, without a hint of his murders for which he was executed in 1879.

Mythical bogeymen from Gothic novels such as the demon-barber Sweeney Todd and the demonically garbed Spring-heeled Jack also haunted long-running penny-a-part serials but were probably too shocking for comics. Both had to wait until adult graphic novels became established. Neil Gaiman began a *Sweeney Todd* graphic novel with American Michael Zulli in the anthology *Taboo*, but it was left unfinished in 1992 after only a promotional poster, preview and prologue. At least in 2005, David Hitchcock completed his trilogy reimagining Spring-heeled Jack, while Alan Moore and Kevin O'Neill weave their grand tapestry of fantasy literature icons in *League of Extraordinary Gentlemen*. Real frontier scout William F. Cody, who became known to the public as Buffalo Bill in 1869, was the

most famous of America's living icons to cross the Atlantic, creating a sensation in person with his Wild West Show. American ten-cent "dime novels" about his exploits were reprinted in "libraries", small text digests for a penny, by the Aldine Publishing Company in London. To these Aldine added from 1901 the derring-do of homegrown heroes Turpin, Duval, Robin Hood and Rob Roy. Their accompanying illustrations by Robert Prowse, F.W. Boyington and others defined how comics and other media have visualised these iconic figures ever since.

There were profits to be made by two publishers of story papers who claimed the moral high ground over the scandalised penny dreadfuls. On the one hand, the pious Religious Tract Society came round to the idea of *The Boys' Own Paper* to compete with the penny dreadfuls head-on, not by preaching overtly but by incorporating their messages into inspirational fiction, a recipe that sustained the weekly, and later monthly, from 1879 to 1967. This was not so different from the strategy taken with *Eagle* by Marcus Morris and his Society of Christian Publicity. On the other hand, competitive publishing magnate Alfred Harmsworth wiped out the dreadfuls by making his story papers more in tune with Britons' turn-of-the-century mood of patriotism and imperialism and by cutting their price to half a penny. For all Harmsworth's lofty claims, he soon brought

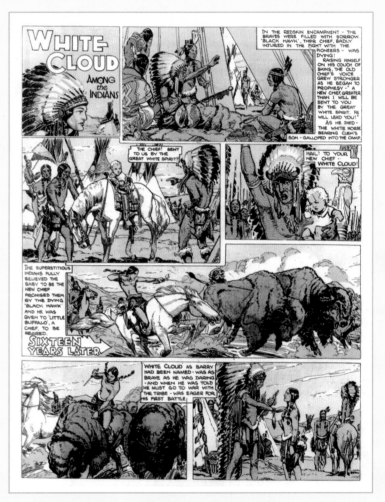

ABOVE: Galvanised by the full-page, full-colour Sunday page adventure strips in American newspapers, Reg Perrott succeeded in introducing a much more dynamic and dramatic approach to British comics, varying his panels' shapes, sizes and viewpoints. His tale of a white baby raised by Native Americans to be their new chief White Cloud ran in colour on the centre spread of *Mickey Mouse Weekly*, this episode dated 1 August 1936.

159

ABOVE: The lazy days of summer camping holidays spent reading your favourite comics. The early 1960s saw a boom in boys' interest in British victories in the Second World War, reflected in pocket-sized picture libraries like *Seek and Strike* in *Air Ace Picture Library* 7, 1960, cover by Giorgio De Gaspari, and in glueing and painting Airfix model kits, which are as popular as ever, today. The painted box illustration is by Roy Cross.

RIGHT: Wulf the Briton, scourge of the invading Romans, drawn by Ron Embleton for the 1961 *TV Express Annual*.

back many of the penny dreadfuls' popular heroes. This prompted the comment from cartoonist and Pooh illustrator A.A. Milne that "Harmsworth killed the 'penny dreadful' by the simple process of producing the 'ha'penny dreadfuller'."

The first significant threat to dent the virtual monopoly of Harmsworth's Amalgamated Press (AP) came from the "Big Five" story papers of Dundee's D.C. Thomson: *Adventure* (1921), *Rover* and *Wizard* (1922), *Skipper* (1930) and *Hotspur* (1933). What set their illustrated adventure yarns apart were the writers' and editorial staff's refreshingly improbable and often outrageous storylines, which truly stood the test of time by being revived, sometimes repeatedly, in strip form for decades after in Thomson's weekly comics. One prime example is Wilson, the Man in Black, the fantasy prototype for a new genre of astonishing sporting prodigies. Barefoot in black knitted long-johns, Wilson burst into the record books in *Wizard* in

1943 by vaulting a fence at an international athletics competition in London and running the first three-minute mile, long before the four-minute barrier had been broken. Once over the finish line, the gaunt mystery man collapsed and looked almost dead. Shortly after, he recovered and raced back to his spartan life on the Yorkshire Moors. Later instalments revealed his rustic origins and the secret herbal brew behind his longevity, claiming to be born in 1795. He later became an RAF pilot, but flying back from one dangerous mission, "Wilson's machine was last seen on fire over the Channel," and he was "officially listed as missing", never to be found. An unassuming, totally dedicated loner, Wilson wanted no glory or publicity. Many British athletes credit their record-breaking feats to being inspired by the tales of his determination, later retold as comics in *Hornet* from 1964 and then *Hotspur*.

In Britain, comics that were not meant to be comical were slow to take off and slow to adapt to the medium's full potential. Walter Booth pioneered the "straight" comic in 1920 in the weekly *Puck* on *Rob the Rover*, about a young lad washed ashore without his memory, whose quest for his identity was never wholly resolved after twenty years of globetrotting. Booth's amnesiac was exported across Europe, and redrawn as a fascist youth hero in Mussolini's Italy. Booth stuck to uniform panels and drew characters head-to-toe from the same angle, as if the reader were watching it all on a stage and sitting immobile in a dead-centre theatre seat.

Reg Perrott deserves much of the credit for energising this static, stagey British style. The varied sizes and "shots" of his panels and his hand-lettered captions may not look remarkable today but at the time, starting in *Mickey Mouse Weekly* in 1936, they finally showed signs of modernisation. Perrott's studio colleague Basil Reynolds recalled the turning point in his friend's career early in 1934. "Reg had been turning out a variety of artwork, the usual puzzles, comics, animal strips, etc. but only drew pin-men because, he said, he couldn't draw human figures. Then one day, he suddenly said, 'I'm going to have a go at a straight strip!' Thereupon, as I watched in growing disbelief, Reg drew six frames in pencil and, without references of any sort, proceeded to fill them in with six pictures of a legionnaire mounted on a black horse, ploughing through the sandy wastes of a desert fort. It was astonishing!" On *Road to Rome*, *White Cloud*, *Golden Arrow* and others, Perrott championed the realistic dynamism and sometimes vertiginous "cinematic shots" of America's new dramatic newspaper strips, in particular his favourite, *Connie* by Frank Godwin. According to Reynolds, "Beneath Reg's rugged exterior there beat the heart of a true romantic, ever thirsting for adventure." Perrott had once seriously suggested that they both drop everything and join the Foreign Legion. When war broke out, Perrott swiftly joined the RAF, but was invalided and died young—not the only remarkable British adventure strip creator whose life would be cut short far too early.

It was tough being a periodical publisher during and after the Second World War, because controls on supplies of paper restricted new comics being launched. Some smaller, independent entrepreneurs, however, found loopholes and established fresh outlets for more modern adventure comics. One was Gerald G. Swan, who was 19 when he set up a market stall for second-hand comics and books in 1921 with a loan from his mother. With business growing briskly, he became a publisher and from 1940 commissioned short strips from freelance British artists, eager for work in the leaner war years and pleased to be given a freer rein to develop their comics in a more modern American style. Swan put together compact 36-page anthologies priced threepence and modelled on American comic books and

"albums"—undated hardback annuals. His *Topical Funnies*, *Dynamic Thrills*, *Slick Fun* and others made up for their sometimes unpolished amateurism by being quirky and enthusiastic. One example is William McCail's scratchily drawn serial compiled into the 52-page *Picture Epics* 1, titled *Back from the Dead*. This told the story of the cadaverous Robert Lovett, buried in 1827, who awoke after more than a century in his tomb and used his deadly eye blasts and other powers in a war against criminals, while adjusting to today's many unfamiliar terms and technology. In one scene, he sees a hoarding marked "Pictures" and enters what he assumes must be an art gallery, only to be directed to a seat in the dark. He is horrified when he watches a woman being tied to a railway track and the complacent audience around him do nothing to save her. When a "monster of steel" roars towards her, a terrified Lovett uses his optical beams to destroy the train and in the process wrecks the cinema or "picture house" he has been in. Former *Bonzo* animator William Ward also worked for Swan, creating Krakos the Egyptian in 1941, a resurrected pharaoh in a fedora prowling foggy wartime London. Swan dropped his comic strip titles in 1955 when paper restrictions were lifted and sold his business in 1964. As W.O.G. Lofts revealed in a tribute, when Swan died in 1980, he left nearly £62,000, "not bad for a poor boy who borrowed 30 bob from his mother to start a second-hand bookstall".

On the heels of his fortnightly *Comet* in 1946, the first new comic after the war, publisher J.B. Allen in Cheshire was eager to launch a companion in the alternate weeks. To get round the paper shortages, he secured the quota alotted to his defunct pre-war health magazine *Fitness and Sun*. To keep up the pretense, at first he had to retain the old title, printing "Fitness and" in small letters, but he soon dropped them and continued it as *Sun* (no relation to the newspaper). According to writer G.H. Beaumont, Allen

ABOVE: Henry Nobbins had been an ordinary labourer until he inherited the title of Earl of Ranworth and five million pounds. Before he could inherit, however, he had to become champion in many different sports, as his ancestors had been. *His Sporting Lordship* appeared in *Valiant* and is drawn here by Geoff Campion.

161

BELOW: As snake-skinned superhero King Cobra attacks in *Hotspur*, he inflates his hood like his reptile namesake. This cover of the 8 March 1980 issue is by Ken Shone.

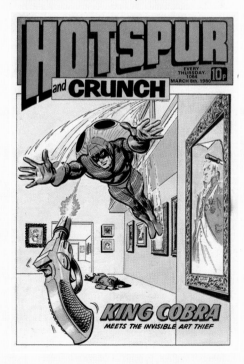

ABOVE: The *P.C. 49* radio serial by Alan Stranks was adapted into a strip for *Eagle* drawn by John Worsley. This nail-biting clifftop scene is from *The Case of the New Member* from *Eagle*, 6 January 1956.

ABOVE: Greedy for treasure, cowardly but kind pirate Captain Pugwash solves *The Secret of the San Fiasco*, mostly thanks to Tom the cabin-boy, in this 1985 book by John Ryan.

was persuaded by Beaumont's artist brother Reg to upgrade *Comet*'s printing to photo-gravure using grey-green and deep-orange inks and *Sun* adopted this from the start. Allen's fine pair of papers were snapped up in May 1949 by AP, which was determined to usurp Thomson in the boys' comics sector. For some while, AP's weekly *Knockout* had been running strip adaptations of famous adventure stories, several drawn by Eric Parker in his fluid, bravura lines, and other serials inspired by or based specifically on the latest western and historical movies. When *Knockout*'s recently promoted editor Leonard Matthews was put in charge of *Sun* as well, he persevered in raising the standard of action comics still higher. He recruited as illustrators such renowned veterans from other fields as painter Septimus Scott and book illustrator H.M. Brock, often writing their adaptations for them. AP's need for more and more new blood prompted adverts seeking artists in the national press, which found them Geoff Campion and Reg Bunn, introductions via writer Ron Clark to Mike Western, Eric Bradbury and others, and the hiring, mostly through agencies, of a wealth of talent from abroad. Following the dawn of the New Elizabethan Age after the Coronation in 1953, adventure comics continued to reflect the renewed enthusiasm for the nation's heroic history, harking back before the days of a fast-fading Empire to the nation's older, illustrious past. So the time was right for the swordsmen, swashbucklers, knights and highwaymen of the dreadfuls and story papers to leap once more back into the fray.

These heroes also battled anew in an innovative compact format called the "library", named after the small story paper magazine the *Sexton Blake Library* offering 64 black-and-white pages within a colour cover, akin to the earlier Aldine libraries. AP's expectations were not high when the first of these comics, two issues of *Cowboy Comics*, were tested in April 1950. The material for these had been originated for Australasian readers who preferred larger comic books starring one hero to the selection box of characters and genres in British anthologies. Editor Edward Holmes wanted to see if these Buck Jones and Kit Carson solo comic books would prove as popular in Britain, where westerns were also all the rage. Finding no AP press to handle

| 1942 | 1955 | 1966 | 1974 | 1982 | 2003 |

their unconventional size, he proposed printing them on their library press and re-packaging the artwork to fit. By a lucky accident, Holmes had hit on an instantly successful format—handy, pocket-sized complete stories, often full-length, "told in pictures", allowing on average two generous, wide panels of rich illustration per page. His was an odd British invention that caught on across Europe and elsewhere, and which back home led to AP's long-running series of *Cowboy*, *Thriller*, *Super Detective*, *War*, *Battle* and *Air Ace Picture Libraries* and others aimed at girls and women. As well as fresh material designed for this size, AP reformatted their previously printed tales and newspaper strips too, like Jack Monk's *Buck Ryan*, the *Daily Mirror* detective. Thomson tried it for size in 1961 with *Commando* and a host of others followed from *Football* to *Starblazer*. Nearly 3,800 issues later, *Commando* is still battling on, while the *Beano* and *Dandy* stars enjoy two-colour libraries of their own.

Other independent publishers mush-roomed after the war into a cumulative explosion of idealists and opportunists, a few of them fly-by-night, others building little empires. T.V. Boardman, Len Miller and his son Arnold, who had each begun by reprinting American comics, branched out into new material by British creators. For Boardman, Denis and Colin McLoughlin crafted the handsome *Buffalo Bill* annuals, while Mick Anglo and his studio solved the crisis facing Miller upon the cancellation of the American *Captain Marvel* titles in 1953 by replacing his reprints with new stories of a rather similar anglicised superhero trio headed by Marvelman, who outlasted the originals by ten years. Even so, The Marvelman Family were really the only big-selling exception to the rule that British

creators did not follow American-style superhero traditions, but had always favoured weirder eccentrics, like the 1930s prehistoric and cowboy strongmen Strang the Terrible and Desperate Dan, or the 1960s high-tech mavericks who were initially not heroes at all, like The Spider and The Steel Claw. The era of Batmania and Marvelmania changed this bias, as did the coming of age of a generation reared on imported costumed crimefighters.

Dez Skinn at Marvel UK oversaw new locally produced stories of Marvel's pantheon, including an Arthurian Black Knight and Captain Britain, first a wholly American product but much improved by British hands. As publisher and editor in 1982, Skinn was also behind the landmark revival in *Warrior* of Marvelman in a very different tone from his light-hearted 1950s roots. Alan Moore and Garry Leach made a superhero who walks among us and is touchingly alien and human at the same time, thereby recharging a genre that many had seen as a spent cliché.

The clichés of all the adventure genres are always ripe for some fresh angles, whether recasting the effete, pipe-smoking detectives as womanising, manly spies or deglamorising war by showing young soldiers' lives and deaths in the trenches. It's because these conventions and archetypes can be slightly tweaked or totally overhauled to suit the shifting zeitgeist that their stories have proved so flexible and so enduring.

ABOVE: Tony Weare drew Britain's longest-running and classiest Western newspaper strip, *Matt Marriott*, in the London *Evening News* from 1955 to 1977. This original strip from the first year shows his mastery of chiaroscuro mood.

LEFT: Staff in hand and garbed in the Union Jack flag, Jack Staff was billed as "Britain's Greatest Hero twenty years ago". Since 2000, Paul Grist has invented a whole history for his brand-new, supposedly forgotten hero.

BELOW: A vinyl figure by James Jarvis of intrepid explorer Mr Waverley, who went on to feature in the 2006 graphic novel *Vortigern's Machine* by James Jarvis and Russell Waterman.

7—Swiftly Morgyn made his way round the lagoon. And as he approached the shining object, a gasp of surprise escaped him—"It's a torpedo!" he muttered. "Some naval ship must have gone down and this is part of the wreckage." And jumping from rock to rock, the big castaway got as near as he could to the reef on which the torpedo lay. He made a noose on one end of the rope he had brought with him. And as the moon began to shine brightly in the black sky, the whales came leaping towards Morgyn. But calmly Morgyn stood and flung the noose.

8—The rope fell short, but patiently Morgyn coiled it and flung it once more. Time after time he did this, and in the end he lassoed the torpedo. He tightened the noose carefully, and then even more carefully he pulled it off the reef, expecting at any moment to hear it explode. He knew that if the firing mechanism had been damaged in any way, the torpedo was liable to blow up. At length, however, he got the torpedo safely to the side of the beach, though the whales jostled it on all sides, thinking it was an enemy of some kind.

9—Carefully the big castaway examined the torpedo. Then, satisfied, he turned to watch the whales with grim face. The whales were swarming in the lagoon and Morgyn hoisted the heavy torpedo on to his shoulder and made his way up the path to the cliffs. Morgyn was the strongest man in the world. His strength was the strength of ten, and even ten ordinary men would have had a great deal of difficulty in carrying the torpedo up those towering cliffs. But Morgyn the Mighty did it with ease.

10—At the top of the cliffs, Morgyn lowered the torpedo carefully to the ground. Then he looked over the edge. Below him was the lagoon, with the whales leaping everywhere in the light of the tropic moon. "They won't be there much longer!" he muttered grimly, and turned to the torpedo once more. Carefully he fixed the mechanism preparing the controls, so that the torpedo would blow up the instant its nose hit anything. Then he hoisted the gleaming torpedo above his head. The huge muscles of his arms and back bulged under the strain.

11—Morgyn walked to the edge of the cliffs, and then, with a tremendous heave, launched the torpedo outwards into the lagoon. The torpedo flashed downwards like a shooting-star and hit the water. Boom! There was a terrific explosion that shook the whole of Black Island. Whales were blasted out of the lagoon, and Morgyn felt the cliffs tremble under his feet. The echoes of that thunderous crash took a long time to die away, and the waves caused by the explosion lashed the beach of the lagoon for almost an hour.

12—With a grim smile Morgyn returned to his shack for some sleep. But at dawn he was up again, spade in hand. He knew what to expect as he made his way straight down to the beach. The shore was littered with dead whales. The torpedo had done its deadly work and had cleared the killers from the lagoon, and the waves had washed the dead bodies far up the beach. But there was still work for Morgyn to do, burying the bodies before they began to rot. But he was happy as he worked. A menace to Black Island had been removed!

Exerting every ounce of his tremendous strength the strong-man heaved—

—and the giant crab soared through the air and crashed on a big rock. It rolled over and lay lifeless on the sand.

Later that day, on the beach, Samson, Trixie and Danny lolled under a sunshade made from the monster crab shell. But not so Gloopy and Horace —they practised their acts under the hot sun. "You never know when circus tricks will come in useful," gasped Gloopy, mopping his brow. "After all, it was a circus trick that saved YOUR life, Horace, m'boy!"

164

MORGYN THE MIGHTY

ABOVE LEFT: Burly Morgyn the Mighty cleans up Shark Island in this decidedly non-environmentally friendly adventure from *The Beano*, 10 September 1938, drawn by George "Dod" Anderson.

ABOVE RIGHT: Stranded on Crusoe Island, an uncharted stretch of the South Seas, are the world's strangest castaways, *The Shipwrecked Circus*. Here, a giant crab is smashed by strongman Samson and its shell turned into a sunshade. Art by Pat Nicolle from the 1958 *Beano Annual*.

LEFT: Dudley Watkins painted Morgyn for this book collection of his stories in 1943.

RIGHT: Watkins drew still stranger tales of another strongman in leopard skins, the prehistoric Strang the Terrible, from *The Beano*, 9 September 1944.

Pile these Waste Paper heaps up high—And soon we'll see old Adolf die!

6—It obviously wasn't enjoying its unsavoury morsel. Strang made the most of his opportunity to escape the horror of the swamp. With swift and powerful strokes he raced for the shore nearest his goal, the mystery mountains. Behind him he could hear the angry roars and splashes as the monster churned the water of the swamp in its rage. With an extra burst of speed the strong man gained dry ground.

7—With his heavy club in one hand he ran for his life across the grass. The monster roared in anger from the centre of the swamp. Luckily for Strang the huge creature did not leave the swamp and chase after him. Strang slackened his mad rush. He noticed that it was growing dusk and that he would soon be having to look for some sort of shelter where he could sleep for the night.

8—Although Strang, who had been carried into this gruesome valley by an underground river, had for some time been past the swamp before, and had little or no idea what lay ahead of him. Past experience had made him realise the grave dangers that might be encountered by sleeping in the open at night. "I'll have to find shelter soon," he muttered. "I can't carry on in the dark."

9—Suddenly he stopped dead in his tracks at the side of a pile of huge boulders. Far away from the top of a small mountain little puffs of smoke were rising. "Smoke signals!" thought Strang. "But who can be sending them?" The sun was sinking faster in the west by now and Strang decided that he would have to find out that secret in the morning. He looked at the pile of rocks at his side.

10—Suddenly he noticed a crack of light between two of the rocks. "Hm!" he murmured thoughtfully. "There must be a space inside." Swiftly he climbed to the top and, sure enough, there was a space large enough for him to crawl inside. "This will make a fine sleeping place for to-night," he thought. "All it needs is a roof." After dropping his club inside Strang looked around for a suitable rock for a roof.

11—In a very short time he found one that suited his purpose perfectly. Lifting the massive flat rock on to his broad back, he lowered himself into the space in the rocks and let the flat rock on his back drop into place as a lid to his den. Strang was now surrounded by boulders and was sure that he was safe from the wild creatures in the valley. In no time at all he dropped off to sleep.

The strongest and strangest strongman in British comics is stubbly-chinned Desperate Dan, desperate because he is a desperado or cowboy, although his hometown Cactusville is as much a British town with lampposts and pillar boxes. As this original artwork reveals, Dudley Watkins was asked to draw some extraordinary flights of fancy, such as this wartime elephant episode from *The Dandy*, 24 January 1942, which includes Dan's attack on a German U-boat.

Starting today—The sensational story of the world's most amazing athlete— and his astounding secret!

THE TRUTH ABOUT WILSON

ABOVE: Later phenomenal sporting eccentrics in comics included *Hot-Shot Hamish*, a hulking footballer with a pile-driver kick, drawn here by Julio Schiaffino in *Tiger*, 16 April 1977, and *The Wild Wonders*, the world's strongest boys, all raised on remote islands in the Scottish Hebrides.

LEFT: He was affectionately known as "Wilson of the Wizard" after the boys' story paper where his tales first appeared in 1943. The exceptional barefoot athlete raced into the record books and into comics on 12 September 1964 in *The Hornet* in the first episode of *The Truth about Wilson* (cover shown BELOW LEFT). Drawn by Spain's Edmond Ripoll, Wilson kept running in *Hornet* and then *Hotspur* until 1980 and was revived again in *Spike* in 1983.

THE TOUGH OF THE TRACK

RIGHT: In the Grand Prix motor sports tradition of Stirling Moss and Jackie Stewart, British race ace Skid Solo roared to the finish in *Hurricane* and *Lion* from 1964 to 1981. In this 1967 story, he solves a mysterious accident by re-enacting the exact same circuit conditions. Art by John Vernon.

ABOVE: Like Wilson, other heroes in Thomson's boys' comics started out in their story papers. Alf Tupper, nicknamed *The Tough of the Track*, first appeared in *Rover* in 1949. His stories were adapted into comics in *Victor* drawn by Pete Sutherland from 1963. This episode is dated 5 June 1963. The "hard-as-nails", working-class runner who loved his fish and chips scored a last victory on 21 November 1992 when he ran against a computer.

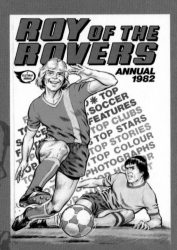

RIGHT: Created by story paper writer Frank S. Pepper, *Roy of the Rovers* kicked off in *Tiger* in 1954. Roy's exceptional goal-scoring skills in a crisis led to the much-used commentators' phrase "Real Roy of the Rovers stuff!" to describe some of real-life football's most thrilling moments. Barrie Mitchell drew this 1982 annual cover.

LEFT: The official signed club portrait of Melchester Rovers from the 1982 Annual.

BELOW LEFT: The last kick in the game goes to Roy Race, who scores a much-needed equaliser. Joe Colquhoun drew this episode in *Tiger* for 23 January 1966.

BELOW RIGHT: Roy's trusty old pair of football boots have gone missing, but this doesn't stop him scoring another last-minute goal in this episode from *Tiger* by Tom Tully and Barrie Mitchell, 16 April 1977.

RIGHT: Writer Frank S. Pepper was asked to give Roy a wife and a son, "Rocky", who grew up to play for Melchester too. Here he is only seventeen and so too young for alcohol, but on a night out clubbing, he gets drunk and assaults a paparazzo photographer, resulting in another press scandal about "footballers behaving badly". Stuart Green and Sean Longcroft created this tabloid-style twist in *Roy of the Rovers Monthly* 15 in November 1994.

Roy turned to drink after he lost a foot in a helicopter crash in 1993. In time, he accepted an offer to manage fallen giants of Italian football, AC Monza, where he came to realise, "Football is my home. Not Melchester, not even England. The packed stadium, the delirious crowd, the winning goal—that's my home." He quit the game after the tragic death of his wife, but returned in 1997 in *Match of the Day* magazine as co-owner and manager of Melchester Rovers. With Roy in charge and son Rocky playing, the team wouldn't languish much longer at the bottom of the First Division.

RIGHT: With a eye for authentic details of weaponry and costume, Patrick Nicolle drew *Bold Robin Hood* for *Sun* in 1952 and 1953, which was adapted into *Thriller Comics* 74, 7 October 1954. The cover below was painted by Septimus Scott.

BELOW: *The King's Musketeers* and *The Man in The Iron Mask* drawn by Chilean illustrator Arturo Del Castillo in *Lion*, this original page dated 28 December 1963.

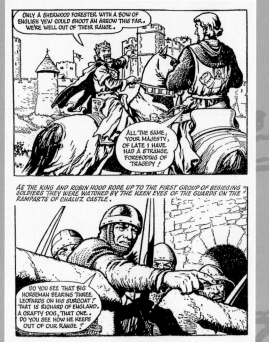

ABOVE: Barry Ford, pen name of Joan Whitford, adapted Rafael Sabatini's novel *Fortunes of Captain Blood* in *Thriller Picture Library* 145, 2 October 1956, drawn with buccaneering panache by John Millar Watt.

BELOW: W. Bryce Hamilton illustrates *Smuggler's Creek*, a weekly serial set in England in 1792 during the French Revolution. This page ran in *Knockout* on 11 July 1953.

169

ABOVE: John Millar Watt of *Pop* fame used special brilliantly coloured inks for this original painting of Dick Turpin, used as the cover of *Thriller Picture Library* 231, dated 21 July 1958.

LEFT: *Dick Turpin's Ride To York* was based on parts of William Ainsworth's novel *Rookwood* and culminated in the death of the highwayman's steed Black Bess. Written by editor Leonard Matthews, it was illustrated by Derek Eyles in nine two-page instalments in *Knockout*, this third part printed on 31 July 1948.

NO EVIL MASTERMIND'S CUNNING MOTIVES, CAN ELUDE THESE BAFFLED DETECTIVES

ABOVE: In *Panther's Moon*, based on the story by Victor Canning, adventurer Roger Quain risks his life by trying to remove the collar of Rajah the panther, in which vital microfilm is hidden. A young Ron Embleton drew this for *Super Detective Library* 58 in July 1955.

ABOVE RIGHT: Second only to Sherlock Holmes, Sexton Blake was Britain's other master detective, whose debut written by Harry Blyth appeared in 1893 in the story paper *The Halfpenny Marvel*. Eric Parker became the definitive illustrator of the many text stories, but when comics about the sleuth finally began in *Knockout* from 1939 to 1960, Parker drew only one, the fourteen-week tale of *The Secret of Monte Cristo* in 1949.

RIGHT: The cover of *Super Detective Library* 131 was painted by James McConnell.

FAR RIGHT: Blackshirt was not some Oswald Mosley-style Nazi sympathiser, but the black-garbed alter ego of crime novelist and master cracksman, Richard Verrell, a man of action invented by writer Roderic Graeme and adapted by him into comics. Here, Blackshirt tussles with a crook who has been impersonating him in the finale of *The Secret of the Devil's Ravine*, drawn by Bill Lacey and published in July 1958.

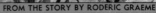

LEFT: Created in 1937 by writer Don Freeman and artist Jack Monk, amateur investigator Buck Ryan was until 1962 the *Daily Mirror*'s answer Dick Tracy by American Chester Gould. Ryan persuaded tough blonde Zola to give up crime and become his assistant, solving mysteries together. In this scene from 1945's *Case of the Broken Thistle*, their presence is detected by mad, masked villain, The Head.

LEFT: *Tug Transom* was written by Peter O'Donnell and drawn by Alfred Sindall for the *Daily Sketch* from 1954 to 1966. In *The Lady in the Tower*, Tug, a burly sea captain, is called in by British Naval Intelligence to expose an arms-smuggling sheikh with officer Gayle Page. Both end up captured and here, Gayle massages Tug after he wins a wrestling bout with the sheikh's bodyguard.

BELOW LEFT: Peter O'Donnell also wrote the much lighter *Romeo Brown*, about a timid, Dirk Bogarde-like detective chased by voluptuous females, drawn by Jim Holdaway in the *Daily Mirror* from 1957 until 1962. *Romeo Brown*'s first artist from 1954 was Dutchman Alfred Mazure. Two tiny paperback comics of his 1942 Dutch private eye, Dick Boss, came out in English in 1947 (BELOW).

171

LEFT: Before Sean Connery played James Bond in the first movie *Dr No* in 1962, artist John McLusky had established 007's rugged looks in the *Daily Express* strip starting in 1958. This strip from the climax of *Goldfinger* in March 1961 was credited to *Bond* creator Ian Fleming but was written by Henry Gammidge. Apart from a break from 1962 to 1964, the strip ran until 1977.

MAGNETO TROUBLE, I FANCY. I'LL FIX IT

HURRY! WE'RE DRIFTING TO THOSE RAPIDS. WE'LL BE SMASHED UP

I'VE JUST FINISHED

THAT CLOUD IS THE SPRAY FROM A WATERFALL!

IT'S O.K. NOW.

HOLD TIGHT, THEN. WE CAN'T RACE AGAINST THE CURRENT, SO I'M GOING TO RACE WITH IT!

As the amphibian tore towards the cloud of spray thrown up by the falls, it seemed that they were rushing to certain doom. Eighty yards—seventy—sixty—would the machine never lift?

LEFT: Captain W.E. Johns based much of his stories on his experiences as a bomber pilot in the RAF. In the First World War, Johns' bomber was hit by enemy aircraft and he went missing. Presumed dead by his family, he survived and surprised them when he returned on Christmas morning, 1918. He created his famous airman James Bigglesworth, known as "Biggles" in the first issue of *Popular Flying*, April 1932. The second Biggles book, *The Cruise of the Condor* in August 1933, was abridged and adapted in 1955 into this 44-page hardback illustrated by Pat Williams. In this scene, his amphibian plane is caught in the rapids and heading for a waterfall.

No. 3768
£1
commando
FOR ACTION AND ADVENTURE

The First ACES

ABOVE: José Maria Jorge drew the cover and inside story of this First World War aerial drama for *Commando* 3768 in 2004.

BELOW: Flying ace Battler Britton comes to the rescue in this scene from *Thriller Picture Library* 204, January 1958, drawn by Gino d'Antonio.

WAR PICTURE LIBRARY No 57
1/-
KILLER SUB

ABOVE AND RIGHT: *Killer Sub* from *War Picture Library* 57, 1 July 1960, cover by Giorgio De Gaspari, art by Graham Coton.

AT A SLIGHT NOD FROM TONY, RAYNOR PICKED UP THE MICROPHONE OF THE LOUDSPEAKER SYSTEM...

THIS IS THE CAPTAIN SPEAKING! I CAN NOW TELL YOU OUR MISSION - *KELLY SOON. 'STRIKER' IS GOING THROUGH THE DEFENCES GUARDING YOSHIMURA NAGASIKO!* ONCE WE GET IN THERE HALF THE IMPERIAL JAPANESE FLEET WILL BE BEGGING FOR OUR TIN FISH! AND I KNOW I CAN DEPEND ON ALL OF YOU TO GIVE 'EM THE LOT WHERE IT HURTS MOST, THAT IS ALL EXCEPT—*GOOD LUCK!*

NOW MAYBE I CAN CHALK UP A DECENT SCORE ON THIS DARNED BOARD!

BABY, YOU'RE GOING TO GET A NICE FAT BATTLEWAGON, ALL TO YOURSELF!

STANDING BESIDE THE CHART TABLE, AND GUIDED BY EVERY TINY DETAIL HE HAD MEMORISED, TONY BEGAN TO GIVE QUIET ORDERS. *STRIKER* GLIDED FORWARD AT QUARTER SPEED ...

...HER SLIM BOWS POINTING AT THE THICKLY SOWN MENACE OF THE MINEFIELD AHEAD!

ONLY BATTLER'S SUPERB SKILL SAVED THEM IN THAT NINTH HOUR! BY HIS WONDERFUL PILOTING HE MANAGED TO BRING THE TATTERED LANCASTER OUT OF THAT NERVE-SHATTERING HAIL OF DEATH. WIPING HIS OILY, SWEAT-STAINED BROW, HE ONCE AGAIN HANDED OVER TO KEN KNIGHT AND CLIMBED BACK TO SEE HOW THE REST OF THE CREW WERE FARING.

HOW'S THE SHOULDER, SMITHY? WE'RE ON THE LAST LAP.

I...I'M FINE, SIR. BUT...BUT TAFFY... HE..HE... A SHELL EXPLODED BACK THERE. I...THINK HE'S HURT.

BATTLER PULLED HIS WAY DOWN THE NARROW FUSELAGE UNTIL HE REACHED THE TAIL. THERE HE FOUND A SCENE OF UTTER CHAOS... TAFFY JONES LAY SPRAWLED IN THE BROKEN WRECKAGE OF THE GUN TURRET, WHICH FLAPPED IN THE SLIPSTREAM, ALMOST SEVERED FROM THE PLANE.

BY JUPITER! WHAT A MESS! COME ON, TAFFY... THAT'S NO PLACE FOR A WELSHMAN.

ABOVE: Tensions rise among the troops in *Strongpoint* when Harry Gravett (no relation) realises who stole his dead friend's lucky coin. Italy's late great comics maestro Hugo Pratt drew this for *War Picture Library 62*, in 1960, while he was working in London.

ABOVE RIGHT: *V for Vengeance* follows a group of masked, anonymous escapees from German prison camps, all called Jack, who carry out revenge killings of top Nazi officers. This was drawn by Frederick Alan Philpott for *Hornet* in 1965.

ABOVE: An atypical multi-racial cover on *Commando Picture Library 11*, painted by Ken Barr who defined the series' tougher attitude from 1961.

RIGHT: Nazis beware! Captain Hurricane is about to explode into one of his "ragin' furies" and go berserk. From *Valiant*, 1 April 1972, drawn by R. Charles Roylance.

RIGHT: An expert in Native American culture and the facts and myths of the American West, Denis McLoughlin documented them in detail for thirteen years in the *Buffalo Bill Wild West Annual* with his writer brother Colin. Here, they tell the story of lawman Bat Masterson (c.1856–1921) in the 1957 annual.

BELOW: The cover for the McLoughlins' 1952 *Buffalo Bill Wild West Annual*.

ABOVE: Shot and left for dead in a violent storm, Rock Kirby is taken by his faithful horse Smokey to shelter in a ghost town called Utopia. Robert Forrest drew *Twisted Trails* in *Wild West Library*, 2 May 1966.

LEFT: Writer Charles Chilton adapted his BBC radio series *Riders of the Range* into comics starting in *Eagle*'s first Christmas issue in 1950. Frank Humphris began a ten-year run on the artwork in 1952. He was often seen riding his horse on an authentic cowboy's saddle around London. Original art dated 22 November 1958.

ABOVE LEFT: Marvelman's apparent theft of some radioactive gold makes him a police suspect so he changes with his magic word Kimota (atomic backwards) into his other identity, young Micky Moran. Don Lawrence wrote and drew this story in the 1950s, early in his career. This colour reprint ran in the 1963 hardback *Marvelman Adventures*.

ABOVE RIGHT: Jerry Siegel, American co-creator of *Superman*, wrote the megalomaniac "King of Crooks", *The Spider*, in *Valiant*, 12 February 1966, drawn by Reg Bunn.

RIGHT: *Young Marvelman* by George Parlett, Reg Parlett's brother, on the cover of a 1963 colour collection.

LEFT: Before Marvel's Norse thundergod *Thor* there was *Thunderbolt Jaxon*, alias orphan boy Jack Jaxon, by Hugh McNeill. Here he is called to a movie lot in the 1958 *Knockout Annual*.

ABOVE: Like Herman Munster, also created in 1964, *Frankie Stein* turned the man-made monster into a laughter-maker in *Wham!* Here, face cream, a mislaid iced lolly and 500 gallons of lemon juice set off a chain of disasters in Ken Reid's "X-certificate" horror comedy for Halloween 1965.

BELOW: *Eagle-Eye Junior Spy* was invented by Leo Baxendale to parody the secret-agent craze, the hero here escaping a lethal exploding haggis hatched by archenemy Grimly Feendish in *Wham!* for 30 October 1965.

ABOVE: A Christmas disaster at sea with naval jinx Jonah drawn by Ken Reid for *The Beano*'s colour back page on 26 December 1959.

ABOVE: Mike Higgs's wacky, noseless "man in black" *The Cloak* spoofed 1960s spy capers in the pages of *Pow!* This mummified thriller is from 16 March 1968.

ABOVE: Cunning arch-rogue of Victorian London and numerous penny dreadfuls, Charlie Peace arrived in comics in *Buster* in 1964. Here, he eludes the authorities once more, but there's a final twist in this tale drawn by Tom Kerr for the 6 May 1967 issue.

RIGHT: With a touch of his control belt, an inventor hunts down a criminal pop band with his brigade of enhanced mechanised puppets. This colour story of *House of Dolmann* was in the 1969 *Valiant Annual*, with painted art by Carlos Cruz.

RIGHT: In *Yellowknife of the Yard*, the Sioux super sleuth Yellowknife narrowly escapes death by catching a whizzing tomahawk in his teeth. Drawn by Doug Maxted in *Valiant*, appropriately for the April Fool's Day issue in 1972.

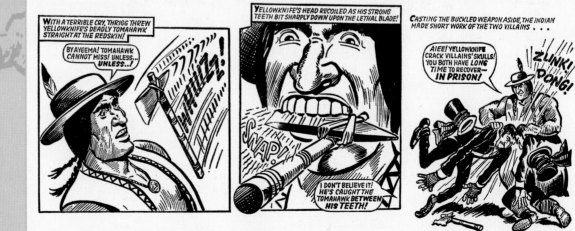

LEFT: Hollywood's action dramas set in ancient times had been filling cinemas and inspiring British comics like *Olac the Gladiator* and *Karl the Viking* in *Lion*, when writer Michael Moorcock and artist Ron Embleton dreamt up *Wrath of the Gods* for *Boys' World* in 1963. In this part from 16 February 1963, our intrepid Greek, Arion, ignores all warnings and boards a cursed galley ship. Nowhere else at the time but in Britain could comics be painted in luscious colours across such widescreen, double-page spreads.

ABOVE: Another classical epic in the comic art equivalent of "Cinemascope" was *Heros the Spartan*, which began in October 1962. Frank Bellamy's final magnum opus for *Eagle* gave him the opportunity to draw warriors in battle and fantastical landscapes and monsters. Written by Tom Tully, this instalment from the centre spread of the 3 April 1965 issue is shot from the original artwork with the lettering and text restored.

Writer Michael Butterworth and artist Ron Embleton collaborated on the stirring saga of *Wulf the Briton* in *Express Weekly* from 1957, and soon after Embleton took over the writing as well. After Wulf, slave to the Roman Lucellus, undertook seven trials to earn his freedom, he went on to lead the struggle against the Roman invaders. Here Wulf tricks Baldur and his mercenaries by drugging an abandoned village feast. This is the rare original art for *Express Weekly* 300, dated 30 July 1960.

ABOVE: In *The Steel Claw* by Ken Bulmer and Jesús Blasco, electric shocks turn Louis Crandell invisible, except for his artificial hand. Here, its power frees him from a sewer, but then it gets caught in the railway points in this gripping cliff-hanger in *Valiant*, 20 April 1963.

ABOVE RIGHT: Tim Kelly is normally impervious to harm thanks to Kelly's Eye, the jewelled Inca relic known as the Eye of Zoltec, but here a hypnotised crocodile makes off with it. Compiled from earlier stories for the 1971 *Valiant Summer Special*, drawn by Solano Lopez.

RIGHT: The freakishly flexible Victorian escapologist Janus Stark squeezes out of another tight spot in *Valiant*, 11 September 1971, drawn by Solano Lopez.

ABOVE: Cursitor Doom, master investigator of the occult and supernatural, senses that his assistant Angus McCraggan is in peril in this tale in the 1975 *Smash! Annual*, drawn with Eric Bradbury's flair for the macabre.

BELOW: William Grange dons his bewhiskered crash helmet to become agile junior superhero *Billy the Cat* in *The Beano* from 1967 to 1974. In this episode from 29 March 1969, drawn by Sandy Calder, he outmanoeuvres a hover-tank.

ABOVE: Starting in 1985, the *Marvelman* series was retitled, "colorised" and continued for America as *Miracleman*. This 1989 cover is by Garry Leach.

LEFT: The secret locked in a recurring nightmare is revealed when the adult Mike Moran speaks the forgotten word "Kimota" and Marvelman returns. Before *Watchmen*, Alan Moore re-charged the superhero genre first here with Leach in *Warrior* 1, March 1982.

BELOW LEFT: *Night Raven: House of Cards* was an original Marvel UK graphic novel about the noir crimefighter by Jamie Delano and David Lloyd in 1991.

BELOW: In the early 1970s, IPC came up with the first superhero called Captain Britain, but although 50 pages were completed, including this cover mock-up by Eric Bradbury, it never appeared. It was left to Anglophile Americans Chris Claremont and Herb Trimpe to create Marvel's first version in 1976.

LEFT: This *Captain Britain* evolved still further in Marvel UK's *The Daredevils* by Alans Moore and Davis in 1983.

181

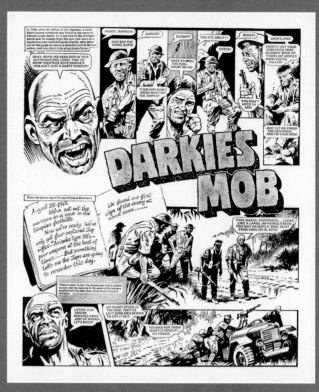

ABOVE: Created by John Wagner and Mike Western for *Battle*, the story of *Darkie's Mob* was told from the bloodstained notebook of a member of a unit of British soldiers stranded in the Japanese jungle and rescued by the enigmatic Captain Darkie. This page ran on 26 February 1977.

ABOVE: Gorier than Steven Spielberg's *Jaws*, giant shark Hookjaw was one of the big draws in *Action*. This is the original art by Ramon Sola for the sixth issue dated 21 March 1976.

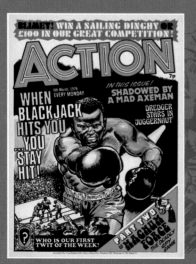

LEFT: In-your-face boxing thrills with *Black Jack*, drawn by Leopoldo Sanchez on the cover of *Action* for 6 March 1976.

RIGHT: Spoiler alert! The truth can now be told that *Hitler Lives*, a serial drawn by Patrick Wright. In 1979 Nazi fanatics have raised Hitler from suspended animation to wage war again. Kurt Lindt vows to end the Führer's life once and for all, even it means losing his own. This dramatic ending ran in *The Crunch*, 14 July 1979.

The horrors of the First World War had never been shown in comics with such shocking accuracy as in *Charley's War* by Pat Mills and Joe Colquhoun in *Battle* from 1978. In this instalment dated 15 April 1989 and shown with the original art, Charley Bourne rescues an injured horse named Warrior from a callous German bombing raid.

RIGHT: The spirit of the penny dreadfuls rises again when Victorian London's dreaded bogeyman Spring-heeled Jack strikes back in this 2005 graphic novel by David Hitchcock.

ABOVE: Dressed in a skintight Union Jack flag, *Jack Staff* began in 2000 as Paul Grist's very British superhero in his affectionate tribute to classic characters. On this page from 2003, Commander Malone uses toy tanks just like those in the old *Beano* series *General Jumbo*. But they fail to subdue the Hurricane, Grist's version of the angry *Valiant* soldier Captain Hurricane, whom he reinvents as Hurricane, a volatile, Hulk-like military experiment gone haywire.

LEFT: Inspired by legends from various ethnic sources, Ed Pinsent has been elaborating the enigmatic mythology of Primitif, a mysterious masked warrior-chieftain, since the late 1980s. This page from *Land of the Dead* was created in 1991 and finally saw print in book form in 2006.

ABOVE: Having made his name in the early 1970s drawing Marvel's *Conan the Barbarian* comic book, Barry Windsor-Smith went on to write and draw graphic novels. *The Freebooters*, compiled in 2005, is his witty, lavish dismantling of the sword-and-sorcery genre. Past his prime, former legend Axus the Great now runs a bar, but here he feels the call to make one last grand heroic gesture.

Celtic history and legend combine in the barbarian fantasy series *Sláine* written by Pat Mills and drawn here by Mike McMahon from 1983 for *2000AD*. This striking original art comes from the opening part of the story "Sky Chariots" and shows Sláine and his dwarf chronicler Ukko riding a mammoth towards a starving village. It was published on 21 January 1984.

ACKNOWLEDGEMENTS

All images are copyright their respective creators or owners acknowledged below and are reproduced for critical and historical purposes. Copyright credits are listed by page number and, where there is more than one image or copyright holder on a single page, in clockwise order starting with A from the top left. Any omission or error should be reported to the publisher so that it can be notified on the website www.greatbritishcomics.com and corrected in future editions.

Associated = Associated Newspaper plc/Solo Syndication
DCT = D.C. Thomson & Co., Ltd
Egmont = Egmont Magazines Ltd/Fleetway
Express = Express Newspapers plc
IPC = IPC Media Ltd
Mirror = Mirror Group Newspapers plc/Mirrorpix
Viz = House of Viz/John Brown Publishing

FRONT COVER: © DCT
1: © IPC
2: © Hulton-Deutsch Collection/Corbis
5: © IPC

CHAPTER 1: LOST WORLDS OF TOPSY-TURVY
6: A © Rodolphe Töpffer; B & C © IPC. **7:** © Mary Evans /Roger Mayne Photographs. **8:** © Mary Evans. **9:** A, B & D © IPC; C © Egmont; E © DCT. **10:** © IPC. **11:** © Mirrorpix. **13:** © IPC. **14:** A © Estate of Frank Hampson; B © Express; C © Estate of Norman Pett; D © Leo Baxendale; E © Liz Lawrence; F © Posy Simmonds; G © Bryan Talbot; H © Alan Clark; I © Express; J © José Villarrubia. **15:** A © Savoy Books; B © Leo Baxendale/Estate of Dudley Watkins; C © Express; D © DCT; E © Estate of Frank Bellamy; F © Eddie Campbell; G © Alan Clark; H © Pat Mills; I © Newcastle Chronicle & Journal Ltd; J © Estate of A.B. Payne.

CHAPTER 2: FOR RICHER, FOR POORER
16: A © Judy magazine; B © V&A Images/Theatre Museum; C © Alfredo Castelli; Text of Frost Report sketch © Estate of Marty Feldman & John Law. **17:** © DCT. **18** © James Sullivan/Fun. **19:** A © Bubbles Inc. S.A.; B © IPC. **20:** A © Respective copyright holder; B © Russell Taylor & Charles Peattie; C © Viz; D © Egmont; F © Mirror; G © DCT; H © Associated. **21:** A © Express; B © Viz. **22:** A, B & C © Judy magazine; D © Ally Sloper's Half-Holiday; E © MGM/MPTV.net. **23:** © IPC. **24:** A © IPC; B © Getty Images; C © IPC. **25:** © IPC. **26:** A © H.M. Bateman Designs; B © Estate of William Heath Robinson; C & D © Punch. **27** © Punch. **28:** A, B & C © Associated; D, E, F & G © Mirror. **29:** © DCT. **30:** A © IPC; B & C © Mirror; D © Express. **31:** A & B © IPC; C © Mirror; D © Phil Elliott. **32:** A & B © Raymond Briggs; C & D © Mirror. **33:** A © Respective copyright holder; B © Frank Dickens; C © Russell Taylor & Charles Peattie; D © Gary Coley. **34:** A & B © Egmont; C © Estate of Arthur Horner; D © Mirror. **35:** A © Clifford Harper; B © Jo Nesbitt; C © Peter Ketley & Dave McNamara; E & F © Mike Weller. **36:** A © Estate of John Glashan; B © Posy Simmonds. **37:** A © Brian Bolland; B © Viz; C © John Fardell & Viz; D © Frank Quitely. **38:** A © Barry Humphries, Nicholas Garland & Private Eye; B © Biff; C © Paul Sample. **39:** A © Kate Charlesworth; B & C © Nabiel Kanan; D © Andi Watson. **40:** A © Eddie Campbell; B © John Bagnall; C © Ilya. **41:** A © Neil Gaiman & Dave McKean; B © Carol Swain; C © Andi Watson; E © Knife, Packer & Private Eye; F © Tony Husband & Private Eye.

CHAPTER 3: SPITTING IMAGES
42: A © James Gillray; B © William Heath & The Mitchell Library, Glasgow. **43:** © IPC. **44:** A © IPC; B © Getty Images; C © James Parsons; D © Egmont; E © IPC; F © Gerald Scarfe & Private Eye; G & H © IPC. **45:** A © Peter Brookes & Times Syndication; B © Damon Albarn & Jamie Hewlett. **46:** © IPC. **47:** © Bubbles Inc. S.A. **48:** A, B & C © IPC; D & E © Egmont/Estate of Shirley Crabtree. **49:** © IPC. **50:** A © IPC; B, C & E © DCT; D © Mick Farren & Dave Gibbons. **51:** A & D © IPC; B © Joe Petagno; C © DCT. **52:** © IPC. **53:** A © Dan Dare Corporation Ltd.; B © GQ magazine; C © Eugene Byrne & Simon Gurr; D © Icon Books; E © Russell-Cotes Museum & Art Gallery, Sean Michael Wilson & Sakura Mizuki. **54:** A © Estate of Edward Barker; B © Penthouse magazine; C © Estate of John Kent; D © Steve Bell; E © William M. Gaines, Agent Inc. **55:** A © Alexei Sayle & Oscar Zarate; B © Spitting Image & Harry North; C © Spitting Image; D © Rebellion A/S.; E © Grant Morrison & Steve Yeowell. **56:** A & B © Peter Milligan & Jamie Hewlett; C © Wayne Massop; D © Omnibus Press; E © Bryan Talbot. **57:** A © Rob Dunlop & Peter Lumby; B © Lucy Sweet; C © Tom Gauld; D © BBC Worldwide.

CHAPTER 4: DOWN ON JOLLITY FARM
58: A © Mirror; B © Respective copyright holder; C © Estate of George Studdy; Song lyrics © Estate of Leslie Sarony. **59:** © IPC. **60:** A © IPC; B © Associated. **61:** A © IPC; B © Respective copyright holder. **62:** A & B © Associated. **63:** A & B © Disney Enterprises Inc.; C © Derek McNally. **64:** A © Estate of George Orwell & The British Foreign Office; B © Aardman Animation; C © Cosgrove Hall Productions Ltd; D & E © DCT; F © Express; G © IPC. **65:** A © Alan Moore & Kevin O'Neill; B © Aardman Animation; **66 & 67:** © Mirror. **68** A, C, D & E © Express; B © Respective copyright holder. **69:** A & B © Liverpool Echo & Estates of Maud Budden & Roland Clibborn; C © Sheffield Evening Telegraph; D & G © Mirror; E & F © Cooper Features, London & Estate of William Timyn. **70:** A, B, C & E © DCT; D © IPC. **71:** A © IPC; B © Estate of Mrs S.G. Hulme-Beaman; C © Disney Enterprises Inc.; D © Alan Clark. **72:** A © Manchester Evening News & Estate of Ken Reid; B © Raymond Briggs; C © Moomin Characters TM/Associated/Bulls; D & E © Associated.

73: A & D © Associated; B © Respective copyright holder; C © Mirror. **74:** © DCT. **75:** A, B & D © IPC; C © Egmont. **76:** A © Cosgrove Hall Productions Ltd/IPC; B © D.A.N.O.T./BBC Worldwide; C, D & E © Egmont. **77:** A © Hunt Emerson; B © Tym Manley & Hunt Emerson; C © Malcolm Livingstone; D © Savage Pencil; E © William Rankin. **78:** A, B & E © Egmont; C © Steven Appleby; D © Alan Grant & Simon Bisley. **79:** A © Aardman Animation; B © Gary Northfield; C © Robin & Laurence Etherington; D © Simone Lia.

CHAPTER 5: WHEEZES IN THE TUCK SHOP
80: A © Look and Learn Ltd; B © Respective copyright holder. **81:** © IPC. **82:** A & C © IPC; B © BBC Worldwide. **83:** © DCT. **84:** A © Estate of Brian White; B & D © DCT; C © Egmont; E & F © IPC; G © Estate of Brian White. **85:** A © Viz; B © DCT. **86:** A, C & D © IPC; B © Respective copyright holder. **87:** © DCT. **88:** A, C & D © IPC; B © Respective copyright holder. **89:** © DCT. **90:** © DCT. **91:** A, C & D © DCT; B © Egmont. **92:** A & B © IPC; C & D © Egmont. **93:** A & B © Egmont; D, E & F © DCT. **94:** © IPC. **95:** © IPC. **96:** A, B & D © Egmont; C © IPC. **97:** A © Steve Bell; B © Leo Baxendale; C, D & E © Viz. **98:** A & B © Egmont; C © Stella Richman Productions Ltd; D © Chris Long. **99:** A & D © DCT; B © Brian Wood; C © Peter Blegvad. **100:** A © IPC; B © Getty Images. **101:** A © Getty Images; B © Dan Dare Corporation Ltd; C © IPC.

CHAPTER 6: THINGS TO COME
102: A © IPC; B = Public domain; C © Merit Games. **103:** © T.V. Boardman. **104:** A © IPC; B © Disney Enterprises Inc. **105:** A © IPC; B © Respective copyright holder. **106:** A & B © Dan Dare Corporation Ltd; C © University of Brighton Design Archives. **107:** © Dan Dare Corporation Ltd. **108:** A © Stephen Hird/Reuters/Corbis; B & D © Rebellion A/S; C © BBC Worldwide; E © Carlton International Media Ltd; F © IPC; G © L. Burn & Co. **109:** © Rebellion A/S. **110:** © Mirror. **111:** © Express. **112:** A, C, D & E © IPC; B © Getty Images. **113:** A © Express; B & C © IPC; D © Estate of Roland Prosper Beamont. **114:** A, B & C © IPC; D & E © DCT. **115:** A © DCT; B © IPC; C © Disney Enterprises Inc. **116 & 117:** © Carlton International Media Ltd. **118:** © IPC. **119:** © BBC Worldwide. Daleks created by Terry Nation. **120–123:** © Rebellion A/S. **124:** A © IPC; B © Dave Huxley & Angus McKie; C © Grant Morrison; D & E © Mick Farren & Chris Welch. **125:** A © Bryan Talbot; B & C © DCT; D © Raymond Briggs; E © Chris Reynolds. **126:** A © ECC Publications; B © Dan Dare Corporation Ltd; C © Warhammer; D © Terry Pratchett. **127:** A © DC Comics; B © Dan Dare Corporation Ltd; C © Warren Ellis & Chris Weston; D © Egmont. **128:** A © Ilya; B © Peter Milligan & Brendan McCarthy; C © Grant Morrison & Philip Bond; D © Dave Gibbons; E © Rebellion A/S. **129:** A & B © Ian Carney & D'Israeli; C © Nick Abadzis; D © Paul Rainey.

CHAPTER 7: JOLLY HOCKEY STICKS TO SHEROES
130: A © IPC; B © Estate of Christabel Leighton-Porter; C © Mirror. **131:** © Associated. **132:** A © Mirror; B © Ronald Searle. **133:** © News Group Newspapers Ltd. **134:** A © IPC; B © Imagination Holdings Ltd; B © Jamie Hewlett, Alan Martin & Deadline Magazine; C © DCT; D & E © IPC; F © Estate of Norman Pett; G © DCT. **135:** A © Lorna Miller; B © Joan Zhou; C © Jamie Hewlett, Alan Martin & Deadline magazine. **136:** A & B © Tatler magazine and Estates of Anne Harriet Fish & Edward Huskinson; C & D © Mirror. **137:** A & D © Mirror; B © V&A Images/Theatre Museum; C © Hulton-Deutsch/Corbis. **138:** A, B & D © DCT; C © IPC. **139:** © DCT. **140:** A © DCT; B, C & D © IPC. **141:** A, B & C © IPC; D © Egmont. **142:** © IPC. **143:** A © Carlton International Media Ltd.; B © DCT; C & D © IPC. **144:** A, B, D & E © IPC; C © DCT. **145:** A & E © IPC; B, C & D © DCT. **146:** A © IPC; B & C © Associated. **147:** A © Associated; B © Getty Images. **148:** A, B & C © Egmont; D © Associated. **149:** A © IPC; B, C & D © Egmont. **150:** A © Suzy Varty; B © Posy Simmonds; C © Julie Hollings; D © Kate Charlesworth. **151:** A & B © Myra Hancock; B © Jeremy Dennis, Sacha Mardou & Lucy Sweet; C © Erica Smith; D © Jeremy Dennis. **152:** A © DCT; B & D © Rebellion A/S.; C © Philip Bond & Deadline magazine. **153:** © Jamie Hewlett, Alan Martin & Deadline magazine. **154:** © Posy Simmonds. **155:** A © London Borough of Lewisham & Steve Marchant; B © Sacha Mardou; C © John Allison; D © BBC Worldwide.

CHAPTER 8: RIPPING YARNS
156: A © Estate of Barry Ono; B = Public domain. **157 & 158:** © IPC. **159:** © Disney Enterprises Inc. **160:** A © Getty Images; B © Express; C © Humbrol/Airfix; D © IPC. **161:** A © IPC; B © DCT. **162:** A © Dan Dare Corporation Ltd; B © Striker 3D Ltd; C © Respective copyright holder; D © DCT; E & F © IPC; G © Alan Clark; H © John Ryan. **163:** A © Associated; B & C © Amos Toys/James Jarvis & Russell Waterman; D © Paul Grist. **164 & 165:** © DCT. **166:** A, C & E © DCT; B © Egmont; D © IPC. **167:** © Egmont. **168, 169 & 170:** © IPC. **171:** A & C © Mirror; B © Associated; D © Estate of Alfred Mazure; E © Express 1987; Goldfinger © Glidrose Productions Ltd, 1959. **172:** A © Estate of Captain W.E. Johns & Junior Publications Ltd; B © DCT; C, D & E © IPC. **173:** A & C © IPC; B & D © DCT. **174:** A & B © T.V. Boardman; C © IPC; D © Dan Dare Corporation Ltd. **175:** A & C © Respective copyright holder; B & D © IPC. **176:** A © Egmont; B © DCT; C & D © IPC. **177:** © IPC. **178:** A © IPC; B © Dan Dare Corporation Ltd. **179:** © Express. **180:** © IPC. **181:** A © DCT; B & C © Respective copyright holder; D © IPC; E & F © Marvel Characters, Inc. **182:** A, B & D © Egmont; C © DCT. **183:** © Egmont. **184:** A © David Hitchcock; B © Paul Grist; C © Ed Pinsent; D © Barry Windsor-Smith. **185:** © Rebellion A/S. **192:** © DCT.

BACK COVER: A © Jamie Hewlett, Alan Martin & Deadline magazine; B © Dan Dare Corporation Ltd; C © Rebellion A/S; D © Express; E © Associated; F © DCT.

Online: www.greatbritishcomics.com
The place to start for updated info, images and links to the ever-changing websites devoted to British comics.

In Print: Explore these books, all published in London unless otherwise stated.

Alderson, Connie *Magazines Teenagers Read*, Pergamon, 1967.

Anglo, Michael *Penny Dreadfuls and Other Victorian Horrors*, Jupiter, 1977.

Ashford, David & McLoughlin, Denis *The Hardboiled Art of D. McLoughlin*, David Ashford, Harrow, 1994.

Atkinson, Diane *Funny Girls: Cartooning for Equality*, Penguin, 1997.

Barker, Martin *A Haunt of Fears: The Strange History of the British Horror Comics Campaign*, Pluto Press, 1984.

— *Comics, Ideology, Power and The Critics*, Manchester University Press, Manchester, 1989.

— *Action: The Story of a Violent Comic*, Titan Books, 1990.

Bateman, Michael *Funny Way To Make A Living*, Leslie Frewin, 1966.

— (ed.) *The Man Who Drew The 20th Century: The drawings & cartoons of H.M. Bateman*, Macdonald, 1969.

Baxendale, Leo *A Very Funny Business*, Gerald Duckworth, 1978.

— *On Comedy*, Reaper, Stroud, 1989.

Bishop, David *Thrill-Power Overload: The Official History of 2000 AD, the Galaxy's Greatest Comic*, Rebellion, Oxford, 2007.

Blackmore, Lawrence *The Modesty Blaise Companion*, Book Palace Books, 2006.

Bleathman, Graham & Denham, Sam *Thunderbirds: Classic Comic Strips from TV21*, Carlton Books, 2001.

Bott, Caroline *The Life and Works of Alfred Bestall*, Bloomsbury, 2003.

Bryant, Mark *Dictionary of Twentieth-Century British Cartoonists and Caricaturists*, Scolar, Aldershot, 2000.

Burns, Mal *Comix Index: The Directory of Alternative British Graphic Magazines (1966–77)*, John Noyce, Brighton, 1978.

Campbell, Alexander (ed.) *Mirror Grange, The book of the Daily Mirror's House of Pip, Squeak and Wilfred*, Daily Mirror, 1930.

Campbell, Eddie *Alec: How To Be An Artist*, Eddie Campbell Comics, Paddington, Australia, 2001.

Cartmell, Deborah (ed.) *Trash Aesthetics: Popular Culture and its Audience*, Pluto Press, 1997.

Carpenter, Kevin *Penny Dreadfuls and Comics*, V&A Museum, 1983.

Castelli, Alfredo (ed.) *Ally Sloper: First Hero of the Comics*, Napoli Comicon, Naples, 2006.

Clark, Alan & Ashford, David *The Comic Art of Roy Wilson*, Midas Books, Tunbridge Wells, 1983.

Clark, Alan *The Comic Art of Reg Parlett*, Golden Fun, Tunbridge Wells, 1986.

— *The Children's Annual*, Boxtree, 1988.

— *The Best of British Comic Art*, Boxtree, 1989.

— **& Clark, Laurel** *Comics: An Illustrated History*, Green Wood, 1991.

— *The Dictionary of British Comic Artists, Writers and Editors*, The British Library, 1998.

Clarke, Phil & Higgs, Mike *Nostalgia About Comics*, Pegasus, Birmingham, 1991.

Cook, William *25 Years of VIZ: Silver-Plated Jubilee*, Boxtree, 2004.

Crompton, Alastair *The Man Who Drew Tomorrow* (biography of Frank Hampson), Who Dares Publishing, Bournemouth, 1985.

Davidson, Steef *The Penguin Book of Political Comics*, Penguin, 1976.

Dierick, Charles & Lefèvre, Pascal (eds) *Forging a New Medium: The Comic Strip in the Nineteenth Century*, VUB University Press, Brussels, 1998.

Dixon, Bob *Catching Them Young 2: Political Ideas in Children's Fiction*, Pluto Press, 1977.

Donald, Chris *Rude Kids: The VIZ Story*, Harper Collins, 2004.

Freeman, Gillian *The Undergrowth of Literature*, Thomas Nelson, 1967.

Gallagher, Brendan *Sporting Supermen*, Aurum Press, 2006.

Garriock, P.R. *Masters of Comic Book Art*, Aurum Press, 1978.

Gifford, Denis *Discovering Comics*, Shire Publications, 1971, revised edn 1991.

— *Stap Me! The British Newspaper Strip*, Shire Publications, 1971.

— *Happy Days, One Hundred Years of Comics*, Jupiter Books, 1975.

— *Run Adolf Run*, Corgi Books, 1975.

— *Victorian Comics*, Allen & Unwin, 1976.

— *The International Book of Comics*, Deans International, 1984.

— *The Complete Catalogue of British Comics*, Webb & Bower, Exeter, 1985.

— *The Encyclopedia of Comic Characters*, Longman, 1987.

— *Comics Go To War*, Hawk, 1988.

— *The Comic Art of Charlie Chaplin*, Hawk, 1989.

— *Best of Eagle Annual 1951–59*, Webb & Bower, 1989.

— *Best of Girl Annual, 1952–59*, Webb & Bower, 1990.

— *Christmas Comic Posters*, H.C. Blossom, 1991.

— *Super Duper Supermen!*, Green Wood, 1992.

— *Space Aces!*, Green Wood, 1992.

Gravett, Paul (ed.) *The 100 British Cartoonists of the Century*, Beer Davies/ The Cartoon Art Trust, 2000.

Harper, Clifford *The Education of Desire: The Anarchist Graphics of Clifford Harper*, Anares, 1984.

Harris, Paul (ed.) *The D.C. Thomson Bumper Fun Book*, Paul Harris Publishing, Edinburgh, 1977.

Hildick, E.W. *A Close Look at Magazines & Comics*, Faber, 1966.

Holland, Steve *The Fleetway Companion*, Bryon Whitworth, Colne, 1991.

— *Look and Learn: A Brief History of the Classic Children's Magazine*, Look and Learn, 2006.

Horn, Maurice (ed.) *World Encyclopedia of Comics*, Chelsea House, New York, 1976, revised edn 1998.

Huxley, David *Nasty Tales: Sex, Drugs, Rock'n'Roll & Violence in the British Underground*, Head Press, Manchester, 2001.

James, Louis *Fiction for the Working Man*, Oxford University Press, Oxford, 1963.

Jarman, Colin M. & Acton, Peter *Judge Dredd: The Mega-History*, Lennard Publishing, Harpenden, 1995.

Kean, Roger *The Fantasy Art of Oliver Frey*, Thalamus Books, Ludlow, 2006.

Khoury, George *Kimota! The Miracleman Companion*, TwoMorrows, Rayleigh, 2001.

— *The Extraordinary Works of Alan Moore*, TwoMorrows, Rayleigh, NC, 2003.

— (ed.) *True Brit: A Celebration of Great Comic Book Artists of the UK*, TwoMorrows, Rayleigh, NC, 2004.

Kibble-White, Graham *The Ultimate Book of British Comics*, Allison & Busby, 2005.

King, Graham & Saxby, Ron *The Wonderful World of Film Fun*, Clarkes New Press, 1985.

Kunzle, David *History of the Comic Strip: The Early Comic Strip*, vol. 1, University of California Press, Berkeley, CA, 1973.

— *History of the Comic Strip: The Nineteenth Century*, vol. 2, University of California Press, Berkeley, CA, 1988.

Mitchell, David M. *A Serious Life*, Savoy Books, Manchester, 2004.

Moore, Ray *The Beano Diaries*, 2 vols, British Comic World, 1992.

Morris, Marcus *Best of Eagle*, Michael Joseph, 1977.

Morris, Sally & Hallwood, Jan *Living With Eagles, Priest to Publisher: The Life and Times of Marcus Morris*, Lutterworth Press, Cambridge, 1998.

Perry, George and Aldridge, Alan *The Penguin Book of Comics*, Penguin Books, 1967, revised edn 1971.

Perry, George & Bestall, Alfred *Rupert: A Bear's Life*, Pavilion, 1985.

Pilcher, Tim & Brookes, Brad *The Essential Guide to World Comics*, Collins & Brown, 2005.

Pumphrey, George *Children's Comics, A Guide for Parents and Teachers*, Epworth Press, 1955.

— *What Children Think of Their Comics*, Epworth Press, 1964.

Robinson, Mark *Doug Maxted: An Interview with a Comics Veteran*, Underclass Publications, Cardiff, 1990.

Sabin, Roger *Adult Comics: An Introduction*, Routledge, 1993.

— *Comics, Comix & Graphic Novels: A History of Comic Art*, Phaidon, 1996.

Saunders, Andy *Jane, A Pin Up at War*, Pen & Sword Books, Barnsley, 2004.

Shirley, Ian *Can Can Rock & Roll Save The World? An Illustrated History of Music and Comics*, SAF, 2005.

Skinn, Dez *Comix: The Underground Revolution*, Chrysalis Books, 2004.

Smith, Howard *Dan Dare at 50*, E.C. Parker, Canterbury, 2000.

Smythe, Reg & Lilley, Les *The World of Andy Capp*, Titan Books, 1990.

Storie, Bill *Garth: A 50th Anniversary Celebration*, Gopherville Argus, Perth, 1993.

Traverso, Giovanni (ed.) *Glamour International: British Girls Special*, vol. 7, Glamour International, Florence, Italy, 1983.

Turner, E.S. *Boys Will Be Boys*, Michael Joseph, 1948, revised edns 1957 & 1975.

White, H. Brian & John D. *I Had An Idea… A Biography of Brian White*, unpublished.

Whitford, Frank *Trog: Forty Graphic Years*, Fourth Estate, 1987.

Wright, Norman & Higgs, Mike *The Dan Dare Dossier*, Hawk, 1987.

Wright, Norman & Ashford, David *Lightning! Swords! Smoking Pistols! A Celebration of the Swashbuckler in Boys' Papers and Comics*, Museum Press, Maidstone, 1995.

Magazines: These magazines from the 1970s to today, cancelled (c) or still running, include coverage of British comics: *A.C.E. (Association of Comics Enthusiasts) Newsletter* (c), *Achtung! Commando*, *AKA* (c), *Arkensword/Ark* (c), *BEM* (c), *Book & Magazine Collector*, *British Comic World* (c), *Comic Art*, *Comic Bits*, *Comic Book Artist*, *The Comic Journal* (c), *Comic Media* (c), *Comic Media News International* (c), *Comics Forum* (c), *The Comics Journal*, *Comics International*, *Comic World* (c), *Eagle Flies Again* (c), *Eagle Times*, *Escape* (c), *Eureka* (c), *Fantasy Advertiser* (c), *Golden Fun* (c), *The Gopherville Argus* (c), *Graphixus* (c), *Head Press*, *Hellfire* (c), *Illustrated Comic Journal* (c), *International Journal of Comic Art*, *Infinity* (c), *Jeff Hawke's Cosmos*, *Judge Dredd Megazine*, *Metamorpho* (c), *Red Eye*, *Zarjaz*. See GBC website for links.

Price Guides: How much are your comics worth? Maybe not as much as you hoped, unless you've found a rarity. Condition, scarcity, demand and keeping those free gifts can make all the difference. Since Denis Gifford's 1985 *Catalogue*, the last major price guide for British Comics was compiled in April 1996 by Steve Holland in Duncan McAlpine's *Comic Book Price Guide* (Titan Books). Martin Hamer updated his *Hamer Guide To Comic Annuals* in 2002. Check *Book & Magazine Collector* for guide prices, auction results on compalcomics.com or vaultauctions.com, and eBay where new records and surprising bargains are being made every second!

187

THANKS

Paul Gravett and Peter Stanbury would like to thank:

Karen Ings at Aurum Press for her initial belief in and unwavering commitment to this book;

Marc Baines, Leo Baxendale, Steve Bell, Chris Beetles, David Bishop, David Britton, Jeremy Brook, Fred Brown, Michael Butterworth, Alfredo Castelli, Phil Clarke, Les Coleman, Victor Collinge, Mike Collins, Craig Conlan, Rufus Dayglo, John Freeman, Colin and Lisa Frewin, Luke Gertler, Ken Harman, Christine Harper, Paul Holder, Brian Hughes, Tony Husband, Nick Jones, Andy Konky Kru, Guy Lawley, Hans Matla, Les McIntyre, Bill McLoughlin, John McShane, Alfons Moliné, Nicholas Morrison, Steven Nicholas, Alan Notton, Malcolm Phillips, Ian Rakoff, Richard Reynolds, Peter Richardson, Desmond Shaw, Howard Smith, Thierry Smolderen, David Staunton Browne, Andy Sumner, Rob van Bavel, Geoff West, Dave Westaway, Paul and Patrick Wright;

and all the other artists, writers, editors, publishers, collectors, dealers, archivists, enthusiasts and friends without whom the book would not have been possible.